C-874
ISBN 0-8373-0874-7

THE PASSBOOK® SERIES

PASSBOOKS®
FOR
CAREER OPPORTUNITIES

SERGEANT, SHERIFF'S DEPARTMENT

National Learning Corporation
212 Michael Drive, Syosset, New York 11791
(516) 921-8888

All rights reserved, including the right of reproduction in whole or in part, in any form or by any means, electronic or mechanical, including photocopying, recording, or by any information storage and retrieval system, without permission in writing from the Publisher.

Copyright © 1998 by

National Learning Corporation

212 Michael Drive, Syosset, New York 11791
(516) 921-8888

PRINTED IN THE UNITED STATES OF AMERICA

PASSBOOK®

NOTICE

This book is *SOLELY* intended for, is sold *ONLY* to, and its use is *RESTRICTED* to *individual*, bona fide applicants or candidates who qualify by virtue of having seriously filed applications for appropriate license, certificate, professional and/or promotional advancement, higher school matriculation, scholarship, or other legitimate requirements of educational and/or governmental authorities.

This book is *NOT* intended for use, class instruction, tutoring, training, duplication, copying, reprinting, excerption, or adaptation, etc., by:

(1) Other Publishers

(2) Proprietors and/or Instructors of "Coaching" and/or Preparatory Courses

(3) Personnel and/or Training Divisions of commercial, industrial, and governmental organizations

(4) Schools, colleges, or universities and/or their departments and staffs, including teachers and other personnel

(5) Testing Agencies or Bureaus

(6) Study groups which seek by the purchase of a single volume to copy and/or duplicate and/or adapt this material for use by the group as a whole without having purchased individual volumes for each of the members of the group

(7) Et al.

Such persons would be in violation of appropriate Federal and State statutes.

PROVISION OF LICENSING AGREEMENTS. — Recognized educational commercial, industrial, and governmental institutions and organizations, and others legitimately engaged in educational pursuits, including training, testing, and measurement activities, may address a request for a licensing agreement to the copyright owners, who will determine whether, and under what conditions, including fees and charges, the materials in this book may be used by them. In other words, a licensing facility *exists* for the legitimate use of the material in this book on other than an individual basis. However, it is asseverated and affirmed here that the materials in this book *CANNOT* be used without the receipt of the express permission of such a licensing agreement from the Publishers.

NATIONAL LEARNING CORPORATION
212 Michael Drive
Syosset, New York 11791

Inquiries re licensing agreements should be addressed to:
The President
National Learning Corporation
212 Michael Drive
Syosset, New York 11791

PASSBOOK SERIES®

THE *PASSBOOK SERIES®* has been created to prepare applicants and candidates for the ultimate academic battlefield—the examination room.

At some time in our lives, each and every one of us may be required to take an examination—for validation, matriculation, admission, qualification, registration, certification, or licensure.

Based on the assumption that every applicant or candidate has met the basic formal educational standards, has taken the required number of courses, and read the necessary texts, the *PASSBOOK SERIES®* furnishes the one special preparation which may assure passing with confidence, instead of failing with insecurity. Examination questions—together with answers—are furnished as the basic vehicle for study so that the mysteries of the examination and its compounding difficulties may be eliminated or diminished by a sure method.

This book is meant to help you pass your examination provided that you qualify and are serious in your objective.

The entire field is reviewed through the huge store of content information which is succinctly presented through a provocative and challenging approach—the question-and-answer method.

A climate of success is established by furnishing the correct answers at the end of each test.

You soon learn to recognize types of questions, forms of questions, and patterns of questioning. You may even begin to anticipate expected outcomes.

You perceive that many questions are repeated or adapted so that you gain acute insights, which may enable you to score many sure points.

You learn how to confront new questions, or types of questions, and to attack them confidently and work out the correct answers.

You note objectives and emphases, and recognize pitfalls and dangers, so that you may make positive educational adjustments.

Moreover, you are kept fully informed in relation to new concepts, methods, practices, and directions in the field.

You discover that you are actually taking the examination all the time: you are preparing for the examination by "taking" an examination, not by reading extraneous and/or supererogatory textbooks.

In short, this PASSBOOK®, used directedly, should be an important factor in helping you to pass your test.

SERGEANT, SHERIFF'S DEPARTMENT

DUTIES

Serves as sergeant in a sheriff's department. Supervises deputy sheriffs in the performance of various law enforcement activities including serving process, transporting prisoners, executing warrants, securing courthouse and courtrooms, criminal identification and investigation and apprehension of violators of the law.

SCOPE OF THE WRITTEN TEST

The written test is designed to test for knowledges, skills, and/or abilities in such areas as:
1. Operation and maintenance of jails and prisoners;
2. Building security;
3. Criminal investigation and identification;
4. Interpreting written material; and
5. Supervision.

HOW TO TAKE A TEST

YOU MUST PASS AN EXAMINATION

A. WHAT EVERY CANDIDATE SHOULD KNOW

Examination applicants often ask us for help in preparing for the written test. What can I study in advance? What kinds of questions will be asked? How will the test be given? How will the papers be graded?

As an applicant for a civil service examination, you may be wondering about some of these things. Our purpose here is to suggest effective methods of advance study and to describe civil service examinations.

Your chances for success on this examination can be increased if you know how to prepare. Those "pre-examination jitters" can be reduced if you know what to expect. You can even experience an adventure in good citizenship if you know why civil service examinations are given.

B. WHY ARE CIVIL SERVICE EXAMINATIONS GIVEN?

Civil service examinations are important to you in two ways. As a citizen, you want public jobs filled by employees who know how to do their work. As a job-seeker, you want a fair chance to compete for that job on an equal footing with other candidates. The best known means of accomplishing this two-fold goal is the competitive examination.

Examinations are widely publicized throughout the nation. They may be administered for jobs in federal, state, city, municipal, town, or village governments or agencies.

Any citizen may apply, with some limitations, such as the age or residence of applicants. Your experience and education may be reviewed to see whether you meet the requirements for the particular examination. When these requirements exist, they are reasonable and are applied consistently to all applicants. Thus, a competitive examination may cause you some uneasiness now, but it is your privilege and safeguard.

C. HOW ARE CIVIL SERVICE EXAMINATIONS DEVELOPED?

Examinations are carefully written by trained technicians who are specialists in the field known as "psychological measurement," in consultation with recognized authorities in the field of work that the test will cover. These experts recommend the subject matter areas or skills to be tested; only those knowledges or skills important to your success on the job are included. The most reliable books and source materials available are used as references. Together, the experts and technicians judge the difficulty level of the questions.

Test technicians know how to phrase questions so that the problem is clearly stated. Their ethics do not permit "trick" or "catch" questions. Questions may have been tried out on sample groups, or subjected to statistical analysis, to determine their usefulness.

Written tests are often used in combination with performance tests, ratings of training and experience, and oral interviews. All of these measures combine to form the best known means of finding the right man for the right job.

II. HOW TO PASS THE WRITTEN TEST
   A. *NATURE OF THE EXAMINATION*
      To prepare intelligently for civil service examinations, you should know how they differ from school examinations you have taken. In school you were assigned certain definite pages to read or subjects to cover. The examination questions were quite detailed and usually emphasized memory. Civil service examinations, on the other hand, try to discover your present ability to perform the duties of a position, plus your potentiality to learn these duties. In other words, a civil service examination attempts to predict how successful you will be. Questions cover such a broad area that they cannot be as minute and detailed as school examination questions.
      In the public service similar kinds of work, or positions, are grouped together in one "class." This process is known as "position-classification." All the positions in a class are paid according to the salary range for that class. One class title covers all these positions, and they are all tested by the same examination.
   B. *FOUR BASIC STEPS*
      1. Study the Announcement.--How, then, can you know what subjects to study? Our best answer is: "Learn as much as possible about the class of positions for which you have applied." The examination will test the knowledge, skills, and abilities needed to do the work.
         Your most valuable source of information about the position you want is the official announcement of the examination. This announcement lists the training and experience qualifications. Check these standards and apply only if you come reasonably close to meeting them.
         The brief description of the position in the examination announcement offers some clues to the subjects which will be tested. Think about the job itself. Review the duties in your mind. Can you perform them, or are there some in which you are rusty? Fill in the blank spots in your preparation.
         Many jurisdictions preview the written test in the examination announcement by including a section called "Knowledge and Abilities Required," "Scope of Examination," or some similar heading. Here you will find out specifically what fields will be tested.
      2. Review Your Own Background.-- Once you learn in general what the position is all about, and what you need to know to do the work, ask yourself which subjects you already know fairly well and which need improvement. You may wonder whether to concentrate on improving your strong areas or on building some background in your fields of weakness. When the announcement has specified "some knowledge" or "considerable knowledge," or has used adjectives such as "beginning principles of ...." or "advanced .....methods," you can get a clue as to the number and difficulty of questions to be asked in any given field. More questions, and hence broader coverage, would be included for those subjects which are more important in the work. Now weigh your strengths and weaknesses against the job requirements and prepare accordingly.
      3. Determine the Level of the Position.-- Another way to tell how intensively you should prepare is to understand the level of the job for which you are applying. Is it the entering level? In other words, is this the position in which beginners in a field of work are hired? Or is it an intermediate or advanced level? Sometimes this is indicated by such words as "Junior" or "Senior" in the class title.Other jurisdictions use Roman numerals to designate the level: Clerk I,

Clerk II, for example. The word "Supervisor" sometimes appears in the title. If the level is not indicated by the title, check the description of duties. Will you be working under very close supervision, or will you have responsibility for independent decisions in this work?

    4. Choose Appropriate Study Materials.-- Now that you know the subjects to be examined and the relative amount of each subject to be covered, you can choose suitable study materials. For beginning level jobs, or even advanced ones, if you have a pronounced weakness in some aspect of your training, read a modern, standard textbook in that field. Be sure it is up-to-date and has general coverage. Such books are normally available at your library, and the librarian will be glad to help you locate one. For entry level positions, questions of appropriate difficulty are chosen -- neither highly advanced questions, nor those too simple. Such questions require careful thought but not advanced training.

    If the position for which you are applying is technical or advanced, you will read more advanced, specialized material. If you are already familiar with the basic principles of your field, elementary textbooks would waste your time. Concentrate on advanced textbooks and technical periodicals. Think through the concepts and review difficult problems in your field.

    These are all general sources. You can get more ideas on your own initiative, following these leads. For example, training manuals and publications of the government agency which employs workers in your field can be useful, particularly for technical and professional positions. A letter or visit to the government department involved may result in more specific study suggestions, and certainly will provide you with a more definite idea of the exact nature of the position you are seeking.

II. KINDS OF TESTS

    Tests are used for purposes other than measuring knowledge and ability to perform specified duties. For some positions, it is equally important to test ability to make adjustments to new situations or to profit from training. In others, basic mental abilities not dependent upon information are essential. Questions which test these things may not appear as pertinent to the duties of the position as those which test for knowledge and information. Yet they are often highly important parts of a fair examination. For very general questions, it is almost impossible to help you direct your study efforts. What we can do is to point out some of the more common of these general abilities needed in public service positions and describe some typical questions.

  1. General Information

    Broad, general information has been found useful for predicting job success in some kinds of work. This is tested in a variety of ways, from vocabulary lists to questions about current events. Basic background in some field of work, such as sociology or economics, may be sampled in a group of questions. Often these are principles which have become familiar to most persons through "exposure" rather than through formal training. It is difficult to advise you how to study for these questions; being alert to the world around you is our best suggestion.

2. Verbal Ability

An example of an ability needed in many positions is verbal or language ability. Verbal ability is, in brief, the ability to use and understand words. Vocabulary and grammar tests are typical measures of this ability. "Reading comprehension" or "paragraph interpretation" questions are common in many kinds of civil service tests. You are given a paragraph of written material and asked to find its central meaning.

3. Numerical Ability

Number skills can be tested by the familiar arithmetic problem, by checking paired lists of numbers to see which are alike and which are different, or by interpreting charts and graphs. In the latter test, a graph may be printed in the test booklet which you are asked to use as the basis for answering questions.

4. Observation

A popular test for law-enforcement positions is the observation test. A picture is shown to you for several minutes, then taken away. Questions about the picture test your ability to observe both details and larger elements.

5. Following Directions

In many positions in the public service, the employee must be able to carry out written instructions dependably and accurately. You may be given a chart with several columns, each column listing a variety of information. The questions require you to carry out directions involving the information given in the chart.

6. Skills and Aptitudes

Performance tests effectively measure some manual skills and aptitudes. When the skill is one in which you are trained, such as typing or shorthand, you can practice. These tests are often very much like those given in business school or high school courses. For many of the other skills and aptitudes, however, no short-time preparation can be made. Skills and abilities natural to you or that you have developed throughout your lifetime are being tested.

Many of the general questions just described provide all the data needed to answer the questions and ask you to use your reasoning ability to find the answers. Your best preparation for these tests, as well as for tests of facts and ideas, is to be at your physical and mental best. You, no doubt, have your own methods of getting into an exam-taking mood and keeping "in shape." The next section lists some ideas on this subject.

IV. KINDS OF QUESTIONS

Only rarely is the "essay" question, which you answer in narrative form, used in civil service tests. Civil service tests are usually of the short-answer type. Full instructions for answering these questions will be given to you at the examination. But in case this is your first experience with short-answer questions and separate answer sheets, here is what you need to know.

1. Multiple-Choice Questions

Most popular of the short-answer questions is the "multiple-choice" or "best-answer" question. It can be used, for example, to test for factual knowledge, ability to solve problems, or judgment in meeting situations found at work.

A multiple-choice question is normally one of three types:

(1) It can begin with an incomplete statement followed by several possible endings. You are to find the one ending which *best* completes the statement, although some of the others may not be entirely wrong.

(2) It can also be a complete statement in the form of a question which is answered by choosing one of the statements listed.

(3) It can be in the form of a problem -- again you select the best answer.

Here is an example of a multiple-choice question with a discussion which should give you some clues as to the method for choosing the right answer.

SAMPLE QUESTION:

When an employee has a complaint about his assignment, the action which will *best* help him overcome his difficulty is

(A) to discuss his difficulty with his co-workers
(B) to take the problem to the head of the organization
(C) to take the problem to the person who gave him the assignment
(D) to say nothing to anyone about his complaint

In answering this question you should study each of the choices to find which is best. Consider choice (A). Certainly an employee may discuss his complaint with fellow employees, but no change or improvement can result, and the complaint remains unsolved. Choice (B) is a poor choice since the head of the organization probably does not know what assignment you have been given, and taking your problem to him is known as "going over the head" of the supervisor. The supervisor, or person who made the assignment, is the person who can clarify it or correct any injustice. Choice (C) is, therefore, correct. To say nothing, as in choice (D), is unwise. Supervisors have an interest in knowing the problems employees are facing, and the employee is seeking a solution to his problem.

2. True-False Questions

The "true-false" or "right-wrong" form of question is sometimes used. Here a complete statement is given. Your problem is to decide whether the statement is right or wrong.

SAMPLE QUESTION:

A person-to-person long distance telephone call costs less than a station-to-station call to the same city.

This question is wrong, or "false," since person-to-person calls are more expensive.

This is not a complete list of all possible question forms, although most of the others are variations of these common types. You will always get complete directions for answering questions. Be sure you understand *how* to mark your answers -- ask questions until you do.

V. RECORDING YOUR ANSWERS

For an examination with very few applicants, you may be told to record your answers in the test booklet itself. Separate answer sheets are much more common. If this separate answer sheet is to be scored by machine -- and this is often the case -- it is highly important that you mark your answers correctly in order to get credit.

An electric test-scoring machine is often used in civil service offices because of the speed with which papers can be scored. Machine-scored answer sheets must be marked with a special pencil, which will be given to you. This pencil has a high graphite content which responds to the electrical scoring machine. As a matter of fact, stray dots may register as answers, so do not let your pencil rest on the answer sheet while you are pondering the correct answer. Also, if your pencil lead breaks or is otherwise defective, ask for another.

Since the answer sheet will be dropped in a slot in the scoring machine, be careful not to bend the corners or get the paper crumpled.

The answer sheet normally has five vertical columns of numbers, with 30 numbers to a column. These numbers correspond to the question numbers in your test booklet. After each number, going across the page, are four or five pairs of dotted lines. These short dotted lines have small letters or numbers above them. The first two pairs may also have a "T" and "F" above the letters. This indicates that the first two pairs only are to be used if the questions are of the true-false type. If the questions are multiple-choice, disregard this "T" and "F" completely, and pay attention only to the small number or letters.

Answer your questions in the manner of the sample that follows. Proceed in the sequential steps outlined below.

Assume that you are answering question 32, which is:
  32. The largest city in the United States is:
     A. Washington, D.C.   B. New York City   C. Chicago
     D. Detroit   E. San Francisco

1. Choose the answer you think is best.
   New York City is the largest, so choice B is correct.
2. Find the row of dotted lines numbered the same as the question you are answering.
   This is question number 32, so find row number 32.
3. Find the pair of dotted lines corresponding to the answer you have chosen.
   You have chosen answer B, so find the pair of dotted lines marked "B".
4. Make a solid black mark between the dotted lines.
   Go up and down two or three times with your pencil so plenty of graphite rubs off, but do not let the mark get outside or above the dots.

VI. BEFORE THE TEST

Common sense will help you find procedures to follow to get ready for an examination. Too many of us, however, overlook these sensible measures. Indeed, nervousness and fatigue have been found to be the most serious reasons why applicants fail to do their best on civil service tests. Here is a list of reminders.

1. Begin Your Preparation Early

   Don't wait until the last minute to go scurrying around for books and materials or to find out what the position is all about.

2. Prepare Continuously

   An hour a night for a week is better than an all-night cram session. This has been definitely established. What is more, a night a week for a month will return better dividends than crowding your study into a shorter period of time.

3. Locate the Place of the Examination

   You have been sent a notice telling you when and where to report for the examination. If the location is in a different town or otherwise unfamiliar to you, it would be well to inquire the best route and learn something about the building.

4. Relax the Night Before the Test

   Allow your mind to rest. Do not study at all that night. Plan some mild recreation or diversion; then go to bed early and get a good night's sleep.

5. Get Up Early Enough to Make a Leisurely Trip to the Place for the Test

   Then unforeseen events, traffic snarls, unfamiliar buildings, will not upset you.

6. Dress Comfortably

   A written test is not a fashion show. You will be known by number and not by name, so wear something comfortable.

7. Leave Excess Paraphernalia at Home

   Shopping bags and odd bundles will get in your way. You need bring only the items mentioned in the official notice sent to you; usually everything you need is provided. Do not bring reference books to the examination. They will only confuse those last minutes and be taken away from you when in the test room.

8. Arrive Somewhat Ahead of Time

   If because of transportation schedules you must get there very early, bring a newspaper or magazine to take your mind off yourself while waiting.

9. Locate the Examination Room

   When you have found the proper room, you will be directed to the seat or part of the room where you will sit. Sometimes you are given a sheet of instructions to read while you are waiting. Do not fill out any forms until you are told to do so; just read them and be ready.

10. Relax and Prepare to Listen to the Instructions

11. If you have any physical problem that may keep you from doing your best, be sure to tell the test administrator. If you are sick, or in poor health, you really cannot do your best on the test. You can come back and take the test some other time.

II. AT THE TEST

The day of the test is here and you have the test booklet in your hand. The temptation to get going is very strong. Caution! There is more to success than knowing the right answers. You must know how to identify your papers and understand variations in the type of short-answer question used in this particular examination. Follow these suggestions for maximum results from your efforts:

1. Cooperate with the Monitor

The test administrator has a duty to create a situation in which you can be as much at ease as possible. He will give instructions, tell you when to begin, check to see that you are marking your answer sheet correctly. He is not there to guard you, although he will see that your competitors do not take unfair advantage. He wants to help you do your best.

2. Listen to All Instructions

Don't jump the gun! Wait until you understand all directions. In most civil service tests you get more time than you need to answer the questions. So don't get in a hurry. Read each word of instructions until you clearly understand the meaning. Study the examples. Listen to all announcements. Follow directions. Ask questions if you do not understand what to do.

3. Identify Your Papers

Civil service examinations are usually identified by number only. You will be assigned a number; you must not put your name on your test papers. Be sure to copy your number correctly. Since more than one examination may be given, copy your exact examination title.

4. Plan Your Time

Unless you are told that a test is a "speed" or "rate-of-work" test, speed itself is not usually important. Time enough to answer all the questions will be provided. But this does not mean that you have all day. An overall time limit has been set. Divide the total time (in minutes) by the number of questions to get the approximate time you have for each question.

5. Do Not Linger Over Difficult Questions

If you come across a difficult question, mark it with a paper clip (useful to have along) and come back to it when you have been through the booklet. One caution if you do this -- be sure to skip a number on your answer sheet too. Check often to be sure that you have not lost your place and that you are marking in the row numbered the same as the question you are answering.

6. Read the Questions

Be sure you know what the question asks! Many capable people are unsuccessful because they failed to *read* the questions correctly.

7. Answer All Questions

Unless you have been instructed that a penalty will be deducted for incorrect answers, it is better to guess than to omit a question.

8. Speed Tests

It is often better *not* to guess on speed tests. It has been found that on timed tests people are tempted to spend the last few seconds before time is called in marking answers at random -- without even reading them -- in the hope of picking up a few extra points. To discourage this practice, the instructions may warn you that your score will be "corrected" for guessing. That is, a penalty will be applied. The incorrect answers will be deducted from the correct ones, or some other penalty formula will be used.

9. Review Your Answers

If you finish before time is called, go back to the questions you guessed or omitted to give further thought to them. Review other answers if you have time.

10. Return Your Test Materials

If you are ready to leave before others have finished or time is called, take *all* your materials to the monitor and leave quietly. Never take any test material with you. The monitor can discover whose papers are not complete, and taking a test booklet may be grounds for disqualification.

III. EXAMINATION TECHNIQUES

1. Read the *general* instructions carefully. These are usually printed on the first page of the examination booklet. As a rule, these instructions refer to the timing of the examination; the fact that you should not start work until the signal and must stop work at a signal, etc. If there are any *special* instructions, such as a choice of questions to be answered, make sure that you note this instruction carefully.

2. When you are ready to start work on the examination, that is as soon as the signal has been given, read the instructions to each question booklet, underline any key words or phrases, such as *least, best, outline, describe,* and the like. In this way you will tend to answer as requested rather than discover on reviewing your paper that you *listed without describing,* that you selected the *worst* choice rather than the *best* choice, etc.

3. If the examination is of the objective or so-called multiple-choice type, that is, each question will also give a series of possible answers: A, B, C, or D, and you are called upon to select the best answer and write the letter next to that answer on your answer paper, it is advisable to start answering each question in turn. There may be anywhere from 50 to 100 such questions in the three or four hours allotted and you can see how much time would be taken if you read through all the questions before beginning to answer any. Furthermore, if you come across a question or a group of questions which you know would be difficult to answer, it would undoubtedly affect your handling of all the other questions.

4. If the examination is of the esssay-type and contains but a few questions, it is a moot point as to whether you should read all the questions before starting to answer any one. Of course if you are given a choice, say five out of seven and the like, then it is essential to read all the questions so you can eliminate the two which are most difficult. If, however, you are asked to answer all the questions, there may be danger in trying to answer the easiest one first because you may find that you will spend too much time on it. The best technique is to answer the first question, then proceed to the second, etc.

5. Time your answers. Before the examination begins, write down the time it started, then add the time allowed for the examination and write down the time it must be completed, then divide the time available somewhat as follows:

(a) If $3\frac{1}{2}$ hours are allowed, that would be 210 minutes. If you have 80 objective-type questions, that would be an average of $2\frac{1}{2}$ minutes per question. Allow yourself no more than 2 minutes per question, or a total of 160 minutes, which will permit about 50 minutes to review.

(b) If for the time allotment of 210 minutes, there are 7 essay questions to answer, that would average about 30 minutes a question. Give yourself only 25 minutes per question so that you have about 35 minutes to review.

6. The most important instruction is *to read each question* and make sure you know what is wanted. The second most important instruction is to *time yourself properly* so that you answer every question. The third most important instruction is to *answer every question*. Guess if you have to but include something for each question. Remember that you will receive no credit for a blank and will probably receive some credit if you write something in answer to an essay question. If you guess a letter, say "B" for a multiple-choice question, you may have guessed right. If you leave a blank as the answer to a multiple-choice question, the examiners may respect your feelings but it will not add a point to your score.

7. Suggestions

   a. <u>Objective-Type Questions</u>

   (1) Examine the question booklet for proper sequence of pages and questions.
   (2) Read all instructions carefully.
   (3) Skip any question which seems too difficult; return to it after all other questions have been answered.
   (4) Apportion your time properly; do not spend too much time on any single question or group of questions.
   (5) Note and underline key words -- *all, most, fewest, least, best, worst, same, opposite*.
   (6) Pay particular attention to negatives.
   (7) Note unusual option, e.g., unduly long, short, complex, different or similar in content to the body of the question.
   (8) Observe the use of "hedging" words -- *probably, may, most likely, etc.*
   (9) Make sure that your answer is put next to the same number as the question.
   (10) Do not second-guess unless you have good reason to believe the second answer is definitely more correct.
   (11) Cross out original answer if you decide another answer is more accurate; do not erase.
   (12) Answer all questions; guess unless instructed otherwise.
   (13) Leave time for review.

   b. <u>Essay-Type Questions</u>

   (1) Read each question carefully.
   (2) Determine exactly what is wanted. Underline key words or phrases.
   (3) Decide on outline or paragraph answer.
   (4) Include many different points and elements unless asked to develop any one or two points or elements.
   (5) Show impartiality by giving pros and cons unless directed to select one side only.
   (6) Make and write down any assumptions you find necessary to answer the question.
   (7) Watch your English, grammar, punctuation, choice of words.
   (8) Time your answers; don't crowd material.

8. Answering the Essay Question

   Most essay questions can be answered by framing the specific response around several key words or ideas. Here are a few such key words or ideas:

M's: manpower, materials, methods, money, management;
P's: purpose, program, policy, plan, procedure, practice, problems, pitfalls, personnel, public relations.

  a. <u>Six Basic Steps in Handling Problems</u>:
     (1) Preliminary plan and background development
     (2) Collect information, data and facts
     (3) Analyze and interpret information, data and facts
     (4) Analyze and develop solutions as well as make recommendations
     (5) Prepare report and sell recommendations
     (6) Install recommendations and follow up effectiveness
  b. <u>Pitfalls to Avoid</u>
     (1) *Taking things for granted*
         A statement of the situation does not necessarily imply that each of the elements is necessarily true; for example, a complaint may be invalid and biased so that all that can be taken for granted is that a complaint has been registered.
     (2) *Considering only one side of a situation*
         Wherever possible, indicate several alternatives and then point out the reasons you selected the best one.
     (3) *Failing to indicate follow-up*
         Whenever your answer indicates action on your part, make certain that you will take proper follow-up action to see how successful your recommendations, procedures, or actions turn out to be.
     (4) *Taking too long in answering any single question*
         Remember to time your answers properly.

IX. AFTER THE TEST

Scoring procedures differ in detail among civil service jurisdictions although the general principles are the same. Whether the papers are hand-scored or graded by the electric scoring machine we have described, they are nearly always graded by number. That is, the person who marks the paper knows only the number -- never the name -- of the applicant. Not until all the papers have been graded will they be matched with names. If other tests, such as training and experience or oral interview ratings have been given, scores will be combined. Different parts of the examination usually have different weights. For example, the written test might count 60 percent of the final grade, and a rating of training and experience 40 percent. In many jurisdictions, veterans will have a certain number of points added to their grades.

After the final grade has been determined, the names are placed in grade order and an eligible list is established. There are various methods for resolving ties between those who get the same final grade: probably the most common is to place first the name of the person whose application was received first. Job offers are made from the eligible list in the order the names appear on it.

You will be notified of your grade and your rank order as soon as all these computations have been made. This will be done as rapidly as possible.

People who are found to meet the requirements in the announcement are called "eligibles." Their names are put on a list of eligibles. An eligible's chances of getting a job depend on how high he stands on this list and how fast agencies are filling jobs from the list.

When a job is to be filled from a list of eligibles, the agency asks for the names of people on the list of eligibles for that job.

When the civil service commission receives this request, it sends to the agency the names of the three people highest on the list. Or, if the job to be filled has specialized requirements, the office sends the agency, from the general list, the names of the top three persons who meet those requirements.

The appointing officer makes a choice from among the three people whose names were sent to him. If the selected person accepts the appointment, the names of the others are put back on the list to be considered for future openings.

That is the rule in hiring from all kinds of eligible lists, whether they are for typist, carpenter, chemist, or something else. For every vacancy, the appointing officer has his choice of any one of the top three eligibles on the list. This explains why the person whose name is on top of the list sometimes does not get an appointment when some of the persons lower on the list do. If the appointing officer chooses the No.2 or No.3 eligible, the No.1 eligible does not get a job at once, but stays on the list until he is appointed or the list is terminated.

X. HOW TO PASS THE INTERVIEW TEST

The examination for which you applied requires an oral interview test. You have already taken the written test and you are now being called for the interview test -- the final part of the formal examination.

You may think that it is not possible to prepare for an interview test and that there are no procedures to follow during an interview.

Our purpose is to point out some things you can do in advance that will help you and some good rules to follow and pitfalls to avoid while you are being interviewed.

A. *WHAT IS AN INTERVIEW SUPPOSED TO TEST?*

The written examination is designed to test the technical knowledge and competence of the candidate; the oral is designed to evaluate intangible qualities, not readily measured otherwise, and to establish a list showing the relative fitness of each candidate, *as measured against his competitors*, for the position sought. Scoring is not on the basis of "right" or "wrong," but on a sliding scale of values ranging from "not passable" to "outstanding." As a matter of fact, it is possible to achieve a relatively low score without a single "incorrect" answer because of evident weakness in the qualities being measured.

Occasionally, an examination may consist entirely of an oral test -- either an individual or a group oral. In such cases, information is sought concerning the technical knowledges and abilities of the candidate, since there has been no written examination for this purpose. More commonly, however, an oral test is used to supplement a written examination.

B. *WHO CONDUCTS INTERVIEWS?*

The composition of oral boards varies among different jurisdictions. In nearly all, a representative of the personnel department serves as chairman. One of the members of the board may be a representative of the department in which the candidate would work. In some cases, "outside experts" are used, and, frequently, a business man or some other representative of the general public is asked to serve. Labor and management or other special groups may be represented. The aim is to secure the services of experts in the appropriate field.

However the board is composed, it is a good idea (and not at all improper or unethical) to ascertain in advance of the interview who the members are and what groups they represent. When you are introduced to them, you will have some idea of their backgrounds and interests, and at least you will not stutter and stammer over their names.

C. WHAT TO DO BEFORE THE INTERVIEW

While knowledge about the board members is useful and takes some of the surprise element out of the interview, there is other preparation which is more substantive. It *is* possible to prepare for an oral -- in several ways:

1. Keep a Copy of Your Application and Review it Carefully Before the Interview

    This may be the only document before the oral board, and the starting point of the interview. Know what experience and education you have listed there, and the sequence and dates of it. Sometimes the board will ask *you* to review the highlights of your experience for them; you should not have to hem and haw doing it.

2. Study the Class Specification and the Examination Announcement

    Usually, the oral board has one or both of these to guide them. The qualities, characteristics, or knowledges required by the position sought are stated in these documents. They offer valuable clues as to the nature of the oral interview. For example, if the job involves supervisory responsibilities, the announcement will usually indicate that knowledge of modern supervisory methods and the qualifications of the candidate as a supervisor will be tested. If so, you can expect such questions, frequently in the form of a hypothetical situation which you are expected to solve. *Never* go into an oral without knowledge of the duties and responsibilities of the job you seek.

3. Think Through Each Qualification Required

    Try to visualize the kind of questions *you* would ask if you were a board member. How well could you answer them? Try especially to appraise your own knowledge and background in each area, *measured against the job sought*, and identify any areas in which you are weak. Be critical and realistic -- do not flatter yourself.

4. Do Some General Reading in Areas in Which You Feel You May be Weak

    For example, if the job involves supervision and your past experience has *not*, some general reading in supervisory methods and practices, particularly in the field of human relations, might be useful. *Do not* study agency procedures or detailed manuals. The oral board will be testing your understanding and capacity, *not* your memory.

5. Get a Good Night's Sleep and Watch Your General Health and Mental Attitude

    You will want a clear head at the interview. Take care of a cold or other minor ailment, and, of course, *no hangovers*.

D. WHAT TO DO THE DAY OF THE INTERVIEW

Now comes the day of the interview itself. Give yourself plenty of time to get there. Plan to arrive somewhat ahead of the scheduled time, particularly if your appointment is in the fore part of the day. If a previous candidate fails to appear, the board might be ready for you a bit early. By early afternoon an oral board is almost invariably behind schedule if there are many candidates, and you may have to wait. Take along a book or magazine to read, or your application to review. But leave any extraneous material in the waiting room when you go in for your interview. In any event, relax and compose yourself.

The matter of dress is important. The board is forming impressions about you -- from your experience, your manners, your attitudes, and from your appearance. Give your personal appearance careful attention. Dress your *best*, but not your flashiest. Choose conservative, appropriate clothing, and be sure it and you are immaculate. This is a business interview, and your appearance should indicate that you regard it as such. Besides, being well-groomed and properly dressed will help boost your confidence.

Sooner or later, someone will call your name and escort you into the interview room. *This is it.* From here on you are on your own. It is too late for any more preparation. But, remember, you asked for this opportunity to prove your fitness, and you are here because your request was granted.

E. WHAT HAPPENS WHEN YOU GO IN?

The usual sequence of events will be as follows: The clerk (who is often the board stenographer) will introduce you to the chairman of the oral board, who will introduce you to each other member of the board. Acknowledge the introductions before you sit down. Do not be surprised if you find a microphone facing you or a stenotypist sitting by. Oral interviews are usually recorded, in the event of an appeal or other review.

Usually the chairman of the board will open the interview by reviewing the highlights of your education and work experience from your application -- primarily for the benefit of the other members of the board, as well as to get the material into the record. Do not interrupt or comment unless there is an error or significant misinterpretation; if so, do not hesitate. But do not quibble about insignificant matters. Usually, also, he will ask you some question about your education, your experience, or your present job -- partly to get you started talking, to establish the interviewing "rapport." He may start the actual questioning, or turn it over to one of the other members. Frequently each member undertakes the questioning on a particular area, one in which he is perhaps most competent. So you can expect each member to participate in the examination. And because the time is limited, you may expect some rather abrupt switches in the direction the questioning takes. Do not be upset by it. Normally, a board member will not pursue a single line of questioning unless he discovers a particular strength or weakness.

After each member has participated, the chairman will usually ask whether any member has any further questions, then will ask you if you have anything you wish to add. Unless you are expecting this question, it may floor you. Or worse, it may start you off on an extended, extemporaneous speech. The board is not usually seeking more information. The question is principally to offer you a last opportunity to present further qualifications or to indicate that you have nothing to add. So, if you feel that a significant qualification or characteristic has been overlooked, it is proper to point it out in a sentence or so. Do not compliment the board on the thoroughness of their examination -- they have been sketchy, and you know it. If you wish, merely say, "No thank you, I have nothing further to add." This is a point where you can "talk yourself out" of a good impression or fail to present an important bit of information. *Remember, you close the interview yourself.*

The chairman will then say,"That is all, Mr. Smith, thank you." Do not be startled; the interview is over, and quicker than you think. Say,"Thank you and good morning," gather up your belongings and take your leave. Save your sigh of relief for the other side of the door.

F. HOW TO PUT YOUR BEST FOOT FORWARD

Throughout all this process, you may feel that the board individually and collectively is trying to pierce your defenses, to seek out your hidden weaknesses, and to embarrass and confuse you. Actually, this is not true. They are obliged to make an appraisal of your qualifications for the job you are seeking, and they *want to see you in your best light*. Remember, they must interview all candidates and a noncooperative candidate may become a failure in spite of their best efforts to bring out his qualifications. Here are fifteen(15) suggestions that will help you:

1. <u>Be Natural. Keep Your Attitude Confident, But Not Cocky</u>

If *you* are not confident that you can do the job, do not exexpect the *board* to be. Do not apologize for your weaknesses, try to bring out your strong points. The board is interested in a positive, not a negative presentation. Cockiness will antagonize any board member, and make him wonder if you are covering up a weakness by a false show of strength.

2. <u>Get Comfortable, But Don't Lounge or Sprawl</u>

Sit erectly but not stiffly. A careless posture may lead the board to conclude you are careless in other things, or at least that you are not impressed by the importance of the occasion to you. Either conclusion is natural, even if incorrect. Do not fuss with your clothing, or with a pencil or an ashtray. Your hands may occasionally be useful to emphasize a point; do not let them become a point of distraction.

3. <u>Do Not Wisecrack or Make Small Talk</u>

This is a serious situation, and your attitude should show that you consider it as such. Further, the time of the board is limited; they do not want to waste it, and neither should you.

4. <u>Do Not Exaggerate Your Experience or Abilities</u>

In the first place, from information in the application, from other interviews and other sources, the board may know more about you than you think; in the second place, you probably will not get away with it in the first place. An experienced board is rather adept at spotting such a situation. Do not take the chance.

5. <u>If You Know a Member of the Board, Do Not Make a Point of It, Yet Do Not Hide It.</u>

Certainly you are not fooling him, and probably not the other members of the board. Do not try to take advantage of your acquaintanceship -- it will probably do you little good.

6. <u>Do Not Dominate the Interview</u>

Let the board do that. They will give you the clues -- do not assume that you have to do all the talking. Realize that the board has a number of questions to ask you, and do not try to take up all the interview time by showing off your extensive knowledge of the answer to the first one.

7. <u>Be Attentive</u>

You only have twenty minutes or so, and you should keep your attention at its sharpest throughout. When a member is addressing a problem or a question to you, give him your undivided attention. Address your reply principally to him, but do not exclude the other members of the board.

8. <u>Do Not Interrupt</u>

A board member may be stating a problem for you to analyze. He will ask you a question when the time comes. Let him state the problem, and wait for the question.

9. <u>Make Sure You Understand the Question</u>

Do not try to answer until you are sure what the question is. If it is not clear, restate it in your own words or ask the board member to clarify it for you. But do not haggle about minor elements.

10. <u>Reply Promptly But Not Hastily</u>

A common entry on oral board rating sheets is "candidate responded readily," or "candidate hesitated in replies." Respond as promptly and quickly as you can, but do not jump to a hasty, ill-considered answer.

11. <u>Do Not Be Peremptory in Your Answers</u>

A brief answer is proper -- but do not fire your answer back. That is a losing game from your point of view. The board member can probably ask questions much faster than you can answer them.

12. <u>Do Not Try To Create the Answer You Think the Board Member Wants</u>

He is interested in what kind of mind you have and how it works -- not in playing games. Furthermore, he can usually spot this practice and will usually grade you down on it.

13. <u>Do Not Switch Sides in Your Reply Merely to Agree With a Board Member</u>

Frequently, a member will take a contrary position merely to draw you out and to see if you are willing and able to defend your point of view. Do not start a debate, yet do not surrender a good position. If a position is worth taking, it is worth defending.

14. <u>Do Not Be Afraid to Admit an Error in Judgment if You Are Shown to Be Wrong</u>

The board knows that you are forced to reply without any opportunity for careful consideration. Your answer may be demonstrably wrong. If so, admit it and get on with the interview.

15. <u>Do Not Dwell at Length on Your Present Job</u>

The opening question may relate to your present assignment. Answer the question but do not go into an extended discussion. You are being examined for a *new* job, not your present one. As a matter of fact, try to phrase *all* your answers in terms of the job for which you are being examined.

G. BASIS OF RATING

Probably you will forget most of these "do's" and "don'ts" when you walk into the oral interview room. Even remembering them all will not insure you a passing grade. Perhaps you did not have the qualifications in the first place. But remembering them *will* help you to put your best foot forward, without treading on the toes of the board members.

Rumor and popular opinion to the contrary notwithstanding, an oral board wants you to make the best appearance possible. They know you are under pressure -- but they also want to see how you respond to it as a guide to what your reaction would be under the pressures of the job you seek. They will be influenced by the degree of poise you display, the **personal traits you show**, and the manner in which you respond.

EXAMINATION SECTION

EXAMINATION SECTION

DIRECTIONS: Each question or incomplete statement is followed by several suggested answers or completions. Select the one that BEST answers the question or completes the statement. *PRINT THE LETTER OF THE CORRECT ANSWER IN THE SPACE AT THE RIGHT.*

1. Physical and mental health are essential to the officer. According to this statement, the officer MUST be
   A. as wise as he is strong
   B. smarter than most people
   C. sound in mind and body
   D. stronger than the average criminal

   1.___

2. Teamwork is the basis of successful law enforcement. The factor stressed by this statement is
   A. cooperation   B. determination
   C. initiative   D. pride

   2.___

3. Legal procedure is a means, not an end. Its function is merely to accomplish the enforcement of legal rights. A litigant has no vested interest in the observance of the rules of procedure as such. All that he should be entitled to demand is that he be given an opportunity for a fair and impartial trial of his case. He should not be permitted to invoke the aid of technical rules merely to embarrass his adversary.
   According to this paragraph, it is MOST correct to state that
   A. observance of the rules of procedure guarantees a fair trial
   B. embarrassment of an adversary through technical rules does not make a fair trial
   C. a litigant is not interested in the observance of rules of procedure
   D. technical rules must not be used in a trial

   3.___

4. One theory states that all criminal behavior is taught by a process of communication within small intimate groups. An individual engages in criminal behavior if the number of criminal patterns which he has acquired exceed the number of non-criminal patterns.
   This statement indicates that criminal behavior is
   A. learned   B. instinctive
   C. hereditary   D. reprehensible

   4.___

5. The law enforcement staff of today requires training and mental qualities of a high order. The poorly or partially prepared staff member lowers the standard of work, retards his own earning power, and fails in a career meant to provide a livelihood and social improvement.

   5.___

According to this statement,
- A. an inefficient member of a law enforcement staff will still earn a good livelihood
- B. law enforcement officers move in good social circles
- C. many people fail in law enforcement careers
- D. persons of training and ability are essential to a law enforcement staff

6. In any state, no crime can occur unless there is a written law forbidding the act or the omission in question, and even though an act may not be exactly in harmony with public policy, such act is not a crime unless it is expressly forbidden by legislative enactment.
   According to the above statement,
   - A. a crime is committed with reference to a particular law
   - B. acts not in harmony with public policy should be forbidden by law
   - C. non-criminal activity will promote public welfare
   - D. legislative enactments frequently forbid actions in harmony with public policy

7. The unrestricted sale of firearms is one of the main causes of our shameful crime record.
   According to this statement, one of the causes of our crime record is
   - A. development of firepower
   - B. ease of securing weapons
   - C. increased skill in using guns
   - D. scientific perfection of firearms

8. Every person must be informed of the reason for his arrest unless he is arrested in the actual commission of a crime. Sufficient force to effect the arrest may be used, but the courts frown on brutal methods.
   According to this statement, a person does NOT have to be informed of the reason for his arrest if
   - A. brutal force was not used in effecting it
   - B. the courts will later turn the defendant loose
   - C. the person arrested knows force will be used if necessary
   - D. the reason for it is clearly evident from the circumstances

9. An important duty of an officer is to keep order in the court.
   On the basis of this statement, it is PROBABLY true that
   - A. it is more important for an officer to be strong than it is for him to be smart
   - B. people involved in court trials are noisy if not kept in check
   - C. not every duty of an officer is important
   - D. the maintenance of order is important for the proper conduct of court business

10. Ideally, a correctional system should include several types of institutions to provide different degrees of custody.
    On the basis of this statement, one could MOST reasonably say that
    A. as the number of institutions in a correctional system increases, the efficiency of the system increases
    B. the difference in degree of custody for the inmate depends on the types of institutions in a correctional system
    C. the greater the variety of institutions, the stricter the degree of custody that can be maintained
    D. the same type of correctional institution is not desirable for the custody of all prisoners

10.___

11. The enforced idleness of a large percentage of adult men and women in our prisons is one of the direct causes of the tensions which burst forth in riot and disorder.
    On the basis of this statement, a GOOD reason why inmates should perform daily work of some kind is that
    A. better morale and discipline can be maintained when inmates are kept busy
    B. daily work is an effective way of punishing inmates for the crimes they have committed
    C. law-abiding citizens must work, therefore, labor should also be required of inmates
    D. products of inmates' labor will in part pay the cost of their maintenance

11.___

12. With industry invading rural areas, the use of the automobile, and the speed of modern communications and transportation, the problems of neglect and delinquency are no longer peculiar to cities but an established feature of everyday life.
    This statement implies MOST directly that
    A. delinquents are moving from cities to rural areas
    B. delinquency and neglect are found in rural areas
    C. delinquency is not as much of a problem in rural areas as in cities
    D. rural areas now surpass cities in industry

12.___

13. Young men from minority groups, if unable to find employment, become discouraged and hopeless because of their economic position and may finally resort to any means of supplying their wants.
    The MOST reasonable of the following conclusions that may be drawn from this statement only is that
    A. discouragement sometimes leads to crime
    B. in general, young men from minority groups are criminals
    C. unemployment turns young men from crime
    D. young men from minority groups are seldom employed

13.___

14. To prevent crime, we must deal with the possible criminal long before he reaches the prison. Our aim should be not merely to reform the law breakers but to strike at the roots of crime: neglectful parents, bad companions, unsatisfactory homes, selfishness, disregard for the rights of others, and bad social conditions.
    The above statement recommends
    A. abolition of prisons   B. better reformatories
    C. compulsory education   D. general social reform

15. There is evidence which shows that comic books which glorify the criminal and criminal acts have a distinct influence in producing young criminals.
    According to this statement,
    A. comic books affect the development of criminal careers
    B. comic books specialize in reporting criminal acts
    C. young criminals read comic books exclusively
    D. young criminals should not be permitted to read comic books

16. Suppose a study shows that juvenile delinquents are equal in intelligence but three school grades behind juvenile non-delinquents.
    On the basis of this information only, it is MOST reasonable to say that
    A. a delinquent usually progresses to the educational limit set by his intelligence
    B. educational achievement depends on intelligence only
    C. educational achievement is closely associated with delinquency
    D. lack of intelligence is closely associated with delinquency

17. There is no proof today that the experience of a prison sentence makes a better citizen of an adult. On the contrary, there seems some evidence that the experience is an unwholesome one that frequently confirms the criminality of the inmate.
    From the above paragraph only, it may be BEST concluded that
    A. prison sentences tend to punish rather than rehabilitate
    B. all criminals should be given prison sentences
    C. we should abandon our penal institutions
    D. penal institutions are effective in rehabilitating criminals

18. Some courts are referred to a *criminal* courts while others are known as *civil* courts.
    This distinction in name is MOST probably based on the
    A. historical origin of the court
    B. link between the court and the police
    C. manner in which the judges are chosen
    D. type of cases tried there

19. Many children who are exposed to contacts and experiences of a delinquent nature become educated and trained in crime in the course of participating in the daily life of the neighborhood.
    From this statement only, we may reasonably conclude that
    A. delinquency passes from parent to child
    B. neighborhood influences are usually bad
    C. schools are training grounds for delinquents
    D. none of the above conclusions is reasonable

20. Old age insurance, for whose benefits a quarter of a million city employees may elect to become eligible, is one feature of the Social Security Act that is wholly administered by the Federal government.
    On the basis of this paragraph only, it may MOST reasonably be inferred that
    A. a quarter of a million city employees are drawing old age insurance
    B. a quarter of a million city employees have elected to become eligible for old age insurance
    C. the city has no part in administering Social Security old age insurance
    D. only the Federal government administers the Social Security Act

21. An officer's revolver is a defensive, and not offensive, weapon.
    On the basis of this statement only, an officer should BEST draw his revolver to
    A. fire at an unarmed burglar
    B. force a suspect to confess
    C. frighten a juvenile delinquent
    D. protect his own life

22. Prevention of crime is of greater value to the community than the punishment of crime.
    If this statement is accepted as true, GREATEST emphasis should be placed on
    A. malingering   B. medication
    C. imprisonment   D. rehabilitation

23. The criminal is rarely or never reformed.
    Acceptance of this statement as true would mean that GREATEST emphasis should be placed on
    A. imprisonment   B. parole
    C. probation   D. malingering

24. The MOST accurate of the following statements about persons convicted of crimes is that
    A. their criminal behavior is almost invariably the result of low intelligence
    B. they are almost invariably legally insane
    C. they are more likely to come from underprivileged groups than from other groups
    D. they have certain facial characteristics which distinguish them from non-criminals

25. Suppose a study shows that the I.Q. (Intelligence Quotient) 25.____
of prison inmates is 95 as opposed to an I.Q. of 100 for a
numerically equivalent civilian group.
A claim, on the basis of this study, that criminals have a
lower I.Q. than non-criminals would be
   A. *improper*; prison inmates are criminals who have been
      caught
   B. *proper*; the study was numerically well done
   C. *improper*; the sample was inadequate
   D. *proper*; even misdemeanors are sometimes penalized by
      prison sentences

Questions 26-45.

DIRECTIONS: Select the letter of the word or expression that MOST
NEARLY expresses the meaning of the capitalized word
in the group.

26. ABDUCT 26.____
    A. lead   B. kidnap   C. sudden   D. worthless

27. BIAS 27.____
    A. ability   B. envy   C. prejudice   D. privilege

28. COERCE 28.____
    A. cancel   B. force   C. rescind   D. rugged

29. CONDONE 29.____
    A. combine   B. pardon   C. revive   D. spice

30. CONSISTENCY 30.____
    A. bravery   B. readiness   C. strain   D. uniformity

31. CREDENCE 31.____
    A. belief   B. devotion   C. resemblance D. tempo

32. CURRENT 32.____
    A. backward   B. brave   C. prevailing   D. wary

33. CUSTODY 33.____
    A. advisement   B. belligerence
    C. guardianship   D. suspicion

34. DEBILITY 34.____
    A. deceitfulness   B. decency
    C. strength   D. weakness

35. DEPLETE 35.____
    A. beg   B. empty   C. excuse   D. fold

36. ENUMERATE 36.____
    A. name one by one   B. disappear
    C. get rid of   D. pretend

37. FEIGN
    A. allow   B. incur   C. pretend   D. weaken   37.___

38. INSTIGATE
    A. analyze   B. coordinate   C. oppose   D. provoke   38.___

39. LIABLE
    A. careless   B. growing   C. mistaken   D. responsible   39.___

40. PONDER
    A. attack   B. heavy   C. meditate   D. solicit   40.___

41. PUGILIST
    A. farmer   B. politician
    C. prize fighter   D. stage actor   41.___

42. QUELL
    A. explode   B. inform   C. shake   D. suppress   42.___

43. RECIPROCAL
    A. mutual   B. organized   C. redundant   D. thoughtful   43.___

44. RUSE
    A. burn   B. impolite   C. rot   D. trick   44.___

45. STEALTHY
    A. crazed   B. flowing   C. sly   D. wicked   45.___

Questions 46-50.

DIRECTIONS: Each of the sentences numbered 46 to 50 may be classified under one of the following four categories:
A. faulty because of incorrect grammar
B. faulty because of incorrect punctuation
C. faulty because of incorrect capitalization or incorrect spelling
D. correct

Examine each sentence carefully to determine under which of the above four options it is best classified. Then, in the corresponding space at the right, write the letter preceding the option which is the BEST of the four suggested above. Each faulty sentence contains but one type of error. Consider a sentence to be correct if it contains none of the types of errors mentioned, even though there may be other correct ways of expressing the same thought.

46. They told both he and I that the prisoner had escaped.   46.___

47. Any superior officer, who, disregards the just complaints of his subordinates, is remiss in the performance of his duty.   47.___

48. Only those members of the national organization who resided in the Middle west attended the conference in Chicago.   48.___

49. We told him to give the investigation assignment to   49._____
    whoever was available.

50. Please do not disappoint and embarass us by not appearing   50._____
    in court.

51. Suppose a man falls from a two-story high scaffold and is   51._____
    unconscious.
    You should
       A. call for medical assistance and avoid moving the man
       B. get someone to help you move him indoors to a bed
       C. have someone help you walk him around until he revives
       D. hold his head up and pour a stimulant down his throat

52. For proper first aid treatment, a person who has fainted   52._____
    should be
       A. doused with cold water and then warmly covered
       B. given artificial respiration until he is revived
       C. laid down with his head lower than the rest of his
          body
       D. slapped on the face until he is revived

53. If you are called on to give first aid to a person who is   53._____
    suffering from shock, you should
       A. apply cold towels   B. give him a stimulant
       C. keep him awake   D. wrap him warmly

54. Artificial respiration would NOT be proper first aid for   54._____
    a person suffering from
       A. drowning   B. electric shock
       C. external bleeding   D. suffocation

55. Suppose you are called on to give first aid to several   55._____
    victims of an accident.
    FIRST attention should be given to the one who is
       A. bleeding severely   B. groaning loudly
       C. unconscious   D. vomiting

56. If an officer's weekly salary is increased from $400.00   56._____
    to $450.00, then the percent of increase is _____ percent.
       A. 10   B. 11 1/9   C. $12\frac{1}{2}$ D. 20

57. Suppose that one-half the officers in a department have   57._____
    served for more than ten years, and one-third have served
    for more than 15 years.
    Then, the fraction of officers who have served between
    ten and fifteen years is
       A. 1/3   B. 1/5   C. 1/6   D. 1/12

58. In a city prison, there are four floors on which prisoners   58._____
    are housed. The top floor houses one-quarter of the in-
    mates, the bottom floor houses one-sixth of the inmates,
    one-third are housed on the second floor. The rest of the
    inmates are housed on the third floor.
    If there are 90 inmates housed on the third floor, the
    total number of inmates housed on all four floors together is
       A. 270   B. 360   C. 450   D. 540

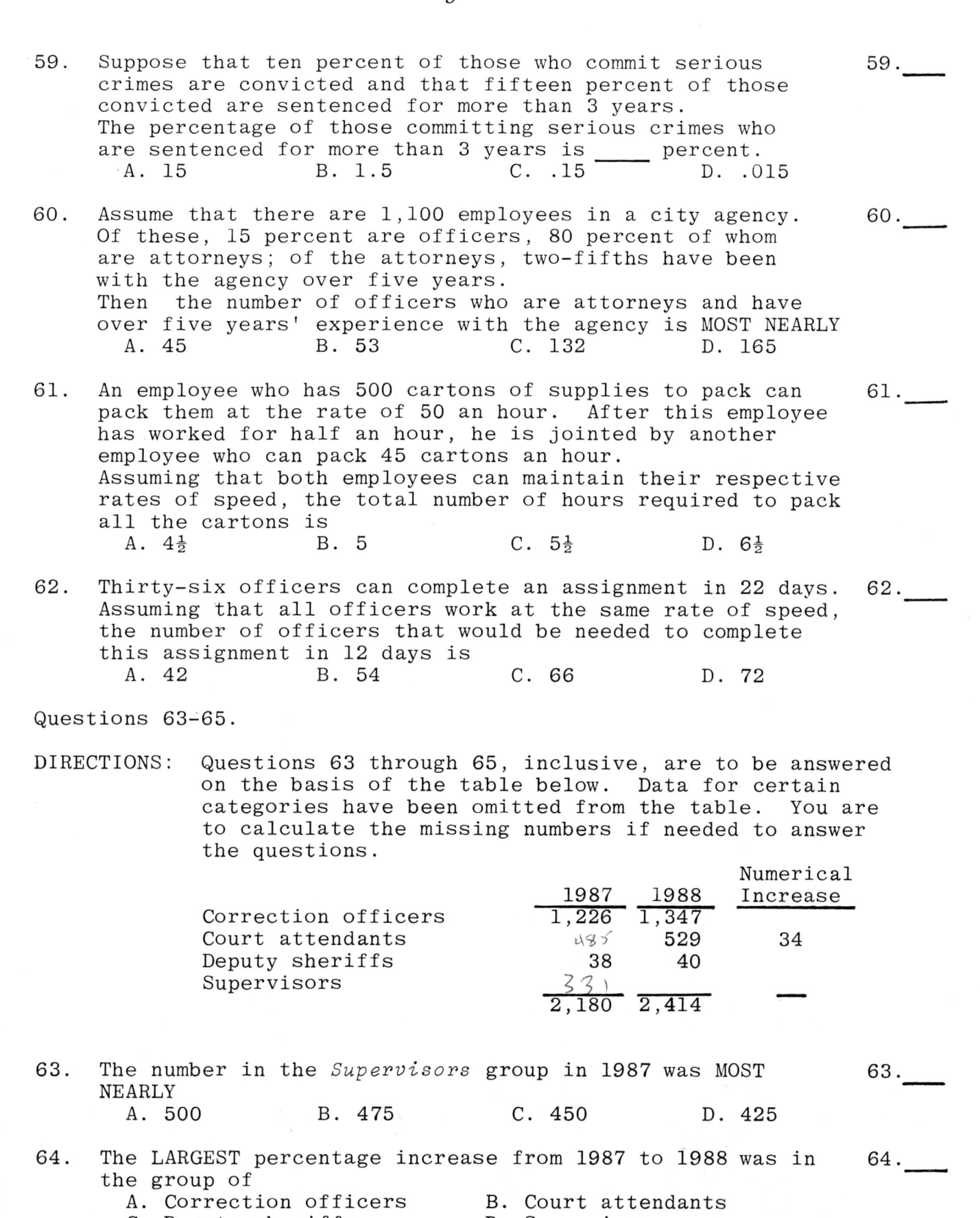

59. Suppose that ten percent of those who commit serious crimes are convicted and that fifteen percent of those convicted are sentenced for more than 3 years.
The percentage of those committing serious crimes who are sentenced for more than 3 years is ____ percent.
   A. 15   B. 1.5   C. .15   D. .015

60. Assume that there are 1,100 employees in a city agency. Of these, 15 percent are officers, 80 percent of whom are attorneys; of the attorneys, two-fifths have been with the agency over five years.
Then the number of officers who are attorneys and have over five years' experience with the agency is MOST NEARLY
   A. 45   B. 53   C. 132   D. 165

61. An employee who has 500 cartons of supplies to pack can pack them at the rate of 50 an hour. After this employee has worked for half an hour, he is jointed by another employee who can pack 45 cartons an hour.
Assuming that both employees can maintain their respective rates of speed, the total number of hours required to pack all the cartons is
   A. 4½   B. 5   C. 5½   D. 6½

62. Thirty-six officers can complete an assignment in 22 days. Assuming that all officers work at the same rate of speed, the number of officers that would be needed to complete this assignment in 12 days is
   A. 42   B. 54   C. 66   D. 72

Questions 63-65.

DIRECTIONS: Questions 63 through 65, inclusive, are to be answered on the basis of the table below. Data for certain categories have been omitted from the table. You are to calculate the missing numbers if needed to answer the questions.

	1987	1988	Numerical Increase
Correction officers	1,226	1,347	
Court attendants	485	529	34
Deputy sheriffs	38	40	
Supervisors	331		
	2,180	2,414	—

63. The number in the *Supervisors* group in 1987 was MOST NEARLY
   A. 500   B. 475   C. 450   D. 425

64. The LARGEST percentage increase from 1987 to 1988 was in the group of
   A. Correction officers   B. Court attendants
   C. Deputy sheriffs   D. Supervisors

65. In 1988, the ratio of the number of Correction officers to the total of the other three categories of employees was MOST NEARLY
    A. 1:1　　　B. 2:1　　　C. 3:1　　　D. 4:1

66. A directed verdict is made by a court when
    A. the facts are not disputed
    B. the defendant's motion for a directed verdict has been denied
    C. there is no question of law involved
    D. neither party has moved for a directed verdict

67. Papers on appeal of a criminal case do NOT include one of the following:
    A. Summons
    B. Minutes of trial
    C. Complaint
    D. Intermediate motion papers

68. A pleading titled *Smith vs. Jones, et al.* indicates
    A. two plaintiffs
    B. two defendants
    C. more than two defendants
    D. unknown defendants

69. A District Attorney makes a *prima facie* case when
    A. there is proof of guilt beyond a reasonable doubt
    B. the evidence is sufficient to convict in the absence of rebutting evidence
    C. the prosecution presents more evidence than the defense
    D. the defendant fails to take the stand

70. A person is NOT qualified to act as a trial juror in a criminal action if he or she
    A. has been convicted previously of a misdemeanor
    B. is under 18 years of age
    C. has scruples against the death penalty
    D. does not own property of a value at least $500

71. A court clerk who falsifies a court record commits a(n)
    A. misdemeanor
    B. offense
    C. felony
    D. no crime, but automatically forfeits his tenure

72. Insolent and contemptuous behavior to a judge during a court of record proceeding is punishable as
    A. civil contempt
    B. criminal contempt
    C. disorderly conduct
    D. a disorderly person

73. Offering a bribe to a court clerk would not constitute a crime UNLESS the
    A. court clerk accepted the bribe
    B. bribe consisted of money
    C. bribe was given with intent to influence the court clerk in his official functions
    D. court was actually in session

74. A defendant comes to trial in the same court in which he had previously been defendant in a similar case.
The court officer should
   A. tell him, *knew we'd be seeing you again*
   B. tell newspaper reporters what he knows of the previous action
   C. treat him the same as he would any other defendant
   D. warn the judge that the man had previously been a defendant

74.___

75. Suppose in conversation with you, an attorney strongly criticizes a ruling of the judge, and you believe the attorney to be correct.
You should
   A. assure him you feel the same way
   B. tell him the judge knows the law
   C. tell him to ask for an exception
   D. refuse to discuss the matter

75.___

76. Suppose a doorman refuses to admit you to an apartment house in which you are attempting to serve a process on a tenant.
Of the following, the BEST action for you to take is to
   A. bribe the doorman to admit you
   B. discard the process since it cannot be served
   C. gain entrance by force
   D. report the matter to your superior

76.___

77. False arrest is an offense for which the deputy sheriff may be held liable.
Therefore, before making an arrest, the deputy sheriff should
   A. be sure a witness is present
   B. be sure it is legal
   C. seek assistance from a patrolman
   D. deputize a private citizen

77.___

78. An arrested person should not be transported upon a public conveyance such as a streetcar, subway, or bus, except in an extreme emergency.
The reason for this regulation is MOST probably the
   A. danger of escape   B. embarrassment to the prisoner
   C. expense involved   D. possible delays

78.___

79. Except in rare emergencies, a deputy should not attempt to make an arrest without a partner.
The BEST reason for this is that the partner may be needed to
   A. arbitrate the matter
   B. lend prestige to the sheriff's office
   C. overcome resistance
   D. provide company for the deputy

79.___

80. At the end of each month, the deputy sheriff must submit   80.____
to his superior officer an activity report covering the
status of his assignments and the extent of his activities
in the service of process during the month.
It is MOST important that such report be
A. accurate   B. brief
C. grammatically correct D. lengthy

81. Deputies are required to hold seized chattels for three   81.____
days after service of the replevin papers. This means
three full 24-hour days, exclusive of the day of service,
and the property should not be turned over earlier than
12:01 A.M. on the fourth day. When one day of the period
falls on a Sunday or a public holiday, that day is
excluded and an additional day must be added to make up
the three.
According to this statement only, if service of replevin
papers is made on Thursday, June 23rd, the property should
be turned over on
A. Sunday, June 26th   B. Monday, June 27th
C. Tuesday, June 28th   D. Wednesday, June 29th

82. Certain property is declared by law to be exempt from   82.____
seizure to satisfy a debt because it is of importance to
the comfort of the family, although of small money value.
On the basis of this law, which of the following would you
MOST expect to be exempt from seizure?
A. Broadloom rug   B. Dining table
C. Marble statuette   D. Modern painting

83. As a general rule, a deputy sheriff is justified in   83.____
refusing to seize an article which differs from the description in the replevin papers, unless the difference is
clearly unimportant in the light of other identifying facts.
According to this statement, which of the following would
a deputy sheriff BEST be justified in seizing where there
is a difference from the description in the papers?
A(n)
A. automobile corresponding in make, year, model, and
   engine number, but differing in color
B. sofa corresponding in upholstery material, color,
   width, and height, but differing in length
C. television set corresponding in year, model, and size
   of screen, but differing in number of tubes required
D. typewriter corresponding in year, model, size of type,
   and color, but differing in name of manufacturer

84. The legal aspect of the sheriff's duties is emphasized by 84.____
his unique personal liability, not only for his own acts
and omissions, but also for those of any deputy or employee
in his office.
According to the foregoing quotation, it would be MOST
correct to state that the sheriff
A. and his employees have unique legal duties to perform
B. is held responsible for actions taken by his subordinates
C. is liable for the acts of his employees only under
   unique circumstances
D. must personally serve many legal papers

85. Which one of the following descriptions of a defendant would help MOST in identifying him?
    A. Age - 31 years; weight - 168 pounds
    B. At time of escape was wearing gray hat, dark overcoat
    C. Deep scar running from left ear to chin
    D. Height - 5 feet, 9 inches; complexion - sallow

86. Which of the following could a deputy sheriff BEST accept as proof of a man's identity?
    A. A personal letter
    B. Automobile driver's license
    C. Automobile registration certificate
    D. Social security card

87. It was formerly the practice to require someone who knew the defendant by sight to accompany the deputy sheriff. It has been learned through experience that the value of such identification is over-rated.
    From this paragraph only, it may be BEST inferred that
    A. circumstantial evidence is not reliable
    B. identifications are sometimes inaccurate
    C. people are usually for the underdog
    D. testimony is often contradictory

88. The depositions must set forth the facts tending to establish that an illegal act was committed and that the defendant is guilty.
    According to this statement only, the one of the following which need NOT be included in a deposition is evidence that establishes the
    A. fact that an illegal act was committed
    B. fact that defendant committed the illegal act
    C. guilt of the defendant
    D. method of commission of the illegal act

89. Each deputy sheriff should understand how his own work helps to accomplish the purpose of the entire agency.
    This statement means MOST NEARLY that the deputy sheriff should understand the
    A. efficiency of a small agency
    B. importance of his own job
    C. necessity for initiative
    D. value of a large organization

90. When X is accused of having cheated Y of a sum of money and Y is proven to have been deprived of the money, there is an additional requirement for a verdict against X.
    The additional requirement is to prove that
    A. the money was stolen from Y
    B. X had the money after Y had it
    C. X had the money before Y had it
    D. X cheated Y of the money

91. To gain a verdict against X in a trial, it was necessary   91.___
    to show that he could have been at Y Street at 5 P.M.
    It was proven that he was seen at Z Street at 4:45 P.M.
    The question that MUST be answered to show whether X is
    guilty is:
    A. How long does it take to get from Z Street to Y Street?
    B. In what sort of neighborhood is Z Street located?
    C. Was X acting suspiciously on the day in question?
    D. Who was with X when he was seen at Z Street at 4:45 P.M.?

92. The deputy sheriff must give the defendant reasonable   92.___
    time to secure the bail fixed in the process before
    confining him to jail.
    The CHIEF purpose of bail is to
    A. permit personnel to act as bondsmen
    B. permit the defendant his liberty while assuring his
       presence at the trial
    C. raise additional money for the general fund of the
       city treasury
    D. relieve the city of the necessity of bringing the
       defendant before a judge

93. When a jury is selected, the attorney for each side has   93.___
    a right to refuse to accept a certain number of prospective
    jurors without giving any reason therefor.
    The reason for this is MAINLY that
    A. attorneys can exclude persons likely to be biased
       even though no prejudice is admitted
    B. persons who will suffer economically by being summoned
       for jury duty can be excused forthwith
    C. relatives of the litigants can be excused, thus
       insuring a fair trial for each side
    D. there will be a greater number of people from which
       the jury can be selected, thus insuring better quality

94. Suppose a deputy sheriff, feeling that the verdict against   94.___
    a judgment debtor was unfair, permits him to escape.
    On the basis of this information only, it is safe to
    assume that the
    A. judge passing sentence was unduly harsh
    B. judgment debtor had possession of a large sum of money
    C. deputy sheriff was recently appointed
    D. deputy sheriff used poor judgment

95. A deputy sheriff shall not receive a gift from any defen-   95.___
    dant or other person on the defendant's behalf.
    The BEST explanation for this departmental rule is that
    A. acceptance of a gift has no significance
    B. favors may be expected in return
    C. gifts are only an expression of good will
    D. litigants cannot usually afford gifts

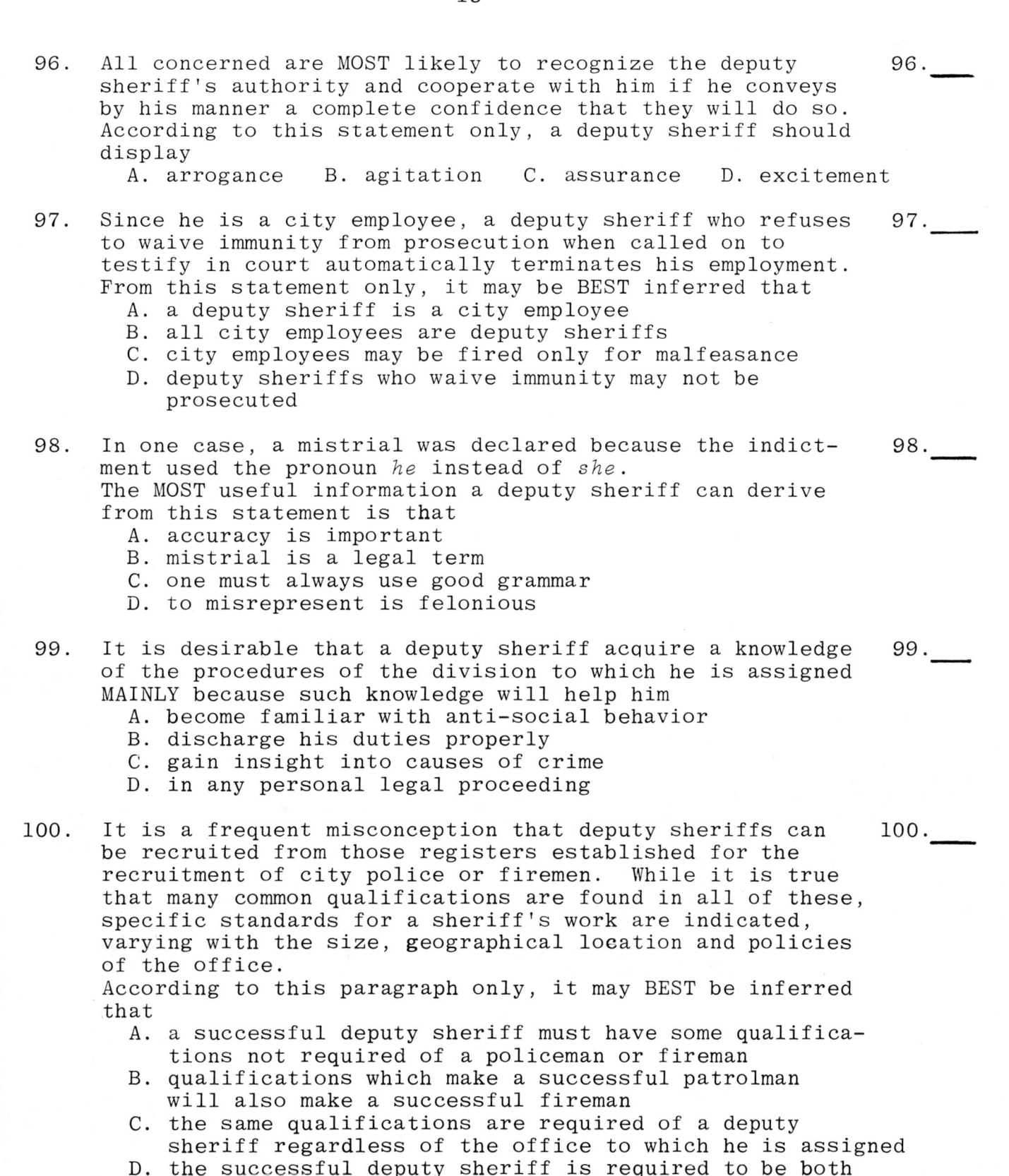

96. All concerned are MOST likely to recognize the deputy sheriff's authority and cooperate with him if he conveys by his manner a complete confidence that they will do so. According to this statement only, a deputy sheriff should display
   A. arrogance   B. agitation   C. assurance   D. excitement

97. Since he is a city employee, a deputy sheriff who refuses to waive immunity from prosecution when called on to testify in court automatically terminates his employment. From this statement only, it may be BEST inferred that
   A. a deputy sheriff is a city employee
   B. all city employees are deputy sheriffs
   C. city employees may be fired only for malfeasance
   D. deputy sheriffs who waive immunity may not be prosecuted

98. In one case, a mistrial was declared because the indictment used the pronoun *he* instead of *she*.
   The MOST useful information a deputy sheriff can derive from this statement is that
   A. accuracy is important
   B. mistrial is a legal term
   C. one must always use good grammar
   D. to misrepresent is felonious

99. It is desirable that a deputy sheriff acquire a knowledge of the procedures of the division to which he is assigned MAINLY because such knowledge will help him
   A. become familiar with anti-social behavior
   B. discharge his duties properly
   C. gain insight into causes of crime
   D. in any personal legal proceeding

100. It is a frequent misconception that deputy sheriffs can be recruited from those registers established for the recruitment of city police or firemen. While it is true that many common qualifications are found in all of these, specific standards for a sheriff's work are indicated, varying with the size, geographical location and policies of the office.
   According to this paragraph only, it may BEST be inferred that
   A. a successful deputy sheriff must have some qualifications not required of a policeman or fireman
   B. qualifications which make a successful patrolman will also make a successful fireman
   C. the same qualifications are required of a deputy sheriff regardless of the office to which he is assigned
   D. the successful deputy sheriff is required to be both more intelligent and stronger than a fireman

KEY (CORRECT ANSWERS)

1. C	26. B	51. A	76. D
2. A	27. C	52. C	77. B
3. B	28. B	53. D	78. A
4. A	29. B	54. C	79. C
5. D	30. D	55. A	80. A
6. A	31. A	56. C	81. C
7. B	32. C	57. C	82. B
8. D	33. C	58. B	83. A
9. D	34. D	59. B	84. B
10. D	35. B	60. B	85. C
11. A	36. A	61. C	86. B
12. B	37. C	62. C	87. B
13. A	38. D	63. D	88. D
14. D	39. D	64. D	89. B
15. A	40. C	65. A	90. D
16. C	41. C	66. A	91. A
17. A	42. D	67. D	92. B
18. D	43. A	68. C	93. A
19. D	44. D	69. B	94. D
20. C	45. C	70. B	95. B
21. D	46. A	71. C	96. C
22. D	47. B	72. B	97. A
23. A	48. C	73. C	98. A
24. C	49. D	74. C	99. B
25. A	50. C	75. D	100. A

SOLUTIONS TO PROBLEMS

56. CORRECT ANSWER: C
Increase = $10.00 ($90.00 - $80.00 = $10.00)

∴ $\frac{\$10}{\$80} = \frac{1}{8} = 12\frac{1}{2}\%$

57. CORRECT ANSWER: C
1/2 + 1/3 = 3/6 + 2/6 = 5/6

∴ 1 - 5/6 = 1/6

58. CORRECT ANSWER: B
1/4 + 1/6 + 1/3 = 3/12 + 2/12 + 4/12 = 9/12 = 3/4

∴ 1 - 3/4 = 1/4 (rest of inmates housed on the third floor)
Since 90 = 1/4, therefore, 4/4 (or 1) = 360.

59. CORRECT ANSWER: B
.10 × .15 = .0150 = 1.5%

60. CORRECT ANSWER: B
Step (1)   1100
           × .15
           ─────
           5500
           1100
           ──────
           165.00 (peace officers)

Step (2)   165
            ×.80
            ─────
            132.00 (attorneys)

Step (3) 132 × 2/5 = 264/5 = 52.8 (peace officers who are
          attorneys and have over five years' experience
          with the agency)

61. CORRECT ANSWER: C
Since the first employee worked for ½ hour, he packed 25 cartons (50 ÷ 2). This leaves 475 cartons to be packed. This first employee packs at the rate of 50 an hour. The second employee, who joins him after ½ hour, packs at the rate of 45 an hour.
50 + 45 = 95 (rate of both employees together)
∴ 475 ÷ 95 = 5 hours (time it takes both employees together)
5 hours + ½ hour = 5½ hours

62. CORRECT ANSWER: C
x:36 = 22:12
12 × x = 36 × 22
    12x = 792
      x = 66

EXAMINATION SECTION

TEST 1

DIRECTIONS: Each question or incomplete statement is followed by several suggested answers or completions. Select the one that BEST answers the question or completes the statement. *PRINT THE LETTER OF THE CORRECT ANSWER IN THE SPACE AT THE RIGHT.*

1. In pleading equitable estoppel, which one of the following is NOT a necessary element?
   A. Deliberate intent on the part of the defendant to mislead the plaintiff
   B. Words or acts of the defendant relied upon by the plaintiff
   C. Reliance by the plaintiff upon the words or acts of the defendant
   D. Change of position by the plaintiff to his injury

2. A motion to dismiss a complaint for legal insufficiency
   A. if granted is res judicata and precludes the losing party from amending his pleadings
   B. may only be made by the defendant before he answers the summons and complaint
   C. may be made either before or after the service of a responsive pleading by either plaintiff or defendant
   D. may be followed by motions to dismiss on grounds other than legal insufficiency, such as release, Statute of Limitations or Statute of Frauds

3. Attachment of a non-domiciliary's property in the State, in a dispute NOT arising concerning that property, gives the courts
   A. in personam jurisdiction over the defendant
   B. quasi-in-rem jurisdiction
   C. in rem jurisdiction
   D. jurisdiction only in matrimonial actions for support

4. Upon the service of a notice for an examination before trial,
   A. a court on motion or on its own initiative may issue a protective order
   B. a non-party witness must appear on the specified date and produce all records in his possession that might have a bearing on the case
   C. any error or irregularity in the notice makes it a nullity
   D. on election the person served may refuse to appear without a confirming court order

5. A and B through their combined negligence in operating their respective vehicles crash and injure C. If C sues A but not B,
   A. A may implead B
   B. A may move to dismiss on the basis that a necessary party has not been joined
   C. A may, if C obtains a judgment from him, sue B for contribution
   D. A has no remedy against B under the stated circumstances

6. Which one of the following statements concerning equity is INCORRECT?
   A. Generally, equity will not intervene if the plaintiff has an adequate remedy at law.
   B. Injunctive relief is an equitable remedy.
   C. If plaintiff elects to sue in equity, he is deemed to have waived any claim for money damages
   D. Restrictive covenants may be enforced in equity.

7. If a judgment creditor files a writ of execution with the sheriff in New York County on a judgment docketed in New York County, the sheriff may levy on all
   A. property in the judgment debtor's possession
   B. personal or real property that is not exempt or subject to perfected security interests or prior liens belonging to the judgment debtor which is in New York County
   C. personal or real property that is not exempt or subject to perfected security interests or prior liens belonging to the judgment debtor wherever it is located
   D. real or personal property belonging to the judgment debtor which is neither exempt nor subject to perfected security interests or prior liens that can be found anywhere in New York State

8. A warrant of arrest has been properly issued to insure the presence of John Roe as a witness at a departmental trial in a city agency. The warrant is issued on June 1. The trial is scheduled for June 4. The MOST appropriate day to make the arrest would be
   A. as soon as possible after June 1
   B. on June 4, if possible
   C. on June 3, if possible
   D. when it is most convenient for the Sheriff's office

9. Upon receipt of an order of civil arrest, the deputy sheriff checked the office file and found that there was a prior order of arrest which had never been executed. Of the following, the one which would NOT be an appropriate course of action for the deputy is to
   A. execute the earlier order of arrest
   B. execute the later order of arrest
   C. execute the earlier order and file a detainer for the later one with the warden of the jail
   D. call counsel for the plaintiff in that action to ascertain the status of the earlier order

10. An order for the civil arrest of John P. Doe is delivered to the Sheriff's office. A photograph of Mr. Doe accompanies the papers. Upon arriving at the home of Mr. Doe, the deputy sheriff finds that there are two men living together: John P. Doe and John Q. Doe. The photograph is that of John Q. Doe. Which of the following is the LEAST appropriate course of action for the deputy to follow?
    A. Arrest John Q. Doe
    B. Take no immediate arrest, but call the attorney for the plaintiff for instructions
    C. Suggest that both men accompany him to the Sheriff's office, if they are willing, to clarify the situation
    D. Arrest both men

11. Executing an order of civil arrest, the deputy sheriff is told by the defendant's wife that the defendant is recuperating from a severe heart attack and is therefore too ill to be moved. The FIRST step which should be taken is to
    A. arrest the defendant
    B. communicate with the attorney for the plaintiff and tell him the facts
    C. call a local hospital and request that a doctor come over and examine the defendant
    D. postpone the execution of the order of arrest for seventy-two hours

12. A deputy sheriff has a proper order for the civil arrest of John Doe. To effect the arrest, the deputy is authorized to
    A. break into Doe's home, if he is certain that Doe is there
    B. break into a warehouse where Doe is working
    C. shoot Doe if, after being arrested, Doe breaks away from the deputy
    D. chase Doe down the street and, if Doe gets inside his house, to break in and arrest Doe in the house

13. While taking Baker to the civil jail in the City, Deputy Sheriff Doe negligently injures Baker. The following are liable to Baker for the negligence of Doe:
    A. Doe and the State
    B. Doe and the Sheriff of the City
    C. only the Sheriff of the City
    D. only Doe

14. An attorney delivers to the Sheriff's office an income execution which states the name of the judgment debtor's employer, but does not state how much money the judgment debtor earns from that employer. The MOST appropriate action which the Sheriff's office should take is to
    A. serve the income execution upon the judgment debtor with a direction that he is expected to pay 10% of his wages to the Sheriff, as those wages are earned
    B. serve the income execution upon the judgment debtor's employer with a direction that he must withhold from the debtor's wages 10% thereof and remit the money to the Sheriff

C. apprise the judgment creditor's attorney that the income execution is defective in form and suggest that the attorney include therein the amount of money which the judgment debtor is expected to earn
D. ignore the income execution as defective in form and wait for an inquiry from the attorney as to why it has not been served

15. Armed with a proper order of civil arrest and all other necessary papers for the arrest of John Doe, a deputy sheriff enters Doe's apartment with the permission of Mrs. Doe. A man, believed by the deputy to be John Doe, is asleep upon the couch in the living room. The deputy states to Mrs. Doe: "I have an order for the arrest of your husband. Consider him under arrest." Mrs. Doe replies: "That man on the couch is my brother, Richard. My husband John is not here."
Which of the following persons now has a cause of action for false arrest?
A. John Doe
B. Richard
C. Mrs. Doe
D. None of the foregoing

16. An order of civil arrest, which states that it is issued in an action for fraud and deceit, is signed for the arrest of "Alex Smith." The only identification which the deputy sheriff has is a badly faded picture of Alex Smith. Taking it to the home of Alex Smith, the deputy sheriff knocks on the door. A woman answers and identifies herself as Alex Smith. Which of the following is NOT an appropriate course of action for the deputy to take?
A. The deputy, upon assuring himself that the woman is the Alex Smith intended to be named in the order, may arrest her
B. The deputy may contact the attorney for the plaintiff to ascertain who Alex Smith is
C. If the attorney for the plaintiff is unavailable, the deputy may contact the plaintiff himself to ascertain who Alex Smith is
D. If it is too late to contact anyone, the deputy may leave without arresting anyone

17. In an action for damages based upon fraud, a defendant who has been arrested
A. may be released upon bail only in the discretion of the court
B. may be released upon bail only after he has served three days in jail
C. may have the order of arrest vacated as unauthorized in an action for fraud
D. has an absolute right to post bail for his release

18. John Doe works as a bank messenger for the Acme Bank in Manhattan. Doe lives in Nassau county. Peters has obtained a judgment against Doe in the Supreme Court, Queens County. Peters now delivers an income execution to the Sheriff's office UNLESS
    A. Peters has already tried unsuccessfully to execute against personal property owned by Doe, the income execution is unauthorized
    B. Peters has already tried unsuccessfully to execute against real property owned by Doe, the income execution is unauthorized
    C. Doe earns in excess of thirty dollars per week, his salary is exempt from an income execution
    D. Doe earns in excess of eighty-five dollars per week, his salary is exempt from an income execution

19. In the preceding question, the appropriate Sheriff's office for Peters to deliver the income execution to would be located in
    A. Nassau County   B. New York County
    C. either Nassau or New York County
    D. any county of the state

Questions 20-25.
DIRECTIONS: Assume the following set of facts for questions 20-25.

Abel commences an action against Dunn in the Supreme Court, Erie County, on January 10, 1982. Baker commences his action against Dunn in Supreme Court, Orange County, on January 20, 1982.

On January 30, 1982, Charles, who also intends to sue Dunn, obtains an order of attachment from the Supreme Court, Bronx County. The same day, levying under this order, a deputy sheriff (1) leaves a copy of the order of attachment and all necessary papers with Dunn's employer; and (2) leaves a copy of the order of attachment and all necessary papers with the person managing "Blackacre," Dunn's palatial summer estate in Jefferson County.

On February 10, 1982, Dunn, who is a resident of Queens County, was properly served with a summons at his home in Charles' action.

On November 2, 1984, the jury in Baker's action returned a verdict in Baker's favor. On November 10, 1984, the jury in Charles' action returned a verdict in Charles' favor. On November 20, 1984, the jury in Abel's action returned a verdict in Abel's favor.

On December 1, 1984, Charles entered and docketed his judgment in the office of the clerk of Bronx County, and on the same afternoon docketed it by transcript in Queens County. On December 10, 1984 Abel entered and docketed his judgment in the office of the clerk of Erie County. On December 21, 1984, Baker entered and docketed his judgment in the office of the clerk of Orange County.

20. Who has FIRST lien on Blackacre?
    A. Abel   B. Baker   C. Charles
    D. None of the foregoing

21. With respect to Dunn's employer, Charles
    A. obtained a lien on January 30, 1982 on 10% of all income which Dunn would thereafter earn from his employer
    B. obtained no lien of any kind on the income which Dunn would earn from his employer
    C. would have obtained a lien on 10% of Dunn's income if the deputy had delivered the order of attachment to Dunn instead of to the employer
    D. has first lien on Dunn's income, but the lien becomes effective only on December 1, 1984

22. With respect to executing upon Charles' judgment of December 1, 1984, Charles' judgment may be satisfied
    A. by levying upon a car owned by Dunn and garaged in Manhattan
    B. only out of the sale of Blackacre
    C. only out of the income Dunn earns from his employer
    D. only out of the sale of Blackacre and the income Dunn earns

23. Without any further procedural steps, Abel may immediately deliver an execution to the sheriff of
    A. Queens County only
    B. Jefferson County only
    C. neither Queens County nor Jefferson County
    D. both Queens County and Jefferson County

24. Assume further that Abel dockets his judgment on August 1, 1985 in Jefferson County. Baker does the same on August 14, 1985, and Charles does it on September 1, 1985. If Charles then delivers an execution to the Sheriff of Jefferson County on January 10, 1986 and if the Sheriff notifies Abel and Baker who deliver similar executions to him on January 20, 1986, the proceeds of the sale of Blackacre will
    A. be prorated equally among Abel, Baker and Charles
    B. go to Charles first; then to Abel; the balance to Baker
    C. go to Charles first; the balance to be prorated between Abel and Baker
    D. go to none of the foregoing

25. If Dunn had sold Blackacre on October 1, 1984, to Y a *bona fide* purchaser for value ignorant of the pending litigations,
    A. Abel could reach Blackacre on execution
    B. Baker could reach Blackacre on execution
    C. both Abel and Baker could reach Blackacre on execution
    D. neither Abel nor Baker could reach Blackacre on execution

KEY (CORRECT ANSWERS)

1.	A		11.	B
2.	C		12.	B
3.	B		13.	B
4.	A		14.	C
5.	A		15.	D
6.	C		16.	A
7.	B		17.	D
8.	B		18.	D
9.	B		19.	A
10.	D		20.	D

21. B
22. A
23. D
24. D
25. D

TEST 2

DIRECTIONS: Each question or incomplete statement is followed by several suggested answers or completions. Select the one that BEST answers the question or completes the statement. *PRINT THE LETTER OF THE CORRECT ANSWER IN THE SPACE AT THE RIGHT.*

1. An attorney delivers a property execution to the Sheriff's office with a direction that it be immediately returned unsatisfied since the attorney has already ascertained that the judgment debtor has no property. The BEST course of action for the sheriff is to
    A. comply with the attorney's request
    B. mail the execution to the judgment debtor's home
    C. mail the execution to the judgment debtor's place of business
    D. make a bona fide attempt to locate the judgment debtor and demand that he pay the judgment

   1. ...

2. Pursuant to an order of attachment, a deputy sheriff has levied upon a Rolls-Royce automobile which, the plaintiff says, belongs to the defendant. Defendant denies that the automobile is his. The automobile has been stored in X's warehouse. Of the following courses of action, the one which would NOT be appropriate is to
    A. publish a notice in the New York Law Journal that the automobile is in storage and inviting the true owner to come forward
    B. get the plaintiff and X to agree that plaintiff will be solely responsible for the storage charges
    C. get the plaintiff's lawyer and X to agree that the lawyer will be solely responsible for the storage charges
    D. get an agreement from the plaintiff's lawyer that he will indemnify the Sheriff in the event the Sheriff is held responsible for the storage charges

   2. ...

3. Assume that in the preceding question, the attorney agrees to advance the foreseeable storage charges. The recommended period of storage for which advance payment should be exacted is
    A. no more than three months   B. no more than six months
    C. at least six months   D. at least a year

   3. ...

4. A deputy sheriff, who has been levying under an order of attachment against John Doe, reads in a trade journal that Doe has filed a petition for bankruptcy. Of the following courses of action, the one which would NOT be appropriate is for the deputy to
    A. continue to levy upon Doe's assets as they are found
    B. call his superiors and notify them of the bankruptcy

   4. ...

    C. notify the plaintiff's attorney of the bankruptcy
    D. seek to determine whether the John Doe he read about is the same John Doe who is the defendant

5. Seeking to make a levy under an order of attachment, a deputy sheriff finds the defendant in possession of a new Cadillac automobile, which the defendant asserts belongs to his brother. The defendant, however, has no registration for the automobile, asserting that the registration is with his brother. Of the following courses of action, the one which would NOT be appropriate is to
    A. drive with the defendant to his brother's house to check the registration
    B. obtain the consent of the plaintiff to let the defendant keep the automobile
    C. levy upon the automobile, if no immediate proof of ownership is available
    D. desist from levying on the auto if no immediate proof of ownership is available

6. In the preceding question, assume that it is proven that the automobile belongs to the defendant, but there is a security interest filed by the Ace Finance Company. Then the automobile may
    A. not be levied on
    B. be levied upon and the purchaser at the eventual execution sale will obtain a clear and free title
    C. be levied upon and the purchaser at the eventual execution sale will obtain a title which is subject to the filed security interest of the Ace Finance Company
    D. be levied upon but the Ace Finance Company may not buy it at eventual execution sale

Questions 7-13.
DIRECTIONS: In questions 7 through 13, select the BEST option.

7. An execution against Doe has been delivered to the Sheriff's office. Doe is found to possess a pawn ticket for a rare Stradivarius violin worth $2,500.00 which he pledged for $50.00.
    A. The court may permit the execution sale of the violin, even though it remains in the custody of the pawnbroker.
    B. The violin may not be sold upon execution unless it is first taken from the pawnbroker.
    C. If Doe is a professional violinist, the violin may not be sold upon execution.
    D. The violin may be sold upon execution only if the pawn ticket can be seized to prevent its negotiation.

8. A judgment has been obtained against John Doe, the president 8. ...
of a corporation. Although an income execution was properly
served upon Doe, he has refused to pay any of his salary to
the Sheriff. A deputy has now been sent to serve the income
execution upon the corporation. In the circumstances,
   A. the deputy must serve the execution upon John Doe as
      president of the corporation
   B. although the deputy may serve any officer of the cor-
      poration, the better practice is to serve John Doe as
      president
   C. if possible, the deputy should serve some other officer
      of the corporation
   D. preferred practice is simply to mail the income execu-
      tion to the corporation

9. Peters obtains a judgment against Doe on June 1. On 9. ...
June 10, Peters learns that Doe, who has been in financial
difficulties, intends to make an assignment for the benefit
of creditors. On June 11, Peters delivers an execution to
the sheriff. On June 15, Doe makes the assignment, in writing,
to X for the benefit of all of Doe's creditors. In the circumstances,
   A. the sheriff may not levy under Peters' execution
   B. the sheriff may levy under Peters' execution and sell
      Doe's property, but must hold the proceeds for the
      benefit of all Doe's creditors
   C. the sheriff may levy under Peters' execution and sell
      the property for the benefit of Peters
   D. the assignment for the benefit of creditors is void
      since no court approval was obtained for it

10. Before the commencement of an action by Peters against 10. ...
Doe, Doe transfers substantial amounts of stocks and bonds
to his wife. This is done as a gift, though it is apparent
that Doe did it to defeat any judgment which Peters might
obtain. Doe continues to control the stocks and bonds.
Peters has now obtained a judgment against Doe and has de-
livered an execution to the sheriff. In the circumstances,
   A. the stocks and bonds may not be levied upon
   B. the stocks and bonds may be levied upon, but only after
      a court has declared the transfer to Doe's wife to be
      fraudulent
   C. if the deputy is convinced that the transfer was
      fraudulent, he should on his own authority proceed to
      levy on the stocks and bonds
   D. if the deputy believes that the transfer was fraudulent,
      the better practice is to refer the question to his super-
      ior who may authorize the levy if there is convincing
      evidence that the transfer was fraudulent

11. An order of attachment has been signed in an action against 11. ...
Doe. Plaintiff's attorney notifies a deputy sheriff that
Smith owes Doe $5,000 which Smith has borrowed from Doe.
In the circumstances,
    A. Smith's debt may be levied upon by serving a copy of
       the order of attachment upon Smith
    B. Smith's debt to Doe may not be levied upon
    C. if Smith's debt is not presently due but is certain
       to become due within six months, it may not be levied
       upon
    D. Smith's debt may be levied upon only if there is a
       negotiable instrument representing the debt

12. An order of attachment has been signed in an action against 12. ...
Doe. Investigation discloses that a friend of Doe named
George has two automobiles belonging to Doe. On June 1,
a deputy sheriff delivers a copy of the order of attachment
to George. In the circumstances,
    A. no valid levy was made on June 1, because no
       automobile was physically seized
    B. no valid levy was made on June 1, unless a special
       order of the court was obtained to dispense the deputy
       sheriff from physically seizing the automobiles
    C. a valid levy was made on June 1, when the order of
       attachment and Sheriff's form S-30 were left with George
    D. a valid levy was made on June 1, and nothing further
       need be done to reduce the automobiles to possession un-
       til the lawsuit is over

13. In the preceding question, assume that a proper levy was 13. ...
made on June 1. Assume further that another of Doe's
automobiles is delivered to George thereafter. In the circumstances, the third automobile
    A. is subject to the levy of June 1 if the automobile
       comes into George's possession on or before November 1,
       even though George delivered the first two auto-
       mobiles to the Sheriff on July 1
    B. cannot be subjected to levy unless there is a new ser-
       vice of the order of attachment upon George
    C. is subject to the levy of June 1 if it comes into
       George's possession within 120 days after June 1
    D. is subject to the levy of June 1 if it comes into
       George's possession within 90 days after June 1,
       and George still has undisputed possession of the first
       two automobiles

14. Doe is the life beneficiary, along with his three brothers, 14. ...
of a trust set up by his father. Doe receives $500.00 per
month from the trust. The Acme Bank is serving as trustee.
Peters has a judgment against Doe. The PROPER way in which
to levy upon Doe's interest in the trust is to
    A. serve the appropriate papers upon Peters
    B. serve the appropriate papers upon the Acme Bank
    C. serve the appropriate papers upon one of Doe's
       brothers
    D. file the papers with the State Dept. of Trusts

15. In the preceding question,
    A. Doe has no interest in the trust which may be levied upon
    B. Doe's entire interest in the trust may be levied upon
    C. 10% of the income earned by Doe from the trust is exempt from levy
    D. 90% of the income earned by Doe from the trust is exempt from levy

16. An order of attachment has been signed in an action against Doe. Investigation reveals that Doe owns 500 shares of IBM stock; the stock certificates are in a safe deposit box in the Acme Bank. The stock may be levied upon by serving the appropriate papers upon
    A. Doe, although the stock certificates are in a safe deposit box in the Acme Bank
    B. the president of IBM Corporation
    C. the Acme Bank which has the certificates and then taking possession of the certificates
    D. the Secretary of State

17. An order of attachment has been signed in an action against Doe. A friend of Doe's is known to possess much valuable property belong to Doe. The order of attachment and the other appropriate papers are served upon the friend on June 1. The friend must then serve upon the Sheriff's office a statement of the property he possesses within
    A. 10 days   B. 15 days   C. 30 days   D. 90 days

18. In the preceding question, the Sheriff's office will send the statement to
    A. the court where the action is pending
    B. the defendant
    C. the plaintiff's attorney
    D. other judgment creditors of Doe

19. Referring back to question 17, which of the following would NOT be an appropriate course of action to follow in the 90-day period after June 1?
    A. The Sheriff may seize all of Doe's property in the friend's possession
    B. The plaintiff may obtain an order extending the 90-day period
    C. The plaintiff may commence a special proceeding to compel the friend to deliver the property to the Sheriff
    D. The Sheriff may commence a special proceeding to compel the friend to deliver the property to the Sheriff

20. In which of the following cases may a deputy sheriff make 20. ...
    a constructive seizure of property simply by leaving the
    appropriate papers with the person in possession of the pro-
    perty? When he is levying
    A. upon personal property capable of delivery, under a
       writ of execution
    B. upon personal property capable of delivery, under an
       order of attachment
    C. under a proper requisition to replevy
    D. under a writ of execution for the delivery of possession
       of a chattel

21. A deputy sheriff has been sent to a warehouse to actually 21. ...
    seize property in execution of a judgment. Upon entering
    the warehouse, he is shown an office with a glass door in-
    side of which is located the property the deputy wants. To
    make a PROPER levy, the deputy
    A. need only peer through the glass door
    B. does not have to enter the office but need only say:
       "That property is now subject to a levy."
    C. must enter the office and touch the property
    D. must enter the office, view the property and have it
       under his immediate ability to control

22. Assuming that the deputy sheriff is certain that the de- 22. ...
    fendant has property, in which of the following cases may
    the deputy break and enter in order to seize the property?
    A. When the property is in the defendant's home
    B. When the property is in the defendant's locker at work
    C. When the property is in a hotel room where the defen-
       dant has been living
    D. In none of the foregoing cases

23. After an order of attachment is signed against Doe, a 23. ...
    deputy sheriff learns that Doe's automobile is in Joe's
    Garage for repairs. Although the deputy presents the ne-
    cessary attachment papers, Joe's Garage is reluctant to re-
    lease the automobile until its repair bill is paid. Which
    of the following courses of action would be LEAST appro-
    priate?
    A. The sheriff may seize and remove the car over the ob-
       jection of Joe's Garage
    B. The sheriff may persuade the plaintiff to pay the
       garage bill
    C. The deputy may persuade the garage to surrender the
       automobile by advising the garage owner that his
       rights will be fully protected
    D. The deputy may persuade the plaintiff's attorney to
       permit a constructive seizure of the car in the hope
       that the case may be settled within 90 days thereafter

24. On September 1, 1978, Peters entered and docketed in Kings County a judgment against Doe. An execution was returned unsatisfied since Doe had no assets in Kings. In January, 1986, Peters learns that Doe had inherited a house worth $60,000 in Kings upon the death of his father in 1984. Peters immediately sends an execution to the sheriff. Of the following, the MOST accurate statement is that the 24. ...
    A. house may not be levied on and sold because Peters has no lien thereon
    B. sheriff may now proceed to sell the house
    C. sheriff must file with the clerk of Kings County a notice describing the judgment, the execution, and the house
    D. buyer at the execution sale will take whatever title and interest Doe had as of January, 1986

25. John Doe bought a house for $50,000 by paying $20,000 in cash and by executing a bond and mortgage to the Acme Bank for $30,000. Eight years later John Doe fell upon hard times and could not pay the mortgage. Acme Bank sued Doe on the bond and got a money judgment for $25,000, the amount then due on the bond and mortgage. Which of the following properties CANNOT be sold in execution of Acme's judgment? 25. ...
    A. Doe's house
    B. Doe's interest in a joint bank account held with his wife
    C. Doe's automobile which he uses to get to and from work
    D. Doe's interest in a boat which he jointly owns with his brother

KEY (CORRECT ANSWERS)

1.	D	11.	A
2.	A	12.	C
3.	C	13.	D
4.	A	14.	A
5.	D	15.	D
6.	C	16.	C
7.	A	17.	A
8.	C	18.	C
9.	C	19.	D
10.	D	20.	B

21.	D
22.	B
23.	A
24.	B
25.	A

TEST 3

DIRECTIONS: Each question or incomplete statement is followed by several suggested answers or completions. Select the one that BEST answers the question or completes the statement. *PRINT THE LETTER OF THE CORRECT ANSWER IN THE SPACE AT THE RIGHT.*

1. The ABC Finance Company intends to bring an action to replevy an automobile which it had sold to John Doe but upon which Doe had failed to make the necessary payments. On December 1, counsel for the Finance Company, without a court order, sends a requisition and the other appropriate papers to the sheriff's office directing the sheriff to seize the automobile before the action is commenced. The APPROPRIATE course of action for the sheriff's office to follow is to
   A. seize the car, but only if it can be found on a public street
   B. seize the car, no matter where it is found, if it can be done without breaking and entering
   C. seize the car, no matter where it is found, even if the sheriff has to break and enter to get the car
   D. apprise counsel for the Finance Company that a court order is required to authorize the seizure of the car

2. A properly issued requisition in a replevin case requires the sheriff to seize a Magnavox television set with a serial number: Q-4289J. Upon arriving at the defendant's home an Admiral television with serial number Q-69452, is the only one found. Which of the following courses of action would be LEAST appropriate? To
   A. ascertain from the defendant whether he ever bought a television from the plaintiff and, if it appears that the Admiral television is the only set he ever bought from plaintiff, to seize it
   B. call the plaintiff's attorney and ask for a clarification
   C. seize the Admiral television because that is the only one found on the premises
   D. leave the defendant's home and return the requisition to the plaintiff's attorney with an explanation as to why it was not executed

3. Defendant purchased a dishwasher from plaintiff and then installed it in his apartment in such a fashion that it became a fixture. It would require major carpentry to remove the dishwasher and to repair the area where the dishwasher had been installed. In an action of replevin, the sheriff is served with a properly issued requisition for the dishwasher. Upon arrival at defendant's home, a deputy discovers that the dishwasher has been installed as described. Which of the following courses of action would be MOST appropriate?
   A. The deputy may pull out the dishwasher and leave the defendant to repair the damage
   B. Without checking with the plaintiff, the deputy may pull out the dishwasher and leave the plaintiff to pay the damage

C. The deputy may seal the dishwasher and direct the defendant to hold on to it "for the account of the plaintiff"
D. Refrain from seizure of the dishwasher since replevin does not lie for fixtures

4. Plaintiff has commenced an action to replevy certain rare wood from the defendant. Pursuant to a properly issued requisition for the wood, a deputy sheriff arrives at defendant's home only to find that the defendant has used the wood to make a magnificent piano. Which of the following statements is TRUE?
   A. Plaintiff is not entitled to replevy the piano.
   B. Plaintiff may replevy the piano, but the deputy should not seize it pursuant to the requisition unless it is specifically described as a piano.
   C. The deputy should seize the piano, although the requisition mentions only wood.
   D. Wood is not the proper subject of a replevin action.

5. After the defendant has appeared in a replevin action, a proper set of papers is delivered to the sheriff requiring the seizure of the chattel. Unless the court orders otherwise, a set of all the papers must be served upon the
   A. defendant in the same manner as a summons
   B. defendant's attorney
   C. defendant's attorney, only if the attorney is in possession of the chattel being replevied
   D. defendant's attorney, only if the defendant is in possession of the chattel

6. Pursuant to a proper set of papers, a deputy sheriff seizes a chattel in a replevin action. The seizure occurs at 2:00 p.m. on Monday, December 14. Before he can deliver the chattel to the plaintiff, the sheriff must wait until
   A. Friday, December 18   B. Thursday, December 17
   C. Wednesday, December 16   D. Tuesday, December 15

7. Pursuant to a proper order of attachment, defendant's automobile is levied upon while it is in a parking lot. The parking lot owner has been served with the correct papers. Which of the following statements is TRUE?
   A. The automobile must be removed from the parking lot within 60 days.
   B. The automobile may be left in the parking lot despite the objections of the parking lot owner, so long as the plaintiff agrees to pay the necessary expenses.
   C. With the consent of the parking lot owner, the car may be left in the parking lot and the plaintiff will pay the parking lot owner's fee.
   D. The automobile may not be left in the parking lot longer than it takes to find another place to store it.

8. When real property is to be sold in execution of a judgment, notice of the sale must be posted in at least three places AT LEAST
   A. 60 days prior to the sale   B. 90 days prior to the sale
   C. 46 days prior to the sale   D. 56 days prior to the sale

3. (#3)

9. When personal property is to be sold in execution of a judgment, notice of the sale must be posted in at least three places AT LEAST
   A. 6 days prior to the sale B. 9 days prior to the sale
   C. 30 days prior to the sale D. 60 days prior to the sale

10. The sheriff intends to sell a parcel of land in execution of a money judgment against its owner. Which of the following is correct?
    A. The sheriff may negotiate a private sale to a customer to whom the land has peculiar value, so long as the sheriff receives a better price than a public auction would have yielded
    B. The sheriff must sell only at a public auction
    C. The sheriff may sell at either a public auction or a private negotiation, so long as he acts in good faith
    D. The sheriff may sell at either a public auction or a private negotiation, so long as he has the permission of the plaintiff

Questions 11 - 16.

DIRECTIONS: For questions 11 - 16, assume the following facts:

Judgments were entered and docketed against a defendant named X in the places and at the times indicated:

    June 1: P-1 v. X in New York County
    June 10: P-2 v. X in Bronx County
    June 19: P-3 v. X in Queens County
    June 30 P-4 v. X in New York County

X owns a Cadillac automobile which he keeps in Putnam County and a bank account with C-M Bank in Kings County. On June 25, X bought a parcel of land known as Blackacre, located in New York County from Y, giving Y $6,000 in cash and executing a purchase money bond and mortgage to Y for $14,000.

Further assume, for question 11 only, that a restraining notice is served on X on behalf of P-4 on September 1; that an execution is delivered to the sheriff in Putnam County on behalf of P-2 on September 10; that an execution is delivered to the sheriff in Queens County on behalf of P-1 on September 15; that the sheriff (Queens) has now levied on the Cadillac which was moved from Putnam County to Queens County on September 12.

11. Who is entitled to the proceeds of the sale of the Cadillac?
    A. P-4 may obtain an order directing the sheriff in Queens to turn over the proceeds to him
    B. P-2 may obtain an order directing the sheriff in Queens to turn over the proceeds to him
    C. P-1 may obtain an order directing the sheriff in Queens to turn over the proceeds to him
    D. P-4, P-2, and P-1 share in proportion to their judgments

Further assume, for question 12 only, that a restraining notice and information subpoena are served on C-M Bank on behalf of P-4 on September 1; that a special proceeding is commenced on September 7 by P-3 to obtain a delivery order against C-M Bank; that P-2 delivers an execution to the sheriff in Kings County on September 10; that P-3 obtains and files his delivery order on September 21; and that the sheriff levies on the account on September 30.

12. Who is entitled to the account?
 A. P-4, P-3, and P-2 share in proportion to their judgments
 B. P-3   C. P-2   D. P-4

Further assume, for question 13 only, that Y obtains a judgment of foreclosure on September 1; that P-3 and P-4 deliver executions to the sheriff in New York County on September 15; that P-1 delivers an execution to the sheriff in New York County on September 30; and that the land is properly sold thereafter.

13. Who is entitled to priority in the proceeds?
 A. Y
 B. P-3 and P-4 share in proportion to their judgments
 C. Y, P-3, and P-4 share in proportion to their judgments
 D. P-1

Further assume, for question 14 only, that P-2 delivers an execution to the sheriff in New York County on September 1; that P-3 delivers an execution to the same sheriff on September 4; that P-4 delivers an execution to the same sheriff on September 10; and that Blackacre is properly sold thereafter.

14. Who is entitled to priority in the proceeds?
 A. P-4   B. P-3   C. P-1
 D. P-1, P-2, and P-3 share in proportion to their judgments

15. In the preceding question 14, the execution buyer takes
 A. title to Blackacre, free and clear of all encumbrances
 B. subject only to P-1's interest
 C. Blackacre subject only to Y's mortgage interest
 D. subject to P-1's and Y's interest

Further assume, for question 16 only, that P-4 delivers an execution to the sheriff in New York County on September 1; that P-2 delivers an execution to the same sheriff on September 10; that P-3 delivers an execution to the same sheriff on September 15; that P-1 delivers an execution to the same sheriff on September 18; and that Blackacre is properly sold thereafter.

16. Who is entitled to priority in the proceeds?
 A. P-1, P-2, and P-3 share the proceeds in proportion to their judgments
 B. P-4 is entitled to priority in the proceeds
 C. P-1 is entitled to priority in the proceeds
 D. P-1 and P-4 share the proceeds in proportion to their judgments

17. Doe, a citizen and resident of the State of Maine, voluntarily agrees to testify in an action by A against B, pending in Supreme Court, New York County. A summons has been left with the sheriff by Peters for service on Doe. The sheriff now learns from Peters that Doe is in the Supreme Court building awaiting his turn to testify. A deputy sheriff serves Doe with the summons while Doe is standing around in the hallway of the courthouse. Doe has moved to set aside the service of the summons. The court should
    A. set aside service of process on the ground that Doe was immune from service
    B. set aside service on the ground that process may not be served in a courthouse
    C. set aside service on the ground that, there being no unusual circumstances in the case, the sheriff's office should not have become involved in serving a summons
    D. deny the motion

18. On June 1, a deputy sheriff makes a proper levy upon an automobile owned by Doe, a defendant in an action wherein an order of attachment has been signed. On July 1, the deputy makes a proper levy upon Doe's bank account. On October 15 Doe files a petition in bankruptcy. The trustee in bankruptcy is appointed on November 10. The bankruptcy court may PROPERLY compel the sheriff to turn over to the trustee
    A. the automobile   B. the bank account
    C. both the automobile and the bank account
    D. neither the automobile nor the bank account

19. Real property has been sold to X in execution of a judgment in favor of the plaintiff. Which of the following statements is TRUE?
    A. The defendant may redeem his property at any time by paying to X the same amount that X paid for the property plus interest.
    B. The defendant may redeem his property within one year after the sale by paying to X the same amount that X paid for the property plus interest.
    C. The defendant may redeem his property within one year after the sale by paying the full judgment to the plaintiff.
    D. The defendant may not redeem his property after the sheriff has delivered a sheriff's deed to X.

20. With the statute of limitations due to expire on June 1, an attorney for the plaintiff delivers a summons on May 15, to the sheriff's office for service upon the defendant. The statute of limitations will NOT be a defense if the summons is served within
    A. 60 days after May 15   B. 60 days after June 1
    C. 90 days after May 15   D. 90 days after June 1

21. A deputy sheriff must serve a Supreme Court summons upon John Doe. Doe, a resident of New York, has carefully avoided being served. The deputy has learned that Doe is in a hotel room in Manhattan. The deputy goes to the hotel, calls from the lobby, and states that he is a former colleague of Doe's and would like to invite Doe for a drink. Doe comes down to the bar where the deputy serves him. Doe now moves to set aside the service of process. The court should
    A. *grant* the motion since the deputy was guilty of deception
    B. *grant* the motion since the deputy never actually touched Doe with the summons
    C. *grant* the motion since the deputy did not serve a complaint with the summons
    D. *deny* the motion since the service was valid

22. In the preceding question(21), assume that John Doe was a citizen and resident of New Jersey who was in New York for a vacation. All other facts are the same. The court should
    A. *grant* the motion since the deputy was guilty of deception
    B. *grant* the motion since as a nonresident, Doe was immune from service
    C. *deny* the motion since the service was valid
    D. *deny* the motion since a nonresident may be served anywhere in the state, anytime including Sunday

23. In the preceding question(22), assume that Doe was spotted on the street racing to his home. The deputy arrives at the home, and is admitted peacefully by Doe's wife. Once in the house the deputy goes from room to room without express permission, locates Doe, and serves him. Of the following, the *MOST* accurate statement is that the
    A. service is void since the deputy committed an illegal search and seizure
    B. deputy could have broken into the house if he had been refused admittance
    C. service is valid
    D. deputy has a legal privilege to effectuate service and is never liable for trespass

24. A deputy sheriff is sent to the headquarters of AAA, Inc. to serve the corporation with a summons. Upon arriving there at 12:30 p.m., he is told by a building employee that everybody in the AAA office is out to lunch. The building employee volunteers to accept the summons and to redeliver it to the President of AAA when the latter returns from lunch. Of the following, the *MOST* accurate statement is that the
    A. service is void even if the building employee does redeliver the summons to the President of AAA, Inc.
    B. service is valid if the building employee does redeliver the summons to the President of AAA, Inc.

C. service upon the building employee was itself a valid service upon AAA, Inc.
D. deputy should have demanded access to the office of AAA Inc. where he should have posted the summons in a conspicuous place

25. Service upon a partnership may be made by serving the summons on   25.___
    A. the managing agent of the partnership
    B. the director of the firm's legal department
    C. any partner at all
    D. only the partner who is designated by the firm to accept process

KEY (CORRECT ANSWERS)

1.	D	11.	B
2.	C	12.	B
3.	D	13.	A
4.	B	14.	A
5.	B	15.	C
6.	A	16.	C
7.	C	17.	A
8.	D	18.	B
9.	A	19.	D
10.	B	20.	B

21.	D
22.	C
23.	C
24.	A
25.	C

EXAMINATION SECTION

TEST 1

DIRECTIONS: Each question or incomplete statement is followed by several suggested answers or completions. Select the one that BEST answers the question or completes the statement. *PRINT THE LETTER OF THE CORRECT ANSWER IN THE SPACE AT THE RIGHT.*

1. The shift from an individual to a formal response of crime resulted in which one of the following:
   A. Elimination of revenge
   B. Made punishment more humane
   C. Lessened the chances of longstanding family feuds
   D. Promoted citizen disinterest in crime and the punishment of criminals
   E. Contributed to the development of a more just method of determining guilt

2. The MOST important trend in corrections today:
   A. Attempt to reinforce any ties between the offender and the community
   B. Long sentences
   C. Less use of confinement if possible
   D. Developing programs for prisoners in prisons
   E. None of the above

3. People commit crimes because
   A. they are mentally ill
   B. they come from poor families
   C. it is their way of trying to solve their problems
   D. they want to
   E. they are born criminals

4. The jail officer's role in the jail is to
   I. represent the sheriff
   II. represent the criminal justice system
   III. assume responsibility for the welfare of prisoners
   IV. punish prisoners for their crimes
   V. appease social pressure

   The CORRECT answer is:
   A. I, II
   B. II, III
   C. I, II, III
   D. II, III, IV
   E. II, V

5. Which one of the following is a *genuine* characteristic of a professional jail officer? He
   A. becomes easily upset by prisoners
   B. wants to punish prisoners for their crimes
   C. tries to treat all prisoners alike without favoritism or emotion
   D. refuses to discuss the prisoners' guilt or innocence
   E. is critical of the courts and the law and says so to prisoners

KEY (CORRECT ANSWERS)

1. E
2. A
3. C
4. B
5. C

TEST 2

DIRECTIONS: Each question or incomplete statement is followed by several suggested answers or completions. Select the one that BEST answers the question or completes the statement. *PRINT THE LETTER OF THE CORRECT ANSWER IN THE SPACE AT THE RIGHT.*

1. From the list below, select the one that is legally proper on which the jail officer can book a prisoner: 1.___
   A. Larceny   B. Hold for Dr. Jones
   C. False identification   D. Suspicion
   E. Hold for investigation

2. The purpose of a strip search is: 2.___
   I. To discover contraband
   II. To let the prisoner know that he is now in jail
   III. To discover if he has lice
   IV. To appraise physical condition
   V. All of the above

   The CORRECT answer is:
   A. I, II   B. II, III   C. I, IV
   D. I, III   E. V

3. Select those statements that are TRUE about strip and frisk searches: 3.___
   I. If you are not certain that you examined an area, return to it
   II. All searches should be systematic
   III. An incomplete search is as bad as no search at all
   IV. Your attitude when conducting the search is as important as the way the search is done
   V. All of the above

   The CORRECT answer is:
   A. I, III   B. II, III   C. II, III, IV
   D. I, III, IV E. V

4. Identification procedures are important because: 4.___
   I. The FBI requires them
   II. It is a method of identifying those persons who are wanted by other jurisdictions
   III. It is a method of identifying prisoners when they are released
   IV. It is necessary for statistical purposes
   V. All of the above

   The CORRECT answer is:
   A. II, III   B. I, IV   C. II, IV
   D. I, II   E. V

5. Physical examinations for all prisoners at the time of   5.___
   admission are
   A. a waste of time since most of them are drunks anyway
   B. necessary to discover the sick and injured
   C. necessary only if a prisoner seems to be obviously
      sick
   D. duplicatory of previous physicals

6. Which of the following are NOT accurate descriptions of   6.___
   personal property and should not be used?
   I. Gold watch
   II. Plaid sport coat, size 40
   III. Yellow metal ring with diamond
   IV. Brown suit, Bonds label, hole in left elbow, trousers
       soiled at right knee, size 40
   V. Timex watch

   The CORRECT answer is:
   A. I, II, V   B. II, III, V   C. I, IV, V
   D. I, II, III   E. I, III, V

7. Bathing of all prisoners when they are admitted to the   7.___
   jail is necessary for the following reasons:
   I. It is good for staff morale to see clean prisoners
   II. Prevent vermin from entering the jail
   III. No one likes dirty people
   IV. It contributes to the health and well-being of
       prisoners
   V. All of the above

   The CORRECT answer is:
   A. I, II   B. II, III   C. III, IV
   D. II, IV   E. V

8. Prisoners should not be permitted to wear long hair   8.___
   because
   A. it is unsightly
   B. it is unsanitary
   C. the jail staff do not like it
   D. all of the above
   E. none of the above

9. All prisoners should wear jail clothing because   9.___
   A. they look neater when they all are dressed alike
   B. it is a good security procedure since it makes
      escape difficult
   C. it is simpler for them to do their laundry
   D. it is cheaper

10. Match the following descriptions of prisoners with the   10.___
    appropriate housing assignment:
    A. Juvenile prisoner   1. dormitory, near   A.___
    B. Elderly or infirm prisoner   infirmary   B.___
    C. Mentally ill prisoner   2. in single cell away   C.___
    D. Hostile aggressive   from all adults   D.___
       prisoner   3. in a single cell
                                  4. in a single cell under
                                     close supervision
                                  5. in a padded cell

11. The PROPER definition of contraband is:
    A. Any item that can be used as a weapon, and all drugs
    B. All items listed as contraband and posted in the jail
    C. All items not issued by the jail and not specifically authorized
    D. Illicit guns

12. Cell searches are necessary for the following reason:
    A. To discover contraband   B. To keep prisoners off balance
    C. To reduce clutter   D. All of the above

13. Identify the two MOST important principles of a cell search:
    I. Examine everything in the cell
    II. Be systematic
    III. Leave the cell in the same condition in which it was found
    IV. Ignore the prisoner when searching his cell
    V. Remain aloof

    The CORRECT answer is:
    A. I, II   B. II, III   C. III, IV
    D. IV, V   E. I, III

14. Indicate whether the following statements are TRUE or FALSE:
    A. Counts are unnecessary if prisoners are locked up at all times.
    B. A jail officer should know how many prisoners he has at all times.
    C. One officer can make an accurate count in a dormitory.
    D. Roll call counts are easy to take and make good sense.
    E. When counting prisoners, the officer must always see flesh.
    F. It is not good practice to permit prisoners to conduct a count.

15. Select the statements that are examples of good key control:
    I. Since minimum security prisoners can be trusted, it is proper to permit them to use keys to unlock and lock all doors
    II. A jail officer should never carry both inside and outside keys
    III. Jail officers should be permitted to exchange keys during shift change
    IV. All security keys should be concealed when carried
    V. None of the above

    The CORRECT answer is:
    A. I, III   B. II, III   C. II, IV
    D. I, IV   E. V

16. The single MOST effective security measure in the jail is 16.____
    A. remote TV camera
    B. tool-hardened steel
    C. metal detectors
    D. the alertness of the jail officer
    E. stoolies

17. Indicate whether the following statements are TRUE or 17.____
    FALSE:
    A. Weapons are needed in the jail in order to protect   A.____
       personnel
    B. Gas in aerosol cans and clubs are not weapons   B.____
    C. The weapon carried in the jail by the officer can   C.____
       be taken away and used against him
    D. Although all jail personnel should be required to   D.____
       check their weapons before entering the jail, FBI
       agents and visiting sheriffs are exempt
    E. The armory should be inside the jail so that weapons   E.____
       will be available to jail officers when they need them

---

KEY (CORRECT ANSWERS)

1. A	11. C
2. D	12. A
3. C	13. B
4. A	14. A. F
5. B	B. T
	C. F
6. E	D. F
7. D	E. T
8. E	F. T
9. B	15. C
10. A. 2	
B. 1	16. D
C. 4	17. A. F
D. 3	B. F
	C. T
	D. F
	E. F

TEST 3

DIRECTIONS: Each question or incomplete statement is followed by several suggested answers or completions. Select the one that BEST answers the question or completes the statement. *PRINT THE LETTER OF THE CORRECT ANSWER IN THE SPACE AT THE RIGHT.*

1. What are the two MOST important changes that occur when a prisoner is admitted to the jail? He
   A. becomes a prisoner
   B. changes status from citizen to prisoner
   C. has to wear jail clothing
   D. begins to lose his identity

   1.___

2. List the *tangible* items that contribute to a prisoner's identity and that are taken from him when he enters the jail. (List six.)
   1. _____ 2. _____
   3. _____ 4. _____
   5. _____ 6. _____

   2.___

3. List the *intangibles* that contribute to a prisoner's identity that he loses when he enters the jail. (List three.)
   1. _____ 2. _____ 3. _____

   3.___

4. Indicate whether the following statements are TRUE or FALSE:
   A. Prisoners are generally not frustrated by their inability to do things for themselves because they have few things bothering them.
   B. Giving a prisoner good conduct time is equal to rewards he would receive in the community such as pay, approval, and responsibility.
   C. Cutting a prisoner's hair at admission does not alter his identity.
   D. A prisoner's sudden dependence on his wife and friends does not change his relationship with them.
   E. There is no similarity between the feelings a prisoner has when confined and the person who is entering military service.

   4.___
   A.___
   B.___
   C.___
   D.___
   E.___

5. The newly admitted prisoner can be assisted in adjusting to the jail by one of the following methods:
   A. Orientation by other prisoners
   B. Written rules and regulations that are given to him
   C. Trial and error and by watching others
   D. Kept in a cell until he learns jail routine

   5.___

6. Although any period in confinement can be considered a critical time, the following times are especially sensitive: (Select two.)
   A. During discharge of the prisoner from the jail
   B. During searches of cells
   C. During strip or frisk searches
   D. Immediately before or after court appearances
   E. During mealtimes
   F. All of the above

6.___

7. What should be done about a prisoner who appears hostile during admission?
   A. Lock him up in a cell immediately
   B. Insist on carrying out the admission procedure and ask the arresting officer to assist you
   C. Be certain to get all the details of the arrest and the prisoner's behavior from the arresting officer. This should be done in the presence of the prisoner so that he knows he can't fool you.
   D. Get rid of the arresting officer as soon as possible. Carry out the admission procedure calmly and quietly.

7.___

8. The BEST procedure to follow when a prisoner is upset from a visit from his wife or girlfriend is to do the following:
   A. Lock him in a cell by himself so that he will not try to escape and where he will not disturb others
   B. Permit him to call his wife or girlfriend and correct the misunderstanding
   C. Talk to the prisoner or at least be a sympathetic and understanding listener
   D. If he is continuously having problems because of argument with visitors, refuse to let further visits to take place

8.___

9. Although many factors are involved in setting and controlling the jail climate, the MOST important is:
   A. The behavior of the prisoners since they can be hostile and manipulative
   B. The attitude and behavior of the staff
   C. The quality of the food
   D. Relaxed security procedures
   E. All of the above

9.___

10. The following technique is useful in avoiding prisoner manipulation:
    A. Refuse to discuss any prisoner's problems with him
    B. Establish good communications with other staff members
    C. Keep good records
    D. Ignore prisoner complaints and refuse to permit any exceptions to jail rules

10.___

11. Indicate whether the following statements are TRUE or FALSE:
    A. A suicide attempt is usually an attempt to manipulate jail staff
    B. Overreacting to prisoners is an indication that the jail officer is conscientious and concerned

11.___

A.___

B.___

C. A jail officer should always act knowledgeable about jail procedures even when he is not

D. Jail rules seldom need to be changed; they do need to be updated by adding new rules from time to time

E. There is nothing wrong with rules made up by prisoners because usually they are tougher than rules developed by the administrator

C.___
D.___
E.___

12. A jail officer who overreacts to prisoners is
    A. alert to prisoner manipulation
    B. demonstrating an interest in his work
    C. lacks confidence and is insecure
    D. all of the above

12.___

13. List characteristics of the trained, professional jailer: (List seven.)
    1. _____   2. _____
    3. _____   4. _____
    5. _____   6. _____
    7. _____

13.___

14. Indicate whether the following statements are TRUE or FALSE:
    A. A jail officer who disagrees with a jail rule and lets prisoners know it will be considered an honest officer and will be contributing to a positive jail climate
    B. The jail officer who gossips with prisoners gets their respect because he is demonstrating that he is just like they are
    C. Discussing dissatisfactions about the jail with prisoners is a good way to get good suggestions for changes in jail policy
    D. Prisoners are quick to interpret differences of opinion between staff members as signs of disunity
    E. Regulations assist prisoners in adjusting to the jail by eliminating confusion
    F. Rigid rules are the most effective way of keeping order and contribute to a well-run jail and few disciplinary reports
    G. Vague regulations are an indication to prisoners that personnel do not have clear understanding or control of the jail
    H. Reasonable rules reduce staff-prisoner conflict

14.___
A.___
B.___
C.___
D.___
E.___
F.___
G.___
H.___

KEY (CORRECT ANSWERS)

1. B, D
2. Street clothing, haircut, jewelry, belt, tie clip, cigarette lighter
3. Work, relations with his family, daily habits
4. A. F
   B. F
   C. F
   D. F
   E. F
5. B
6. C, D
7. D
8. C
9. B
10. B
11. A. F
    B. F
    C. F
    D. F
    E. F
12. C
13. Flexibility, self-confidence, willingness to make decisions, impartiality, refusal to respond in a hostile manner to prisoner hostility, respect for himself and his work, willingness to perform all necessary tasks
14. A. F
    B. F
    C. F
    D. T
    E. T
    F. F
    G. T
    H. T

TEST 4

DIRECTIONS: Each question or incomplete statement is followed by several suggested answers or completions. Select the one that BEST answers the question or completes the statement. *PRINT THE LETTER OF THE CORRECT ANSWER IN THE SPACE AT THE RIGHT.*

1. Select the one statement that completes the following sentence.
   The OVERALL objective of supervision is
   A. achievement of security
   B. protection of prisoners
   C. teaching prisoners how to work
   D. the development of an orderly environment

   1.___

2. Another IMPORTANT goal of supervision is control.
   This means:
   A. Making certain that each prisoner is either locked in his cell or under the direct physical control of the jail officer
   B. That jail officers closely supervise prisoner activities, especially where trusties are in charge of other prisoners
   C. That jail personnel supervise all prisoners, develop procedures, set standards, and evaluate results
   D. All of the above

   2.___

3. An officer is placed on a new assignment where he will be supervising prisoners.
   Which of the following is the proper FIRST step he should take in assuming this assignment?
   A. Call the prisoners together and tell them what kind of work he expects from them.
   B. Ask the prisoners for suggestions on how this particular operation can be improved.
   C. Ask each prisoner for a description of his work so that he can seek ways to revise procedures and make them more effective.
   D. Read post orders, familiarize himself with policies and procedures, and learn all he can about the assignment.

   3.___

4. Officer P assigned four prisoners to a small empty cell block and gave them the following instructions. *I want this place cleaned up. I'll be back before the end of the day to check on your work.*
   List the errors made by Officer P. (List three.)
   1. _____
   2. _____
   3. _____

   4.___

5. A supervisor is responsible for making an accurate and honest evaluation of a prisoner's performance. In order to do this, he must
   A. know a great deal about the prisoner, including his offense, his family life, and his education
   B. have supervised him long enough to know him well
   C. recognize and account for individual differences
   D. evaluate all prisoners as working equally hard or satisfactorily
   E. recognize either improvement or a change for the worse and, if possible, explain it

5.___

6. Select the two statements that demonstrate a supervisor's objectivity in evaluating a prisoner:
   A. This man is lazy
   B. This man is always at the end of the line when picking up tools and first in line when turning them in
   C. Prisoner J is one of the slowest moving men in the crew
   D. Prisoner A is hard working, energetic, and always on the go
   E. Prisoner S listens carefully, asks questions when he does not understand, and makes few mistakes

6.___

7. Officer R is trying hard to do a good job. He feels that it is important for jail officers to communicate with prisoners. In this way, he can keep in touch with them and their problems and, as a result, will be a more effective supervisor. This morning he came in and in talking to some of the prisoners commented that he certainly was tired; he should not have stayed out so late. Not only was he tired, but his wife was angry with him because of the late hours he keeps when bowling.
One of the prisoners asked him about his score. He replied that he averaged 105. One of the prisoners commented that this was a lady's score, and the other prisoners laughed. What errors did Officer R make? (List three.)
   1. _____
   2. _____
   3. _____

8. Officer S has been talking to Prisoner O. During the conversation, O says, *"Don't you think that Idiot T would know better than to loan I cigarettes when he knows I is leaving before commissary day?"* Officer S replied, *"I never did think T had too many brains and now I'm certain of it. But then, I doesn't have too many smarts either."* What do you think Prisoner O is thinking of Officer S's remarks? (Select one.)
   A. Well, we seem to agree about some things.
   B. Gee, Officer S is pretty sharp about who is smart or dumb.
   C. I wonder what he says about me to other prisoners.
   D. He is right about T but I think I is a smart old bird. But I'm not going to argue with him.

8.___

9. Prisoner B is having problems with his wife. She wants   9.___
   to have their eight-year-old boy's tonsils removed, and
   B wants her to wait until he is released. He is discussing
   the problem with Officer R who tells him, *"Listen, let her
   have them removed. The sooner the better; it's like pulling
   a tooth, fast and simple."*
   Do you think this advice was good or bad? (Select one.)
   - A. *Good*; it will keep the wife occupied while Prisoner B
     is in jail.
   - B. *Good*; the boy should have his tonsils removed.
   - C. *Bad*; Officer R knows nothing about the family situation
     or the boy's medical condition.
   - D. *Bad*; he is taking the wife's side in the argument.
   - E. *Good*; he is giving the prisoner advice, and the
     prisoner needs it if he is to resolve his problem.

10. The Lockmeup County Jail is run simply and with little   10.___
    fuss or bother. The sheriff has found that the prisoners
    can pretty well take care of themselves. The jail is
    fairly clean and seems to be quite orderly. It seems,
    however, that some prisoners never do any work and always
    have money, cigarettes, and commissary.
    What is going on here?
    - A. The prisoners are probably a well-behaved, cooperative
      group who are interested in getting along with the
      sheriff.
    - B. It is highly probable that prisoners are running the
      jail and have established a sanitary court.
    - C. Both of the above
    - D. None of the above

11. Officer J has assigned three prisoners to the kitchen   11.___
    detail to wash pots, mop the floor, and wipe tables. He
    will not be available to supervise them at all times. He
    has, therefore, given one of the prisoners responsibility
    for organizing the work and giving out assignments.
    Is Officer J making any supervisory errors?
    - A. *No*; a good supervisor learns to delegate responsibility.
    - B. *Yes*; prisoners should never have any supervisory
      responsibility over other prisoners.
    - C. *No*; he will be checking them from time to time so
      there is little chance that anything will go wrong.
    - D. *Yes*; he has not been clear in his assignment of work.

12. Officer P is responsible for the supervision of a cell   12.___
    block during the evening hours when there is little
    activity in the jail. His post is at the door to the
    cell block, but he makes it a habit to make rounds of
    the cell block once every hour. His tour always takes
    place during the last 15 minutes of the hour. Officer P
    believes in being systematic and organized. This evening
    Prisoner S asked him for a light and engaged him in con-
    versation. S is usually not talkative. The other
    prisoners lounging in the bullpen area between cells seemed
    somewhat noisier than usual, but not to the point where
    it would be disturbing.

What do you think could be happening in the cell block?
- A. Nothing; it is not unusual for prisoners to change and become friendly. In fact, S's desire to talk should be encouraged; perhaps in time he may want to discuss his problems with Officer P.
- B. An escape is in progress, and the prisoners are trying to provide a distraction.
- C. These distractions could cover an escape attempt or sexual assaults in another part of the jail.
- D. Nothing; the prisoner usually becomes a little noisy as the evening progresses.

13. Referring to Question 12 above, do you think Officer P is making any errors?
    - A. *No*; he is responding to a prisoner's need to talk to someone.
    - B. *Yes*; he should not make his tours through the cell block according to such a rigid schedule.
    - C. *No*; he seems to be alert and is actively supervising the cell block.
    - D. *Yes*; he should not be giving S a light.

14. The television set for prisoners is located in the dayroom. Although it had been possible to buy the set with remote controls, this was not done.
    How do you think the jail staff can ensure that they will exercise control over the set?
    - I. The threat of losing the television will be enough to keep the prisoners in line.
    - II. The on-off switch should be controlled by the jail staff.
    - III. The prisoners should be permitted to set up a committee to develop rules for television use.
    - IV. Jail staff should set viewing hours and have the final approval over programs.

    The CORRECT answer is:
    A. I, II B. II, III C. I, IV
    D. III, IV E. II, IV

15. The jail is switching over to dining room feeding. This has been made possible by the addition of eight jail officers.
    Where should the posts be located to cover the trouble spots?
    - A. Along the walls of the dining room
    - B. Circulating in the dining room
    - C. One watching the line entering the dining room, one in the kitchen, and the other circulating
    - D. One at the line entering the dining room, one at the serving line, one at the silverware collection and tray scraping can, and three either along the wall or circulating

16. List the important points in supervising the feeding of   16. ____
    prisoners in their cells. (List four.)
    1. _____
    2. _____
    3. _____
    4. _____

17. Although the jail has a routine procedure for handling   17. ____
    sick call, Officer P has worked out a much simpler system.
    Whenever a prisoner requests to see the doctor, Officer P
    questions him; and if the prisoner complains of a headache
    or cold, he is given two aspirin. This has reduced the
    sick call line substantially. Officer P prides himself in
    his ability to handle sick call requests and to spot the
    chronic complainers.
    Do you feel that Officer P's behavior is proper?
      I. No; jail officers should not give out medication.
     II. Yes; doctors are busy and reducing the number of
         sick call requests will help them give more time to
         those who are really sick.
    III. No; Officer P is diagnosing prisoner medical complaints,
         and he is not qualified to do this.
     IV. Yes, as long as he limits his medical activity to those
         who have colds and headaches.
      V. Yes; after all, the prisoners are diagnosing their
         condition by telling Officer P that they have colds
         or headaches. Furthermore, aspirin is not medicine.

    The CORRECT answer is:
      A. I, III   B. I, II   C. III, IV
      D. I, IV   E. III, V

18. List the five BASIC principles of supervising prisoners   18. ____
    on sick call and during their medical care.
    1. _____
    2. _____
    3. _____
    4. _____
    5. _____

19. Supervising visiting is a dull assignment to Officer K.   19. ____
    He manages to pass the time by concentrating on the
    visiting couple who are seated nearest him. Usually, he
    overhears some interesting conversations. Visiting in
    this jail is done in a room with tables that have a four-
    inch partition running through their center. Today,
    Officer K became so interested in the visit of the prisoner
    and his girlfriend seated near him that he didn't realize
    that he was permitting them and other prisoners to visit
    longer than regulations allowed.
    Do you think Officer K has made any errors?
      I. No; he was giving close supervision to the visitors.
     II. Yes; it is not his responsibility to eavesdrop on
         visitors' conversations.
    III. No; permitting visiting to last longer than regulations
         allow is not an error.

        IV. Yes; he was distracted by one visitor and did not
            pay any attention to other visiting taking place.

   The CORRECT answer is:
      A. III, IV   B. III, V   C. II, IV
      D. I, II   E. II, III

20. Which of the following descriptive statements are
    included in a definition of a trusty. A trusty
       A. is a prisoner who can be trusted to work without
          supervision
       B. is a prisoner who can work under minimum supervision
       C. can be depended on not to escape
       D. is a prisoner who because he can be trusted can be
          given responsibility to supervise the work of other
          prisoners and lock and unlock cells. He thus makes
          the work of jail personnel much easier.

21. What *special* privileges should trusties have that are
    NOT permitted to other prisoners?
       A. Freedom to move about in the jail without special
          permission
       B. Extra food because they work
       C. Permitted to run errands for jail personnel
       D. They should not have any special privileges

22. A prisoner being considered for trusty status should be
    evaluated in three areas. Indicate by writing in the
    kinds of information that should be examined. (List three
    kinds.)
       1. _____
       2. _____
       3. _____

23. Why must juveniles be kept separate from adult prisoners?
    (List two reasons.)
       1. _____
       2. _____

24. In what way is supervision of women DIFFERENT from super-
    vision for men?

    _____
    _____
    _____
    _____

25. Officer W has been supervising the recreation periods
    recently. Yesterday, he overruled the umpire's decision
    even though there had been no argument from either team.
    There was little doubt that the umpire had made a bad
    call. Today, he took part in a volleyball game in order
    to even sides.
    Do you feel Officer W has made any errors?
       A. *No*; he is correcting the umpire and thus avoiding
          complaints or arguments from prisoners.

B. *Yes*; it seems that the prisoner did not contest the call.
C. *Yes*; he is becoming involved with prisoner recreation activities when there is no need to do so, and he is ignoring his supervisory responsibility.
D. *No*; a supervisor should be alert to possible problems and try and solve them before they become serious. Correcting the umpire was correct. He is also contributing to the recreation period by participating in the game.

26. List the BASIC principles of supervising a prisoner at a funeral or other social activity outside the jail. (List three.)
    1. _____
    2. _____
    3. _____

26. ___

KEY (CORRECT ANSWERS)

1. D
2. C
3. D
4. Poor directions - too general; did not take into account the possibility that some of the prisoners may not have understood his orders; is not making periodic checks.
5. C
6. B, E
7. A. Discussed his off-duty activities with prisoners.
   B. Discussed his relationship with his wife with prisoners.
   C. Mention of the bowling score was not important, but this was an opening for the prisoners to make an insulting remark.
8. C
9. C
10. B
11. B
12. C
13. B
14. E
15. D
16. A. Deliver food while it is hot
    B. Supervisor must accompany the prisoner who is serving food
    C. Count utensils to and from prisoners
    D. Make seconds available as a means of preventing stronger prisoners from stealing food from the weak.
17. A
18. A. Do not diagnose.
    B. Supervise prisoners closely when they are taking medication.
    C. Never give out more than one dose of medication at one time.
    D. Keep accurate medical records.
    E. Permit all prisoners' sick call requests.
19. C
20. B

21. D
22. A. Escape record and detainers
    B. Work habits
    C. Behavior in confinement
23. A. To prevent adults from possibly sexually assaulting them.
    B. To keep juveniles from being exposed to hardened criminal types
24. There is no basic difference. The same principles and techniques can be used. Women must be kept separate from male prisoners.
25. C
26. A. Do not remove cuffs unless prior approval has been given by the jail administrator.
    B. Keep the prisoner in sight at all times.
    C. No special visits or other requests to be granted.

TEST 5

DIRECTIONS: Each question or incomplete statement is followed by several suggested answers or completions. Select the one that BEST answers the question or completes the statement. *PRINT THE LETTER OF THE CORRECT ANSWER IN THE SPACE AT THE RIGHT.*

1. The GOAL of discipline in jail is to
    A. teach prisoners absolute obedience to orders
    B. teach acceptable behavior
    C. teach prisoners self-control
    D. control prisoners

2. Written rules serve the following purposes:
    I. To inform prisoners what not to do
    II. To inform prisoners about what is expected of them
    III. To establish standards for evaluating prisoners' conduct
    IV. Take authority away from jail officers who should be responsible for establishing standards of conduct

    The CORRECT answer is:
    A. I, II
    B. I, III
    C. II, IV
    D. III, IV
    E. II, III

3. Officer O has a temper that he displays whenever a prisoner gets on his nerves. He insists that prisoners do what they are told and that they follow the rules to the letter. It is his opinion that generally people get into trouble with the law because they lack discipline. He feels that it is his responsibility to teach prisoners discipline.
    Do you feel that Officer O is CORRECT?
    A. *Yes*; prisoners will generally take advantage of an officer who is not very strict.
    B. *No*; Officer O is too strict. He probably antagonizes prisoners by his attitude.
    C. *Yes*; all jail officers have a responsibility to teach prisoners discipline.
    D. *Yes*; however, he certainly sets a poor example by his display of temper.

4. Officer A caught two prisoners horsing around and decided to punish them by making them run in place. He reasoned that this would tire them so that they would not have the energy for horseplay.
    Do you think his actions were PROPER?
    A. *Yes*; prisoners learn a lesson from immediate punishment.
    B. *No*; the officer who sees the infraction should not, as a rule, also decide the punishment.
    C. Both of the above
    D. None of the above

5. Officer S is a firm believer in keeping order. He practices this belief and, as a result, turns in a high number of disciplinary reports.
   Do you think that S is acting properly?
   A. *Yes*; all infractions of rules should be reported.
   B. *No*; he should only report infractions that are serious and that cannot be handled informally.
   C. Both of the above
   D. None of the above

5.___

6. The following is a list of rule violations. Indicate those that require formal action and those that may be handled informally. (Use letter F for formal and letter I for informal.)
   A. Loud and continuous noise
   B. Talking after lights out
   C. Horseplay in sick call line
   D. Arguing with waiter in serving line
   E. Evidence of bar tampering
   F. Contraband (knife)
   G. Contraband (money)
   H. Contraband (book)
   I. Holding up line when returning to cells

6.___

A.___
B.___
C.___
D.___
E.___
F.___
G.___
H.___
I.___

7. Officer D has taken Prisoner E out of line for horseplay and is correcting him before a group of interested prisoners. What do you think are the possible consequences of this action?
   A. Prisoner E will learn a lesson.
   B. Prisoner E may become angry at being embarrassed in front of other prisoners.
   C. Officer D has realized that this was an excellent opportunity to teach E proper behavior and will make a positive impression on the prisoner.
   D. The other prisoners will also have an opportunity to learn from Prisoner E's experience.

7.___

8. Prisoner O became abusive toward another prisoner, and they were on the edge of fighting when Officer C arrived on the scene. Both prisoners continued to argue, and a shoving contest began.
   What should Officer C do?
   A. Step between the prisoners and separate them.
   B. Grab Prisoner O and pull him away.
   C. Shout to both prisoners to stop.
   D. He had better call another officer for assistance and then step in.

8.___

9. Officer S is a large man and quite sure of himself. Today, when Prisoner N refused to come out of his cell to take a shower, Officer S went in and took him out.
   Do you think this was the proper method?
   A. *Yes*; prisoners should do what they are told.
   B. *No*; the prisoner should have been permitted to remain in his cell until he decided to come out.

9.___

C. *Yes*; prisoners must conform to all schedules.
D. If it was necessary that Prisoner N come out of his cell, the officer should not have gone in alone to take him out.

10. Prisoner N has declared that he is on a hunger strike and has refused to eat three meals in a row. A number of officers are upset by N's behavior and feel that something should be done about him.
Which do you feel is the PROPER procedure?
   A. Force feed him; all prisoners should eat three meals a day.
   B. Ignore him; he will eat when he is hungry.
   C. Wait a few days; and if he continues to refuse food, he should be force fed.
   D. Refer him to the doctor who can make a decision if and when he will require any medical care and forced feeding.

10.___

KEY (CORRECT ANSWERS)

1. C
2. E
3. D
4. B
5. B

6. Formal: E, F, G, H
   Informal: A, B, C, D
7. B
8. D
9. D
10. D

TEST 6

DIRECTIONS: Each question or incomplete statement is followed by several suggested answers or completions. Select the one that BEST answers the question or completes the statement. *PRINT THE LETTER OF THE CORRECT ANSWER IN THE SPACE AT THE RIGHT.*

1. A prisoner is brought to the jail with the following symptoms: shakiness, staggering, thick speech, and a blank glassy-eyed look.
    Select the PROPER action to be taken.
    A. He is drunk; place him in the drunk tank.
    B. Although he may be drunk, it is possible that he may have a serious injury or illness. He should be referred to a doctor.
    C. Both of the above
    D. None of the above

    1.___

2. Shortly after being admitted, a prisoner begins to shake, does not talk clearly, and claims to see bugs crawling over him.
    The jailer should do one of the following:
    A. The prisoner is obviously psychotic and should be referred to the doctor
    B. The prisoner is having *DTs*; the doctor should be called immediately
    C. Although the prisoner is acting strangely, he should be observed for a time until it is obvious that he is sick
    D. None of the above

    2.___

3. Prisoner E has been in jail two weeks waiting trial. Lately, he has been acting strangely. He has been talking to an imaginary person, laughing and arguing. Today he accused Officer T of trying to *get him*.
    What should the officer do?
    A. Observe Prisoner E and submit a report to the administrator for medical referral
    B. Warn E to quiet down because he is disturbing others
    C. Try to prove to Prisoner E that the officer is not trying to get him
    D. None of the above

    3.___

4. Prisoner L seems to have a habit of talking to himself, especially when he is playing solitaire. During the last week, he has also been complaining about his physical condition, claiming that he has a bad heart and that he is afraid it will stop one of these days soon.
    What should the officer do?
    A. It seems that L is becoming psychotic; he should be referred to the doctor.

    4.___

B. L's talking to himself is not a symptom of psychosis, but his physical complaint is; write a report and refer him to the doctor.
C. There is nothing wrong with L; and since he has not requested medical attention, he should be left alone.
D. Write a report on his complaints and refer him to the doctor. He may not be psychotic, but his medical complaint should be referred.

5. Prisoner V is charged with petty theft. Apparently, he absent-mindedly walked out of a store with a pair of gloves. Now he claims that he is innocent because he had money to pay for the gloves. Furthermore, he says that he has a bank account with ten thousand dollars. The other prisoners laugh at him, which only makes him angry. Since he has no money and no family, he has not called anyone. Now he wants an attorney and wants to call the largest bank in town for a release of funds.
What should the officer do?
    A. It is obvious that V is senile. He demonstrated this by forgetting he had the gloves when he left the store. Refer to the doctor.
    B. V is hallucinating; he certainly does not behave as though he has money. Refuse him permission to call the bank and refer to the doctor.
    C. Have V give his account number or other method of identifying himself and call the bank. If he has no account, refer to the doctor.
    D. None of the above

5.___

6. Officer Y has been watching Prisoner O for the last few days because he felt that O was acting strange. He finally sent a referral memo to the jail administrator that contained the following information: *Prisoner O has been acting strangely the last few days. He seems frightened, mumbles to himself, and walks the floor of his cell a lot. I think he should be seen by the doctor.*
Do you think this report contains sufficient information?
    A. *Yes*; it tells the doctor that the prisoner is acting strangely.
    B. *No*; there is not enough information.
    C. *Yes*; even though there is little information, there is enough for a doctor to know that something is wrong with the prisoner.
    D. *No*; there is very little description. It does not describe how the prisoner acts when frightened, how much walking is a lot, or contain any information that might show if the prisoner is talking to himself or hallucinating.

6.___

7. Prisoner G is very forgetful; he can't remember simple rules or follow instructions too well. He is a disciplinary problem because he always seems to be involved in some kind of illegal activity. Yesterday, he was caught with a knife. He claimed he was only carrying it for Prisoner B and claimed he did not know it is contraband. G is a youthful appearing 25 years.

7.___

What action should be taken?
- A. G is suffering from extreme advanced senility; refer him for a medical exam.
- B. G is a good liar and is only trying to get out of trouble now that he has been caught.
- C. G seems to be mentally deficient. Rather than harsh punishment, he needs to have someone explain rules to him more clearly. He also needs closer supervision.
- D. None of the above

8. Prisoner J appeared normal when he was admitted to the jail two days ago. Now he seems to be ill. He complains of aching muscles, is weak, and has lost his appetite, and is vomiting.
What seems to be his problem and what should the officer do?
- A. Sounds like flu; refer to the doctor.
- B. J is having drug withdrawal symptoms. He should be referred to the doctor, kept isolated from others, and closely supervised.
- C. J is suffering from insulin shock. He should be kept in a cell away from others until he calms down in a few days.
- D. Sounds like nothing. None of the above.

9. A person on drug withdrawal requires special care, including isolation and close supervision because
- A. drug addicts are usually dangerous and should always be housed in maximum security conditions
- B. he needs to be closely supervised to keep him away from drugs
- C. to prevent him from bothering others, to make it easier to control him, provide close supervision in case he attempts to injure himself
- D. all of the above

10. Officer D has on a number of occasions referred to *sex fiends* and how it is necessary to exercise care when around them because they are dangerous.
Do you agree?
- A. *Yes*; it is not possible to predict just what a sex offender will do.
- B. *No*; sex offenders are not dangerous while in jail, but I wouldn't want to meet one on the street.
- C. *Yes*; anyone who would commit sex crimes must be untrustworthy and dangerous.
- D. *No*; there are all types of sex offenders, and only a few are violent or dangerous.

11. Officer H has worked in the jail for many years. He is rightfully proud of his ability and experience. He claims that he can always spot a homosexual by his walk and feminine behavior.
Do you think that Officer H is CORRECT?
- A. *Yes*; all homosexuals walk like girls and act feminine.
- B. *No*; it is not possible to identify a homosexual without interviewing him.

C. *Yes*; it's very simple. They are usually slim and have delicate features.
D. *No*; some masculine-appearing men are homosexual, and often slim delicately-built men are not. It is not appearance but behavior that must be examined.

12. Prisoner Y is slim and has a limp-wristed feminine appearance. Prisoner W is husky and aggressive. Y pretty much minds his own business and does his time. W is loud and is trying very hard to become friends with Y. He keeps offering Y cigarettes and candy which Y refuses. What do you suspect is happening?   12.___
    A. Nothing; W is just trying to be friendly.
    B. Obviously Y is homosexual and W doesn't seem to realize it.
    C. Y may or may not be a homosexual; his behavior so far does not indicate that he is. W, however, is acting like an aggressive homosexual and trying to get close to Y.
    D. None of the above

13. Indicate whether the following statements are TRUE or FALSE: 13.___
    A. Homosexuals can be easily identified.   A.___
    B. A person who talks to himself is psychotic.   B.___
    C. People who threaten suicide will not attempt it.   C.___
    D. People who threaten suicide are just trying to get sympathy.   D.___
    E. Young people have a high suicide rate.   E.___
    F. The best method of handling a person who threatens suicide is to call his bluff.   F.___
    G. Keeping suicide risks isolated from others is the best way to manage them.   G.___

14. Prisoner K appears sick. His face is flushed, his skin is dry, and his mouth is dry. His breath is noticeably sweet.   14.___
    What should you do?
    A. Give him some aspirin and permit him to go on sick call.
    B. Give him orange juice or something else with sugar in it because he is having insulin shock.
    C. Call the doctor immediately; he is suffering from inadequate insulin.
    D. Ignore the matter.

15. Prisoner P complains of not feeling well. He is pale and weak, his skin is moist, and he seems to be quite shaky as though he were intoxicated. P claims he is diabetic and is in need of something with sugar in it to correct this condition.   15.___
    What would you do?
    A. Check the records and, if they show he is diabetic, call the doctor and ask for instructions.
    B. Ignore him because this is just another way for some prisoners to get something extra to eat.

C. Give him candy or orange juice; he is showing symptoms of insulin shock. If he does not feel better almost at once, call the doctor.
D. Give him the back of your hand.

16. Prisoner J is having a seizure in his cell. What should the officer do? (Select five.)
    A. Hold him down so that he does not injure himself.
    B. Remove nearby objects so that he does not injure himself.
    C. Sit him up and give him water to drink.
    D. Wait until the seizure is over and then give him his medication.
    E. Loosen clothing around neck and place a padded object between his teeth to prevent his biting his tongue.
    F. Place coat or pillow beneath prisoner's head to prevent injury.
    G. Turn his face to one side.
    H. Notify the doctor immediately.
    I. The doctor should be routinely informed.

16.___

17. Prisoner J has had four seizures in the last hour. You have followed the proper procedure in helping him in each instance.
    What do you do NEXT?
    A. Make certain that he is taking his medication.
    B. Restrain him on his bed so that he does not injure himself during the next seizure.
    C. Call the doctor immediately in order to provide emergency care.
    D. All of the above

17.___

18. As a result of a seizure, Prisoner J has received a head injury. The wound located above the right ear is bleeding. In addition, there seems to be watery fluid flowing from his nose. His breathing is slow and difficult. As yet, he has not regained consciousness as he usually does immediately after a seizure.
    What should you do?
    A. Let him sleep; he must be tired from the seizure.
    B. Apply a pressure bandage to stop the bleeding.
    C. Call the doctor; there seems to be evidence that he may have a serious head wound.
    D. Call the warden.
    E. Nothing; he's trying to divert your attention.

18.___

19. The jail officer's responsibility in managing special prisoners includes the following areas: (Select four.)
    A. Diagnosing prisoners' physical and mental condition and referring to the doctor.
    B. Giving first aid whenever it is needed.
    C. Noticing strange or unusual behavior and referring to the doctor.
    D. Developing the ability to describe the physical and emotional condition of prisoners objectively.

19.___

E. Prepare records that describe prisoners' injuries and record their medical complaints.
F. Evaluate prisoner medical complaints, prescribe medication when required, and keep the chronic complainers from sick call.
G. Closely supervise the taking of medication, keep careful records of all medicine distributed to and taken by prisoners.

KEY (CORRECT ANSWERS)

1.	B	11.	D	
2.	B	12.	C	
3.	A	13.	A.	F
4.	D		B.	F
5.	C		C.	F
			D.	F
6.	D		E.	T
7.	C		F.	F
8.	B		G.	F
9.	C	14.	C	
10.	D	15.	C	

16. B,E,F,G,I
17. C
18. C
19. C,D,E,G

EXAMINATION SECTION
TEST 1

DIRECTIONS: Each question or incomplete statement is followed by several suggested answers or completions. Select the one that BEST answers the question or completes the statement. *PRINT THE LETTER OF THE CORRECT ANSWER IN THE SPACE AT THE RIGHT.*

1. Which of the following is the LEAST important factor to consider in surveying the physical layout of a building for traffic flow?
    A. Location of windows
    B. Number of entrances
    C. Number of exits
    D. Location of First Aid room

2. The major purpose of any security program in a large organization is to prevent unlawful acts. If adequate patrol coverage is provided at a given location, it is MOST likely that
    A. crimes will not be committed
    B. undesirables will not enter the building
    C. unlawful acts will increase in the long run
    D. there will be less opportunity to commit a crime

3. The MOST frequent cause of fires in public facilities is
    A. incinerators
    B. vandalism
    C. electrical sources
    D. smoking on the job

4. After bomb threats are received, it is sometimes necessary to evacuate a facility. How long BEFORE the threatened time of explosion should a facility be evacuated?
    A. At least 15 minutes
    B. At least 25 minutes
    C. At least 50 minutes
    D. At least 60 minutes

5. Once a facility is evacuated because of a bomb threat, how much time should pass before the public and employees are allowed to enter the building?
    A. 10 minutes
    B. 20 minutes
    C. 40 minutes
    D. 60 minutes

6. Of the following locations in public buildings, the one which is the LEAST likely place for bombs to be planted is in
    A. storerooms
    B. bathrooms
    C. cafeterias
    D. waste receptacles

7. The one of the following that is the surest means of establishing positive identification of someone entering a facility is by
    A. personal recognition
    B. I.D. badge
    C. social security card
    D. driver's license

8. The one of the following which most probably would NOT be included in a police record report concerning an incident at a facility is the
    A. name of complainant or injured party
    B. name of the investigating officer
    C. statement of each witness
    D. religion of complainant or injured party

9. Preventing trouble is one of the primary concerns of special officers. When dealing with unruly groups of people who threaten to become violent, which of the following is a measure which should *NOT* be taken?
   A. Maintain close surveillance of such groups
   B. Try to contact the leaders of the group regardless of their militancy
   C. Keep the officer force alerted
   D. Have the officer force deal aggressively with provocations

10. Of the following, the *MOST* important factor to consider in the deployment of officers dealing with a client population is the officers' ability to
   A. remain calm
   B. look stern
   C. evaluate personality
   D. take a firm stand

11. Assume that an offender is struggling with a group of officers who are trying to arrest him. What force, if any, can be used to overcome this resistance?
   A. The amount of force acceptable to the public
   B. The amount of force necessary to restrain the offender and protect the officers
   C. Any amount of force that is acceptable to the officers at the scene
   D. No force may be used until the police arrive

12. Assume that a fire is discovered at your work location. The one of the following actions which would be *INAPPROPRIATE* for you to take is to
   A. notify the telephone operator
   B. station a reliable person at the entrance
   C. open all windows and doors in the area
   D. start evacuating the area

13. If a person has an object caught in his throat or air passage but is breathing adequately, which one of the following should you do?
   A. Probe for the object
   B. Force him to drink water
   C. Lay him over your arm and slap him between the shoulder blades
   D. Allow him to cough and to assume the position he finds most comfortable

14. The one of the following methods which should *NOT* be used to report a fire is to
   A. call 911
   B. pull the handle in the red box on the street corner
   C. call the Fire Department county numbers listed in each county directory
   D. call 411

15. Assume that an officer, alone in a building at night, smells the strong odor of cooking or heating gas. In addition to airing the building and making sure that he is not overcome, it would be *BEST* for the officer to call
    A. his superior at his home and ask for instructions
    B. for a plumber from the department of public works
    C. 911 for police and fire help
    D. the emergency number at Con Edison

16. Of the following situations, the one that is *MOST* dangerous for an officer is when he
    A. investigates suspicious persons and circumstances
    B. finds a burglary in progress or pursues burglary suspects
    C. attempts an arrest or finds a robbery in progress
    D. patrols on the overnight shift

17. An officer on security patrol generally should spend *MOST* of his time
    A. checking doors and locks
    B. helping the public and answering questions
    C. chasing criminals and looking for clues
    D. writing reports on unusual incidents

18. The one of the following that is an *ACCEPTABLE* way to arrest a person is to
    A. tell him to report to the nearest police precinct
    B. send a summons to his permanent address
    C. tell him in person that he is under arrest
    D. show him handcuffs and ask him to come along

19. A carbon dioxide fire extinguisher is *BEST* suited for extinguishing
    A. paper fires   B. rag fires
    C. rubbish fires   D. grease fires

20. A pressurized water or soda-acid fire extinguisher is *BEST* suited for extinguishing
    A. wood fires   B. gasoline fires
    C. electrical fires   D. magnesium fires

21. The one of the following statements that does *NOT* apply to the use of handcuffs is that they
    A. are used as temporary restraining devices
    B. eliminate the need for vigilance
    C. cannot be opened without keys
    D. are used to secure a violent person

22. The one of the following that is *GENERALLY* a crime against the person is
    A. trespass   B. burglary
    C. robbery   D. arson

23. Of the following, the SAFEST way of escape from an office in a burning building is generally the
    A. stairway
    B. rooftop
    C. passenger elevator
    D. freight elevator

24. In attempting to control a possible riot situation, an officer pushed his way into a crowd gathered outside the building and tried to cause confusion by arguing with members of the group. This procedure NORMALLY is considered
    A. *desirable*; any violence that occurs will remain outside the building
    B. *desirable*; the crowd will break into smaller groups and disperse
    C. *undesirable*; to maintain control of the situation, the officer must not become part of the crowd
    D. *undesirable*; the supervisor should stay clear of the scene

25. Which one of the following is MOST effective in making officers more safety-minded?
    A. Maintaining an up-to-date library of the latest safety literature
    B. Reading daily safety bulletins at roll-call
    C. Holding informal group safety meetings periodically
    D. Offering prizes for good safety slogans and displays

KEY (CORRECT ANSWERS)

1.	A	11.	B
2.	D	12.	C
3.	C	13.	D
4.	A	14.	D
5.	D	15.	D
6.	C	16.	C
7.	A	17.	A
8.	D	18.	C
9.	D	19.	D
10.	A	20.	A

21.	B
22.	C
23.	A
24.	C
25.	C

TEST 2

DIRECTIONS: Each question or incomplete statement is followed by several suggested answers or completions. Select the one that *BEST* answers the question or completes the statement. *PRINT THE LETTER OF THE CORRECT ANSWER IN THE SPACE AT THE RIGHT.*

1. Assume that an angry crowd of some 75 to 100 people has built up in one of the hallways of a center and that only one superior officer and two subordinate officers are on duty in the building. A glass panel in one of the stairway doors has just been broken under the pressure of the crowd and a bench has been hurled down a flight of stairs. The one of the following actions that the superior officer *SHOULD* take in this situation is to
   A. push his way into the crowd and try to reason with them
   B. order the two other officers to try to quiet the crowd
   C. call the police on 911 and meet them outside the building
   D. do nothing at this point in order to avoid a riot

1.____

2. One of the duties and responsibilities of a supervisor is to test the knowledge of the officers concerning their post conditions. This should be done if the officer's assignment is
   A. fixed only   B. roving only
   C. roving only in a troublesome post
   D. either fixed or roving

2.____

3. An officer discovers early one morning that an office in the building he guards has been burglarized. Of the following, it is important for the officer to *FIRST*
   A. go through the building and look for suspects
   B. call the police and protect the area and whatever evidence exists until they arrive
   C. allow people into their offices as they come to work
   D. examine, sort and handle all evidence before the police get there

3.____

4. Assume that two officers are interrogating one suspect. How should these officers position themselves during the interrogation?
   A. One officer should stand on either side of the suspect.
   B. One officer should stand to the right of the suspect, and the other officer should stand behind the suspect.
   C. Both officers should stand to the right of the suspect.
   D. One officer should stand to the right of the suspect, and the other officer should stand in front of the suspect.

4.____

5. A witness who takes an oath to testify truly and who states as true any matter which he knows to be false is guilty of
   A. perjury   B. libel   C. slander   D. fraud

5.____

6. An officer checking a substance suspected of containing narcotics should, GENERALLY,
   A. taste it in small amounts
   B. send it to a laboratory for analysis
   C. smell it for its distinctive odor
   D. examine it for its unusual texture

7. A certain center is situated in an area where frequent outbreaks of hostilities seem to be focused on the center itself. Which of the following BEST explains why the center may be a target for hostile acts? It
   A. serves community needs
   B. represents governmental authority
   C. represents all ethnic groups
   D. serves as a neutral battlefield

8. An officer often deals with people who might be addicted to drugs. The one of the following symptoms which is NOT generally an indication of drug addiction is
   A. dilation of the eye pupils
   B. frequent yawning and sneezing
   C. a deep, rasping cough
   D. continual itching of the arms and legs

9. In emergency situations, panic will MOST probably occur when people are
   A. unexpectedly confronted with a terrorizing condition from which there appears to be no escape
   B. angry and violent
   C. anxious about circumstances which are not obvious, easily visible or within the immediate area
   D. familiar with the effects of the emergency

10. The one of the following actions on the part of a person that would NOT be considered "resisting arrest" is
    A. retreating and running away
    B. saying, "You can't arrest me."
    C. pushing the officer aside
    D. pulling away from an officer's grasp

11. Which of the following items would NOT be considered an APPROPRIATE item of uniform for an officer to wear while on duty?
    A. Reefer type overcoat
    B. Leather laced shoes with flat soles
    C. White socks
    D. Cap cover with cap device displayed

12. What can happen to an officer if the leather thong on his night stick is NOT twisted correctly? The
    A. baton may be taken out of tee officer's hand
    B. officer's wrist may be broken
    C. leather will tear more easily
    D. officer's arm may be injured

13. The one of the following kinds of information which SHOULD be included in the log book is
    A. any important matter of police information
    B. an item noted in Standard Operating Procedures only
    C. everything of general interest
    D. a crime or offense only

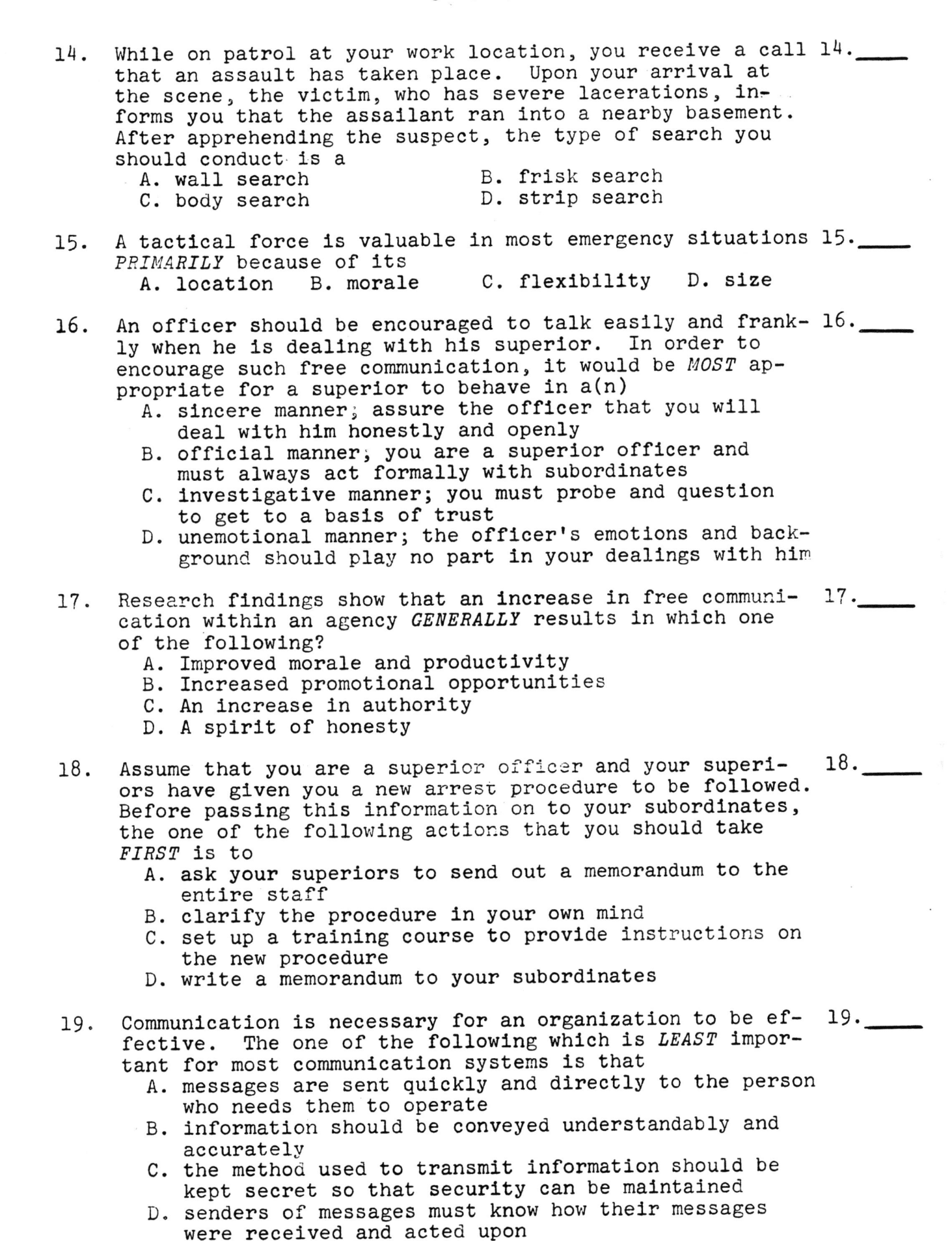

14. While on patrol at your work location, you receive a call that an assault has taken place. Upon your arrival at the scene, the victim, who has severe lacerations, informs you that the assailant ran into a nearby basement. After apprehending the suspect, the type of search you should conduct is a
    A. wall search
    B. frisk search
    C. body search
    D. strip search

15. A tactical force is valuable in most emergency situations PRIMARILY because of its
    A. location   B. morale   C. flexibility   D. size

16. An officer should be encouraged to talk easily and frankly when he is dealing with his superior. In order to encourage such free communication, it would be MOST appropriate for a superior to behave in a(n)
    A. sincere manner; assure the officer that you will deal with him honestly and openly
    B. official manner; you are a superior officer and must always act formally with subordinates
    C. investigative manner; you must probe and question to get to a basis of trust
    D. unemotional manner; the officer's emotions and background should play no part in your dealings with him

17. Research findings show that an increase in free communication within an agency GENERALLY results in which one of the following?
    A. Improved morale and productivity
    B. Increased promotional opportunities
    C. An increase in authority
    D. A spirit of honesty

18. Assume that you are a superior officer and your superiors have given you a new arrest procedure to be followed. Before passing this information on to your subordinates, the one of the following actions that you should take FIRST is to
    A. ask your superiors to send out a memorandum to the entire staff
    B. clarify the procedure in your own mind
    C. set up a training course to provide instructions on the new procedure
    D. write a memorandum to your subordinates

19. Communication is necessary for an organization to be effective. The one of the following which is LEAST important for most communication systems is that
    A. messages are sent quickly and directly to the person who needs them to operate
    B. information should be conveyed understandably and accurately
    C. the method used to transmit information should be kept secret so that security can be maintained
    D. senders of messages must know how their messages were received and acted upon

20. Which one of the following is the *CHIEF* advantage of listening willingly to subordinate officers and encouraging them to talk freely and honestly? It
    A. reveals to superiors the degree to which ideas that are passed down are accepted by subordinates
    B. reduces the participation of subordinates in the operation of the department
    C. encourages officers to try for promotion
    D. enables officers to learn about security leaks on the part of officials

21. A superior may be informed through either oral or written reports. Which one of the following is an *ADVANTAGE* of using oral reports?
    A. There is no need for a formal record of the report.
    B. An exact duplicate of the report is not easily transmitted to others.
    C. A good oral report requires little time for preparation.
    D. An oral report involves two-way communication between a subordinate and his superior.

22. Of the following, the *MOST* important reason why officers should communicate effectively with the public is to
    A. improve the public's understanding of information that is important for them to know
    B. establish a friendly relationship
    C. obtain information about the kinds of people who come to the center
    D. convince the public that services are adequate

23. Officers should generally *NOT* use phrases like "too hard," "too easy" and "a lot" principally because such phrases
    A. may be offensive to some minority groups
    B. are too informal
    C. mean different things to different people
    D. are difficult to remember

24. The ability to communicate clearly and concisely is an important element in effective leadership. Which of the following statements about oral and written communication is *GENERALLY* true?
    A. Oral communication is more time-consuming.
    B. Written communication is more likely to be misinterpreted.
    C. Oral communication is useful only in emergencies.
    D. Written communication is useful mainly when giving information to fewer than twenty people.

25. Rumors can often have harmful and disruptive effects on an organization. Which one of the following is the *BEST* way to prevent rumors from becoming a problem?
    A. Refuse to act on rumors, thereby making them less believable
    B. Increase the amount of information passed along by the "grapevine"
    C. Distribute as much factual information as possible
    D. Provide training in report writing

KEY (CORRECT ANSWERS)

1.	C		11.	C
2.	D		12.	A
3.	B		13.	A
4.	B		14.	A
5.	A		15.	C
6.	B		16.	A
7.	B		17.	A
8.	C		18.	B
9.	A		19.	C
10.	B		20.	A

21. D
22. A
23. C
24. B
25. C

POLICE SCIENCE
EXAMINATION SECTION

DIRECTIONS FOR THIS SECTION:
Each question or incomplete statement is followed by several suggested answers or completions. Select the one that BEST answers the question or completes the statement. *PRINT THE LETTER OF THE CORRECT ANSWER IN THE SPACE AT THE RIGHT.*

TEST 1

1. The sergeant is the key man in the enforcement of discipline.
   Of the following, the BEST justification for this statement is that
   A. the sergeant, as compared with other supervisory officers, has a more rounded view of the operation of the Force as a whole
   B. the sergeant was most recently a patrolman himself, and so is more likely to view minor violations sympathetically
   C. the sergeant, as compared with other supervisory officers, is in closer contact with the men in the field
   D. there must be proportionately more sergeants than other supervisory officers if a police organization is to be well balanced

2. Sergeants may find that it is the older members of the Force who require the most attention on their part.
   This statement assumes MOST directly that
   A. competence in police work will increase with experience
   B. strict supervision may increase the tendency on the part of patrolmen to break minor regulations
   C. the need for supervision may have little relationship to the amount of experience
   D. young members of the Force are usually less well acquainted with detailed regulations

3. In the clinical approach to disciplinary problems, attention is focused on the basic causes of which the overt reactions are merely symptomatic rather than on the specific violations which have brought the employee unfavorable notice.
   The MOST accurate implication of this statement is that the clinical approach
   A. results in prompt and more uniform treatment of violators
   B. does not evaluate the justice and utility of penalties which may be applied in each case
   C. provides for greater insight into the underlying factors which have led to the infractions of discipline
   D. avoids the necessity for disciplinary action

4. It is generally agreed that an individual conference with a patrolman is MOST effective when the sergeant
   A. limits the discussion to one particular problem and takes no initiative in the discussion except for answering specific questions
   B. opens the discussion with brief comment on some of his own personal problems so as to put the patrolman at ease
   C. has had the same problem brought to his attention recently by other patrolmen under his supervision

1

    D. discusses specific problems with the patrolman and the progress made, with a view to stimulating self development of skills

5. In disciplining men, the one of the following which is NOT a *good* principle to follow is to
    A. administer disciplinary measures in a quiet way, varying penalties as individual cases warrant
    B. reprimand them sharply when they deserve it so that others can hear it and will be more careful themselves
    C. lecture the men as a group at regular intervals to prevent disregard of rules and procedures
    D. make your criticisms immediately after something wrong is done

6. In order to build a spirit of cooperation among his staff, a supervisor must call attention to correct as well as incorrect behavior in a manner that subordinates will feel is consistent and reasonable.
Of the following, the BEST rule for the supervisor to follow is:
    A. Call attention to incorrect behavior only if it is significant, but give praise for any form of correct behavior
    B. In discussing deficiencies, treat them as problems to be overcome rather than as personal criticisms
    C. Never single out one subordinate for praise in front of the entire staff
    D. All instances of criticism should be preceded by instances of commendation of equal significance

7. In using praise as a motivating force for good work, the sergeant should realize that praising his men too frequently is *undesirable* CHIEFLY because
    A. the patrolmen will become too impressed with their own competence
    B. the praise is likely to lose its value as an incentive
    C. well organized criticism of patrol performance is better than praise
    D. praise is only effective when coupled with criticism

8. It is generally agreed that evaluating subordinate's work performance should be a continuing process.
The PRIMARY purpose of such evaluation by the sergeant would be to
    A. arrive at a mutual understanding of how well the patrolman is performing his assigned duties
    B. create a proper working relationship between the sergeant and the patrolman
    C. discover new work methods which can be useful to the patrolman in improving his job performance
    D. enable the sergeant to establish accurate performance standards to use in appraising the work of all the men under his supervision

9. It has been suggested that a sergeant should strive constantly to develop each of his patrolmen to the limit of the latter's ability and skills.
This suggestion is, *generally*,
    A. *advisable;* although basically alike, individuals possess widely different backgrounds and each patrol-

man must be given training in the specific duties of his immediate job
- B. *inadvisable;* individuals differ from each other and urging an unambitious employee to greater effort against his will may make him a reluctant and less satisfactory worker
- C. *advisable;* only by full utilization of each patrolman's talents can maximum service be obtained
- D. *inadvisable;* assisting patrolmen to develop themselves may result in their dissatisfaction when insufficient opportunities for promotion are available

10. One of the patrolmen under your supervision presents minor disciplinary problems. Investigation discloses that he has had a good record under several other sergeants.
Under these circumstances, the BEST course of action to follow is to
- A. discuss this matter with your superior officer inasmuch as the other sergeants appear to have been much too lenient
- B. ask a sergeant who formerly supervised this patrolman to advise the man to change his attitude
- C. exercise strict close supervision until the condition is corrected
- D. review your treatment of the man to determine if the fault lies with you

10. ...

11. Most police departments of large American cities decentralize their police organization by establishing precinct stations which operate almost independently of central headquarters. Occasionally, however, specialized units, requiring special skills, such as the homicide squad or identification experts, are on orders from central headquarters even though assigned to local precincts.
Of the following, the MOST valid reason for such exceptions is that
- A. these specialized functions are of the greatest importance among police functions and require the direct supervision of central headquarters
- B. it would be unlikely to find sufficient numbers of superior officers in the various local precincts who could give qualified supervision and guidance to the men in these specialized units
- C. such specialized units are probably not needed in each of the police precincts
- D. personnel assigned to specialized units should receive uniform training and instructions

11. ...

12. It is universally recognized that superior officers play a very important role in maintaining employee morale and in guiding their subordinates so as to avoid problems of discipline.
The one of the following methods of basic supervision which would be LEAST useful to a superior officer in this connection is for him to inform each of his subordinates of the
- A. exact tasks he is to perform
- B. comparison of his job performanue with that of the other officers in his unit
- C. standards of performance for each aspect of his job

12. ...

3

D. objectives of his job and of the unit in which he works

13. Orders cannot be carried out properly by a subordinate unless he understands them.
Therefore, in the process of giving orders, it is generally BEST for the sergeant to
    A. give orders covering only the smallest possible part of a job at one time, so as to correct any misunderstanding before starting on the next part
    B. rely upon the common sense of the subordinate to ask questions if he does not understand the orders
    C. ask whether the orders are understood
    D. ask sufficiently probing questions to determine whether the orders are being understood

13. ...

14. Assume that a newly-appointed sergeant finds that several of his subordinates have greater seniority in the department, but ranked much lower than he on the list for promotion to sergeant and may not be promoted for some years.
The BEST way for the sergeant to handle this situation is to
    A. ask his captain to transfer these men to different locations or apply for a transfer himself
    B. assert his authority immediately so that they will accept his supervision
    C. gain their cooperation by being particularly friendly and treating them as equals
    D. treat them the same as the other men, but make a point of consulting them on matters on which they are well informed

14. ...

15. A police sergeant has adopted the practice of spending a considerable amount of time accompanying each of his subordinates in their patrol cars and, in the course of normal motorized patrol, giving them training in observation and patrol techniques. For a sergeant to make *regular* use of this method of training his subordinates is
    A. *inadvisable*, MAINLY because the subordinates will be ill at ease
    B. *advisable*, MAINLY because the sergeant will be able to develop an informal, friendly relationship with his subordinates
    C. *inadvisable*, MAINLY because it would be wasteful to give such training on an individual basis rather than in groups
    D. *advisable*, MAINLY because of the benefits to be derived from on-the-spot training by an experienced superior officer with specific knowledge of the area

15. ...

16. A subordinate who is one of the most capable and efficient patrolmen in your squad is continually complaining about his assignments, although he is given his fair share of undesirable and desirable tasks. You have noticed that his complaints are undermining the morale of the other men.
The BEST of the following actions for you to take is to
    A. make him your unofficial assistant so that he will get more satisfaction from his work
    B. request his transfer to a squad where there will be more opportunity for him to use his capabilities
    C. have a confidential talk with him, explain the bad effect of his complaints, and ask him to curb them

16. ...

D. have a confidential talk with the other men and ask them not to pay attention to his complaints

17. Soon after he was promoted to the rank of captain and assigned to a precinct, Captain Doe discovered that his command was poorly organized and that many men in it hardly knew their own jobs, and little concerning the jobs of their fellow officers on any level. He therefore, instituted an intensive training program, in which a selected group of officers on each level were required to learn their own duties as well as the duties of the next higher level in the chain of command. Thus, in the absence of the desk lieutenant, a specific sergeant could be assigned to the desk. In the absence of the captain himself, a specific lieutenant could serve as acting captain.
This program instituted by the captain to improve the efficiency of both the men and the command as a whole is *generally* known by experts as 17. ...
  A. the understudy system   B. executive training
  C. retraining   D. on-the-job training

18. The attitudes and actions of the sergeants will, in a large measure, determine the future development of new patrolmen while getting on-the-job training in the field and also the general climate of the precincts. They meet the patrolmen on a face-to-face basis daily and their attitudes will, to a certain extent, be adopted by their subordinates.
Of the following, the attitude which BEST fosters the *proper* climate in the organization is that 18. ...
  A. group discussion and individual development should be operating at all points of decision-making
  B. supervision is a constant process of development and the supervisor willingly accepts new concepts of proven worth
  C. supervision has as its chief goal the subordinate's immediate and unquestioning acceptance of others
  D. no one under supervision has any authority for unrestricted action or decision

19. To conform with directions from headquarters, a change is adopted in a certain procedure. A sergeant finds, after a short period, that the old procedure was discinctly superior.
Of the following, the BEST action for him to take is to 19. ...
  A. have one of his experienced patrolmen broach the matter by bringing it to the attention of the commanding officer
  B. follow the new procedure without comment because the reasons for doing so will probably become self-evident
  C. follow the new procedure until superior officers learn of its drawbacks and **amend it**
  D. follow the new **procedure and assemble** definite facts and figures to prove its inadequacy to his superior officer

20. Your superior officer notifies you, the patrol sergeant, that several of the patrolmen have complained to him about your harsh supervisory methods.
Of the following, the FIRST reply you should make is to 20. ...

5

A. tell him that in doing your job you have always considered only the welfare of the department and the citizens it protects
B. ask him what specific acts have been considered harsh
C. ask him to refuse to listen to such complaints and to instruct these men to observe the chain of command
D. promise to ease up on the men

21. The one of the following which is LEAST descriptive of the appropriate functions of a supervisor with respect to his subordinates is a responsibility to
    A. guide and motivate their behavior to fit the plans and jobs which have been established
    B. understand their feelings and the problems they face as they translate plans into completed action
    C. reconcile equitable treatment of all subordinates with differences in individual needs
    D. emphasize attention to the downward flow of orders from higher executives and minimize attention to the upward flow of information and attitudes from the rank and file

22. For a sergeant to encourage competition among patrolmen under his supervision is, *generally*,
    A. *advisable*, MAINLY because the patrolmen would be motivated to perform more efficiently
    B. *inadvisable*, MAINLY because the pressures of competition would adversely affect the performance of certain patrolmen
    C. *advisable*, MAINLY because competition would provide a concrete basis for evaluating patrolmen's performance
    D. *inadvisable*, MAINLY because the patrolmen would probably concentrate on tasks which are likely to get recognition and neglect other essential but less spectacular tasks

23. Assume that a police sergeant has just assigned a routine task to a patrolman under his supervision. After telling the patrolman what he wants done, the BEST course of action for the sergeant to take, in order to develop the patrolman's self confidence, would be to
    A. supervise the patrolman very closely as he proceeds with the task, in order to prevent him from making a mistake
    B. ask the patrolman for a detailed description of how he plans to do the job and make corrections, if necessary, before he proceeds
    C. allow the patrolman to proceed independently, leaving the method to his discretion and interfering only if necessary
    D. describe the exact method the patrolman should follow, before allowing him to proceed with the task

24. Police sergeants are sometimes transferred from one branch of police work to a radically different and unfamiliar field.
The one of the following that would contribute MOST to the sergeant's *successful* assumption of his supervisory responsibilities in his new assignment would be his ability to
    A. devote himself tirelessly to the new field for the first few months until he becomes more expert in it

B. select dependable assistants from among his new subordinates and confer with them before acting on difficult or technical problems with which he is unfamiliar
C. assert his authority during the period in which he must learn from his subordinates
D. admit to his subordinates that he is inexperienced, and not exercise his authority until he becomes expert in the new field

25. In assigning various functions to the patrolmen under his supervision, a sergeant should go on the assumption that a patrolman will be able to
    A. learn many different types of work
    B. perform one type of work much better than other types
    C. perform well in a type of work only if he has had considerable experience in it
    D. perform any type of work in which he is given training

TEST 2

1. A police department can attempt to obtain compliance with law either by developing a public willingness to conform to the desired pattern of behavior or by compelling people to conform by threat of punishment.
Proponents of compliance with a minimum of enforcement claim as a CHIEF argument in its favor that
    A. it is a less costly process than a policy of strict enforcement
    B. strict enforcement procedures will tend to lead our country towards a totalitarian government
    C. it is the most effective means of achieving immediate results in controlling crime waves or eruptions
    D. only a favorable attitude of the public to law observance can bring about real and lasting progress in the development of order and security

2. Recent years have seen a growing antagonism between the middle-class citizenry and the police.
The CHIEF reason for this has been the
    A. tremendous growth in demands for civil rights, coupled with the police duty to maintain order
    B. constant rise in the number of automobiles, coupled with the need to enforce the motor vehicle laws
    C. expanded use of repressive tactics by the police in their attempts to restrain thrill-seeking youths and adults with too much leisure time
    D. failure of the police to stamp out corruption in their own ranks while demanding total civilian adherence to law and order

3. The *basic* purpose of patrol is MOST effectively implemented by police activity which
    A. makes use of unmarked cars
    B. increases the potential offender's expectation of arrest
    C. emphasizes apprehension of offenders
    D. de-emphasizes routine police duties and emphasizes special services

4. Experts state that the need for supervision of motorized patrols is of paramount importance in the modern police department.
   This statement is *true* PRIMARILY because motorized patrols
   A. bear the chief load of police activity and must cope with varied calls for assistance and other duties
   B. furnish police services to outlying and sparsely populated area more quickly than foot patrol
   C. provide patrol services over large geographic areas with varying crime rates
   D. employ highly trained staff and very costly mechanical equipment

5. The statement has been made that the motorized beat should overlap the foot beats and calls for service should be assigned to the motorized officer.
   This statement is *generally*
   A. *true;* motorized and foot-patrol beats can be organized on each shift so that all will contain equal needs for the various patrol services
   B. *false;* motorized beats should provide a shorter average distance between points than the foot-patrol beats
   C. *true;* the foot patrolman thus devotes his time primarily to his inspectional duties
   D. *false;* each motorized beat should contain a proportionate share of the community territory

6. When transporting a prisoner in a four-door sedan, it would be BEST for the two-man crew to handcuff
   A. the prisoner's wrists in front of him, seat him in the front of the car and have one officer seated in the rear
   B. the prisoner's wrists behind his back, and seat him in the rear of the car with one of the officers
   C. the prisoner's wrists in front of him, and seat him in the rear of the car with one of the officers
   D. one of the prisoner's wrists to one of the officer's wrists and seat him in the rear of the car

7. The disguise worn by a patrolman-decoy dressed as a woman should be complete and consistent with the environment he is patrolling, so as to attract a minimum of attention. He must not, however, carry his firearm and his shield in his handbag or purse.
   The CHIEF reason for taking this precaution is that
   A. the patrolman must have his shield more readily available should the need arise for prompt identification
   B. there would be less likelihood of the criminal's suspicions being aroused by the patrolman's excessively careful handling of the handbag or purse
   C. a sudden successful purse snatching could result in providing the criminal with ready means to commit other crimes
   D. his firearm should be more readily accessible since that may make the difference between safety and danger for the patrolman

8. The one of the following which states the BEST plan for an officer on patrol to follow when patrolling his post is for him to

A. give equal coverage to all parts of his post or area of patrol
B. patrol all quiet areas of his post first and then spend the rest of his tour of duty in potential high-hazard areas
C. cover all parts of his post but without using any fixed schedule or route
D. patrol in such a manner as to be visible on post only about half of each tour and seek inconspicuous locations the rest of the time

9. Proper selective patrolling entails combining time and location factors.
   From a crime prevention point of view, the CHIEF implication of this statement for a superior officer in charge of officers on patrol posts is that he should
   A. arrange the assignments of his subordinates to insure their being in the places of greatest potential danger to the peace at the times of greatest potential hazard to life and property
   B. personally visit the places of greatest incidence of crime at unannounced and irregular intervals in order to observe the type of patrol performed by his subordinates
   C. strive to improve the efficiency of his subordinate officers to insure their responding to the scene of a crime with a minimum of delay
   D. rotate the hours and assignments of all his subordinate officers on patrol to give them experience at times and places of greatest incidence of crime

9. ...

10. Proper police patrol is considered basic to an effective juvenile crime prevention program.
    The one of the following plans which would be LEAST conducive to proper and effective patrol is to
    A. place most emphasis on areas attractive to juveniles during the night and after school hours
    B. place great emphasis on joint patrol activities with attendance officers during normal school hours
    C. assign definite responsibility for specific areas to specific officers
    D. emphasize first-hand observation of conditions which may contribute to delinquency

10. ...

11. The one of the following which is NOT an advantage of motor patrol is that of
    A. providing an officer with an element of surprise by enabling an irregular and not easily predictable patrol
    B. enabling an officer to cover a larger area with greater efficiency
    C. enabling an officer to reach the scene of action rapidly and in better condition to cope with the situation
    D. providing an officer with maximum opportunity for observation within range of the senses

11. ...

12. The one of the following situations in which it would generally be MOST advisable for a police department to maintain and use a call-box system in its law-enforcement work is one in which the department has

12. ...

A. a small number of superior officers assigned to supervise their subordinates on patrol
B. a disproportionate number of relatively inexperienced officers assigned to patrol duties
C. a large number of officers assigned to foot patrol
D. only one officer assigned to each radio motor patrol car

13. Experience has shown that MOST burglaries reported to the police between 8:30 a.m. and 10 a.m. involve burglaries committed   13. ...
A. in commercial or industrial establishments
B. in homes or apartments   C. by household servants
D. by dishonest employees

14. A recent development in patrol practice has been the use of motor scooters.   14. ...
Of the following, the CHIEF advantage in the use of motor scooters over other vehicles for patrol purposes is that they are a valuable supplement to
A. motor patrol   B. foot patrol
C. horse control of crowds   D. supervisory inspection

15. Of the following, the MOST important factor in deciding which areas require two-men automobile patrol rather than one-man automobile patrol is the   15. ...
A. frequency of anticipated incidents in relation to the geographic extent of the patrol sector
B. need to insure greater attentiveness to duty
C. frequency of discovery by patrolmen of incidents that require more than one man to deal with them safely and effectively
D. provision for more frequent relief periods and greater diversification of patrol duties

16. The commanding officer of a certain precinct, which has had a rising crime rate, has reorganized his patrol force in such a manner as to create a public impression that the uniformed force is frequently and conspicuously patrolling all sections of the precinct at all times.   16. ...
The MOST likely result of this new plan of patrol is that
A. the public will feel more secure although the actual number of crimes is likely to remain unchanged
B. would-be offenders who have already planned a crime will not be deterred from going ahead with their plans
C. it will not in any way affect the extent to which would-be offenders believe their crime, if executed, will be detected
D. would-be offenders will tend to feel that the likelihood of their successfully executing crimes will be lessened

17. The patrol force is the backbone of the police department, and its effective use is an important consideration.   17. ...
The one of the following which is the MOST accurate statement regarding the effective use of foot and auto patrol is that
A. in the largest cities auto patrol should completely replace foot patrol
B. there is no necessity for auto patrol in the smaller communities
C. nearly all foot patrol can be replaced by auto patrol in the smaller cities

D. the size of a city is not a factor in determining the type of patrol to be used

18. It has been suggested that a corps of dogs be trained to serve on patrol service with regular officers because the animals are especially capable of getting in and out of narrow alleys much more quickly, thoroughly and safely than the officers can.
The one of the following which is the CHIEF drawback to their use in such work is the
    A. comparatively long period of training required to accustom them to narrow spaces
    B. general presence of cats in such areas
    C. high cost of upkeep and care
    D. possibility of the animal attacking the officer

18. ...

Questions 19-22.
DIRECTIONS: Questions 19 through 22 are based on the following paragraph.

During actual pursuit of a traffic offender and particularly in speed cases when the operator of the police vehicle is maneuvering for clocking, there is a need for haste so that the clocking may be applied when the motorist is traveling in violation of the speed laws. However, necessary haste cannot include rashness. The pursuit, for whatever purpose, must not be at the expense of the safety of other users of the road. When changing lanes to get ahead, the police operator must do it safely or not at all. Giving proper and clear signals as to his intentions is a must but should not be construed as a guarantee of completing the maneuver safely. He must use good judgment in determining whether his "S" pass can be made safely. If there is a possibility that **the motorist to be passed would be forced to apply his brakes to avoid a collision** the passing should be delayed. Instead, he should be notified by hand signal of the police vehicle operator's intention to pass and directed to reduce speed so that the police vehicle can be driven past safely. In other than emergencies, sudden stops should be avoided. In a situation where law-enforcement needs require a sudden reduction in speed, consideration must be given to the vehicles behind to preclude rear-end collisions. A gradual reduction in speed, coupled with a sufficient warning to convey the intention to stop or turn is the preferential course of action. Similarly, if at all possible, the police operator should avoid turning at locations that are clearly unfavorable for turning, such as through safety zones or between stanchions placed to prohibit passage, since such maneuvers increase the probability of an accident.

19. The one of the following which MOST adequately describes the central theme of the paragraph is: The
    A. essentiality of maintaining maximum speed during the pursuit of motorized traffic offenders
    B. danger of passing intervening vehicles while pursuing motorized traffic offenders
    C. precautions to take in the pursuit of motorized traffic offenders
    D. methods of attaining greater speed while pursuing motorized traffic offenders

19. ...

20. According to the above paragraph, when the operator of a police vehicle is pursuing an offender in the same lane, and approaches another vehicle which is between him and the offender's vehicle, it would be MOST correct to state

20. ...

TEST 2

that the operator of the police vehicle
- A. may attempt to by-pass the vehicle between him and the offender with complete safety so long as he has given proper and clear automatic and hand signals to its operator
- B. may attempt to by-pass the vehicle between him and the offender even if it would be necessary for him to make an "S" pass to do so
- C. must not attempt to by-pass the vehicle between him and the offender until he has directed its operator to reduce speed
- D. must not attempt to by-pass the vehicle between him and the offender unless he can do so safely without leaving the lane

21. According to the above paragraph, when the operator of a police vehicle notices a motorist driving along and suspects that the motorist may have just violated some traffic law, he MAY
    - A. not exceed the posted speed limit except when he is attempting to get into position to clock the offender's speed
    - B. travel at whatever speed he deems necessary in order to catch up with and clock the speeding suspect but only as long as both remain in the same lane and the lane remains clear
    - C. not exceed the posted speed limit unless he feels certain that the offender has exceeded or can be reasonably expected to exceed the posted speed limit
    - D. exceed the posted speed limit in order to apprehend the violator but must never do so if there is any possibility of danger to anyone else using the road

22. A police vehicle is in pursuit of a motorized traffic offender who is attempting to evade capture by alternating between weaving in and out of slower-moving traffic, making sudden stops, and going through safety zones or stanchions placed to prohibit passage.
    According to the above paragraph, the operator in pursuit should, *generally*,
    - A. follow right behind the offender through all these maneuvers but keep alert for sudden changes in tactics
    - B. avoid engaging in such of these maneuvers as he can without increasing the distance between him and the offender
    - C. refrain from engaging in driving maneuvers similar to the offender's without duly considering the inherent dangers
    - D. anticipate the offender's actions and take the steps necessary to cut him off when he emerges from safety zones

23. According to the Penal Law, it would be MOST correct to state, with respect to the carrying of a switchblade knife by a person other than a peace officer or prison official, that such a weapon
    - A. can be carried by a validly licensed hunter while on a hunting trip

B. can be carried by a uniformed member of a recognized scout or militia organization
C. cannot be carried legally by any such person at any time
D. can be carried and used by a person in his own home in self-defense

24. "Policy" or "Numbers Game" is a scheme of chance wherein the player selects a number containing three figures which are written on a slip of paper, and given with the amount bet to a collector. The winning number is determined each day by chance. In this game, the winner gets 600 times the amount bet and the loser gets nothing.
According to the Penal Law of the State, it would be MOST correct to state that
A. anyone contriving, drawing, or participating in any way in policy can be charged as a common gambler
B. every lottery is legally classified and triable as "policy"
C. a "policy" collector cannot be prosecuted for lottery under PL 970 (common gambler) or PL 1372 (assisting in a lottery) because the lottery laws were enacted before "policy" came into being
D. every "policy" is a lottery and collectors may be prosecuted under PL 970 (common gambler) or PL 1372 (assisting in a lottery)

25. Tom Brown has been taken into custody by the police as the prime suspect in a holdup murder. The victim had been a beloved local physician noted for his benevolent and charitable nature. Rumors spread rapidly and a mob quickly surrounds the police vehicle in which Brown is about to be transported to the station house. There are cries of "kill him" from the crowd which is trying to break into the vehicle.
According to the Penal Law of the State, the members of the mob can be charged with lynching if
A. their actions cause any injury to the persons or equipment of the police
B. their actions actually cause the death of Brown
C. they commit any act of physical violence against Brown's person
D. they forcibly obtain custody of Brown from the police

TEST 3

1. Officer Peters has arrested J. Doe for a violation of law. The arresting officer should inform the desk officer, for appropriate notification, if Doe
A. has $7,000 in his possession, which is not the proceeds of the current crime with which he is charged
B. is charged with a gambling offense and has $1,000 in his possession
C. owns a four-year-old automobile which is seized as evidence
D. is charged with a gambling offense and the sum of $400 "in the pot" is seized as evidence

TEST 3

2. Patrolman Fred Ford of Precinct A, while on foot patrol, observes John Grant, who appears to be about 14 years of age, playing shuffleboard in the Friendly Tavern. John, who came in alone, is playing with three young men, who are estimated to be about 22 years of age. Patrolman Ford confirms from an exiting patron that John is actually 14 years of age and learns that he lives eight blocks away, in Precinct B. The owner of the Friendly Tavern is serving as bartender when Patrolman Ford observes Grant.
Accordingly, Patrolman Ford should
   A. take Grant into custody, and arrest the owner of the Friendly Tavern
   B. arrest Grant and the owner of the Friendly Tavern
   C. take Grant into custody and issue a summons to the owner of the Friendly Tavern
   D. arrest Grant and issue a summons to the owner of the Friendly Tavern

2. ...

3. A member of the force may make an arrest for crimes and offenses NOT committed in his presence
   A. when a person is charged with operating a motor vehicle erratically while intoxicated and in a condition likely to cause an accident
   B. when requested orally by an election inspector to arrest a person for refusing to obey the lawful commands of the election inspector
   C. upon receipt of a complaint from a member of a municipal agency, while wearing an insignia of authority in the course of his duties, that the person has violated a regulation of the State Civil Defense Emergency Act
   D. upon verbal order of a judge

3. ...

4. Officers on patrol duty are often called upon to deal with aided cases.
In dealing with such cases, the officer involved must
   A. accompany the patient to the hospital if the latter is suffering from a communicable disease
   B. accompany the person involved to a municipal shelter if the person is a lost adult
   C. unload his revolver when bringing a mental patient into the psychiatric ward of a hospital
   D. use restraining equipment on any mental patient on orders from any ambulance attendant

4. ...

5. Radio Patrol Car No. 586, assigned to the 104th Precinct, is responding to a call for police at the scene of a homicide which occurred three blocks inside the boundary of the 83rd Precinct. At a point two blocks from the scene of the homicide, Car 586 is struck on the left side by a taxi which failed to make a required full stop. Officer Wynn, who is driving Car 586, suffers a broken left arm and two rib fractures; Officer Loos, the recorder, is unhurt.
Accordingly, this accident must be reported on Form MV 104A which MUST be prepared by the
   A. recorder of Car 586
   B. first member of the force who arrives at the scene of the vehicular accident
   C. radio motor patrol sergeant of the 83rd Precinct
   D. radio motor patrol sergeant of the 104th Precinct

5. ...

6. The Family Court Act authorizes any member of the force to take into protective custody any runaway child who, in the opinion of the member of the force, has left home without just cause.
   Accordingly, this Act applies to
   A. girls and boys under the age of 16, and the officer's action is recorded on the proper form
   B. girls under 18 and boys under 16, and the officer's action is recorded on the proper form
   C. girls and boys under 18, and the officer's action is recorded on the proper form
   D. girls under 16 and boys under 18, and the officer's action is recorded on the proper form

7. A patrolman who is asked to get aid for a sick person on his patrol post may summon an ambulance if he deems it necessary. Furthermore, if the sick person's condition seems to indicate the need for a doctor in addition, the decision to request a doctor MUST be made by the
   A. borough communications unit operator who received the call from the patrolman
   B. desk officer of the precinct concerned after being notified of the incident by the borough communications unit
   C. ambulance attendant after his arrival at the scene and his examination of the sick person
   D. patrolman who requested the ambulance

8. When immediate additional help is required at any location, the one of the following who is NOT authorized to request or order the transmission of a Signal 10-41, to which three sergeants and fifteen patrolmen would respond, is the
   A. superior officer in charge at the borough communications unit on the basis of information received from a member of the force on the scene
   B. desk officer of the precinct of occurrence on the basis of information received from a member of the force on the scene
   C. radio patrol car recorder who initially reports to the scene of the occurrence in response to a radio call from the borough communcations unit
   D. sergeant on the scene of the occurrence

9. Sergeant Robert Thomas reports to his designated mobilization point in response to the implementation of the unusual disorder plan. He then proceeds to his assigned sector with his detail. Accordingly, Sergeant Thomas should do *all* of the following EXCEPT
   A. assign men to vulnerable points as listed on the proper form (assignment sneet - unusual disorder)
   B. instruct the patrolmen to call the mobilization point for vehicles to transport prisoners
   C. return triplicate copy of the form to the mobilization point when the detail is dismissed
   D. issue an order to restrict the sale of alcoholic beverages in his sector

10. A prisoner must be informed of his right to contact his family or friends and the desk officer is required to telephone such persons free within the city limits at the request of the prisoner.

TEST 3/KE

The MAXIMUM number of such free phone calls which the desk officer is required to make is
   A. one   B. two   C. three   D. four

11. A sergeant on patrol is required to supervise the performance of duty of patrolmen on foot and radio motor patrol. In connection with this, he is required to
   A. indicate each visit to a patrolman on post by signing the patrolman's memorandum book
   B. notify the desk officer by telephone of all visits to each patrolman on post for entry in the telephone switchboard record
   C. visit every post within the patrol precinct once each tour
   D. call the station house every hour while patrolling to the right and every thirty minutes at any other time

12. A patrolman on patrol duty encounters an intoxicated sixteen-year-old boy. After questioning the boy, the patrolman informs the precinct desk officer of the exact location where the boy secured the alcoholic beverages. Accordingly, the IMMEDIATE investigation will be conducted by the
   A. patrolman on whose post the premises are located
   B. patrol sergeant of the precinct in which the premises are located
   C. precinct detective squad member assigned
   D. plainclothes squad member assigned

13. A sergeant assigned to a patrol precinct wants to visit, on police business, a prisoner in an institution operated by the Department of Correction. Accordingly, the sergeant should apply for a DD 21 (pass to visit prisoner) to the
   A. precinct commander   B. detective borough commander
   C. Chief Inspector   D. Chief of Detectives

KEYS (CORRECT ANSWERS)

TEST 1		TEST 2		TEST 3	
1. C	11. B	1. D	11. D	1. A	7. D
2. C	12. B	2. A	12. A	2. A	8. C
3. C	13. C	3. B	13. A	3. D	9. D
4. D	14. D	4. A	14. B	4. C	10. C
5. B	15. C	5. C	15. C	5. C	11. A
6. B	16. C	6. B	16. D	6. B	12. D
7. B	17. A	7. D	17. C		13. B
8. A	18. B	8. C	18. C		
9. C	19. D	9. A	19. C		
10. D	20. B	10. B	20. B		
	21. B		21. D		
	22. D		22. C		
	23. C		23. A		
	24. B		24. B		
	25. B		25. B		

EXAMINATION SECTION
TEST 1

DIRECTIONS: Each question or incomplete statement is followed by several suggested answers or completions. Select the one that BEST answers the question or completes the statement. *PRINT THE LETTER OF THE CORRECT ANSWER IN THE SPACE AT THE RIGHT.*

1. If S, the subject that investigator H is tailing, enters a large department store, H should
    A. wait outside the store in a concealed place until S comes out
    B. follow S into the store
    C. enter the store, but wait by the door
    D. wait outside the store but in a position near the door S entered

    1.___

2. Which of the following is MOST likely to indicate an attempt at falsification of a particular document?
    A. Change in style of handwriting within the document
    B. Illegible writing
    C. Erasures or alterations
    D. Folds or creases in the document

    2.___

3. A subject being tailed during a foot surveillance quickly turns and confronts the shadower and states, *Say Bud, are you tailing me?*
Of the following, the MOST appropriate action for the shadower to take is to
    A. ignore the question and keep on walking
    B. admit that he is shadowing the subject but refuse to tell him why
    C. deny the accusation but give no explanations
    D. give some excuse for his presence in the form of a cover-up

    3.___

4. K, an investigator, has been given the assignment of tailing S, a suspect, who will be traveling by car at night in the city.
Of the following, the SIMPLEST way for K to carry out this surveillance would be to
    A. mark S's car beforehand so it is identifiable at night
    B. memorize the model, color, and style of S's car
    C. memorize the license plate of S's car
    D. mechanically disable S's car so it will be unusable

    4.___

5. The United States Treasury Department may prove to be a valuable source of information in specialized instances. Which of the following types of information usually would NOT be in the custody of that Federal agency?
    A. Immigration records
    B. Records of licensed manufacturers of narcotics
    C. Importers and exporters records
    D. Records of persons or firms manufacturing alcohol

    5.___

6. Which of the following is a writ directing that documents or records be produced in court?
   A. Writ of habeas corpus
   B. Subpoena habeas corpus
   C. Order, pro hoc vice
   D. Subpoena duces tecum

7. *Modus Operandi* is a phrase frequently used in investigative work to refer to a
   A. specific type of investigation
   B. particular policy in tracing missing persons
   C. manner in which a criminal operates
   D. series of crimes committed by more than one person

8. P, an investigator, has been assigned to interview W, a witness, concerning a minor automobile accident. Although P has made no breach of the basic rules of contact and approach, he nevertheless recognizes that he and W have a personality clash and that a natural animosity has resulted.
   Of the following, P MOST appropriately should
   A. discuss the personality problem with W and attempt to resolve the difference
   B. stop the interview on some pretext and leave in a calm and pleasant manner, allowing an associate to continue the interview
   C. ignore the personality problem and continue as though nothing had happened
   D. change the subject matter being discussed since the facts sought may be the source of the animosity

9. Assume that an investigator desires to interview W, a reluctant witness to a bribery attempt that took place several weeks previously. Assume further that the interview can take place at a location to be designated by the interviewer.
   Of the following, the place of interview should PREFERABLY be the
   A. office of the interviewer
   B. home of W
   C. office of W
   D. scene where the event took place

10. Assume that T, an investigator, is testifying in court. He does not clearly remember the details of the incident about which he is testifying.
    Of the following, the MOST appropriate action for T to take is to
    A. admit he does not remember the details and go on to the next question
    B. look at his statement previously given to the attorney interviewing him before trial
    C. refresh his memory by referring to his notebook
    D. testify to only those items he can recall

11. Assume that as an investigator you are interviewing W, 11.___
    a witness. During the interview, it becomes apparent
    that W's statements are inaccurate and at variance with
    the facts previously established.
    In these circumstances, it would be BEST for you to
    A. tell W that his statements are inaccurate and point
       out how they conflict with previously established
       facts
    B. reword your questions and ask additional questions
       about the facts being discussed
    C. warn W that he may be required to testify under oath
       at a later date
    D. ignore W's statements if you have other information
       that support the facts

12. Assume that W, a witness being interviewed by you, an 12.___
    investigator, shows a tendency to ramble. His answers
    to your questions are lengthy and not responsive.
    In this situation, the BEST action for you to take is to
    A. permit W to continue because at some point he will
       tell you the information sought
    B. tell W that he is rambling and unresponsive and
       that more will be accomplished if he is brief and
       to the point
    C. control the interview so that complete and accurate
       information is obtained
    D. patiently listen to W since rambling is W's style
       and it cannot be changed

13. Assume that an investigator is to interview a witness. 13.___
    Of the following, the BEST procedure for the investigator
    to follow in regard to the use of his notebook is to
    A. take out his notebook at the start of the interview
       and immediately begin taking notes
    B. memorize the important facts related during the
       interview and enter them after the interview has
       been completed
    C. advise the witness that all his answers are being
       taken down to insure that he will tell the truth
    D. establish rapport with the witness and ask permission
       to jot down various data in his notebook

14. The first duty of the investigator who has in his posses- 14.___
    sion a document which may be used in evidence is to
    preserve it in its original condition.
    Following are three actions which might constitute rules
    for the handling of a document:
      I. Pick up the document with tweezers or a pin
     II. Staple the document to a folder so that it is
         protected
    III. Photograph or photocopy the document
    Which one of the following choices MOST accurately classi-
    fies the above statements into those which are APPROPRIATE
    and those which are NOT APPROPRIATE as procedures for
    handling such documents?

A. I and III are appropriate, but II is not appropriate.
B. I and II are appropriate, but III is not appropriate.
C. II is appropriate, but I and III are not appropriate.
D. III is appropriate, but I and II are not appropriate.

15. Of the following, which one would be the CLEAREST indication that a suspicious check is a forgery?   15.___
    A. There are smudges from carbon paper at the edges of the back of the check.
    B. The signature on the check is an exact duplicate of an authentic signature.
    C. The amount of the check has been crossed out and a new amount written in.
    D. Two different color inks were used in making out the check.

16. Assume an investigator is making an inspection of a desk and finds a writing pad on which a suspect may have written. The top page of the pad has indentations which were formed when the previous page was written on. Following are three procedures which might be appropriate in order to read the indentation: 16.___
    I. Hold the paper in such a manner that a single light source falls along the sheet at a parallel or oblique angle.
    II. Soak the pad in water and thoroughly dry it in the sun.
    III. Rub a piece of carbon paper lightly across the underside of the paper in question.
   Which one of the following choices classifies the above statements into those which are APPROPRIATE procedures and those which are NOT APPROPRIATE?
    A. I and II are appropriate, but III is not appropriate.
    B. II and III are appropriate, but I is not appropriate.
    C. I and III are appropriate, but II is not appropriate.
    D. II is appropriate, but I and III are not appropriate.

17. In order to conduct an effective interview, an interviewer's attention must be continuously directed in two ways, toward himself as well as toward the interviewee. Of the following, the PRIMARY danger in this division of attention is that the   17.___
    A. interviewer's behavior may become less natural and thus alienate the interviewee
    B. interviewee's span of attention will be shortened
    C. interviewer's response may be interpreted by the interviewee as being antagonistic
    D. interviewee's more or less concealed prejudices will come to the surface

18. X and Y go into a vault together and close the door. A shot is heard, and Y rushes out with a smoking gun in his hand.   18.___
    A witness to his event who said *Y shot X* would be offering
    A. direct evidence   B. real evidence
    C. circumstantial evidence D. hearsay evidence

19. Assume that an investigator is attempting to get a suspect to agree to take a lie detector or polygraph test.
    Which of the following actions on the part of the investigator would be LEAST appropriate?
    A. Describe the test to the suspect in simple language so that he understands the procedure.
    B. Suggest that the test is a means for the suspect to indicate his innocence.
    C. Discuss the test's capability of indicating whether a person is telling the truth.
    D. Suggest that a refusal to take the test indicates guilt.

20. The term *corpus delicti* is MOST appropriately used to refer to
    A. a body of criminal law   B. the body of a person
    C. a body of civil law   D. the body of a crime

21. Which of the following is considered the BEST type of permanent ink to use in preparing documents?
    A. Ball point   B. Nigrosine
    C. Log wood   D. Iron gallotannate

22. An important aspect of investigative work is the preservation of materials which may be used as evidence. Following are three statements which might constitute rules for the proper handling of blood in a fluid condition found at a crime scene:
      I. The blood should be removed with an eye dropper and placed in a test tube.
     II. Saline solution should be added to the blood sample in a ratio of 1 to 4.
    III. The sample blood should be frozen and delivered to the laboratory as soon as possible.
    Which of the following choices classifies the above actions into those which are APPROPRIATE and those which are INAPPROPRIATE?
    A. I and II are appropriate, but III is inappropriate.
    B. I and III are appropriate, but II is inappropriate.
    C. I is appropriate, but II and III are inappropriate.
    D. III is appropriate, but I and II are inappropriate.

23. The term *entrapment* refers to the act of
    A. peace officers or agents of the government in inducing a person to commit a crime not contemplated by him for the purpose of instituting a criminal prosecution against him
    B. private individuals inducing a person to commit an act not contemplated by him for the purpose of bringing a civil action against him
    C. peace officers or agents of the government in observing a person engaged in the commission of a criminal act and, therefore, obtaining direct evidence against the person
    D. private individuals or investigators in interrupting a person engaged in committing a criminal act

24. Assume you are investigating a person who is alleged to be an officer in a manufacturing corporation doing business in New York City.
Which of the following sources of information is the LEAST appropriate source to consult in checking whether this is true?
   A. POOR'S REGISTER OF DIRECTORS AND EXECUTIVES
   B. POLK'S BANKER'S ENCYCLOPEDIA
   C. MOODY'S MANUAL OF INVESTMENTS, AMERICAN AND FOREIGN
   D. POLK'S COPARTNERSHIP AND CORPORATION DIRECTORY

25. If an investigator is assigned to the surveillance of a suspect which requires the use of an automobile, it would generally be LEAST advisable for him to use a car
   A. rented from a rental agency
   B. personally owned by the investigator
   C. bearing special unregistered plates
   D. borrowed by someone who is trustworthy but has no official associations

KEY (CORRECT ANSWERS)

1. B
2. C
3. D
4. A
5. A

6. D
7. C
8. B
9. A
10. C

11. B
12. C
13. D
14. A
15. B

16. C
17. A
18. C
19. D
20. D

21. D
22. A
23. A
24. B
25. B

TEST 2

DIRECTIONS: Each question or incomplete statement is followed by several suggested answers or completions. Select the one that BEST answers the question or completes the statement. *PRINT THE LETTER OF THE CORRECT ANSWER IN THE SPACE AT THE RIGHT.*

1. Following are three statements regarding writing instruments:
    I. The hardness of the lead and the sharpness of the point affect the appearance of pencil writing.
    II. The ballpoint pen obscures the writer's ability to exhibit his characteristic habits of quality, rhythm, and shading.
    III. An examination of writing performed with a ballpoint pen easily reveals the angle at which the pen was held with relation to the writer's body and the paper.
   Which of the following choices classifies the above statements into those which are generally CORRECT and those which are generally INCORRECT?
     A. I is correct, but II and III are incorrect.
     B. II is correct, but I and III are incorrect.
     C. I and II are correct, but III is incorrect.
     D. I and III are correct, but II is incorrect.

   1.___

2. Following are three statements regarding procedures to be followed in obtaining exemplars from a suspect which may or may not be appropriate:
    I. After the suspect is seated and provided with writing materials, the investigator should dictate the comparison text, always indicating punctuation and paragraphing.
    II. The material should be dictated several times, the speed of the dictation being increased each time so that the suspect will be inclined to lapse into his normal handwriting habits.
    III. As each sheet is completed, it should be removed from the suspect so that he will not be able to imitate the first exemplars he has prepared.
   Which of the following choices classifies the above procedures into those which are APPROPRIATE and those which are INAPPROPRIATE?
     A. I and II are appropriate, but III is inappropriate.
     B. I and III are appropriate, but II is inappropriate.
     C. I is appropriate, but II and III are inappropriate.
     D. III is appropriate, but I and II are inappropriate.

   2.___

3. During an investigation, it may be necessary to take a *deposition*.
   The one of the following which BEST describes a *deposition* is
     A. a record made of the case progress
     B. a statement made by a witness in which he agrees to give testimony in court without resort to subpoena

   3.___

C. testimony of a witness reduced to writing under oath or affirmation, in answer to interrogatories
D. another name for an *affidavit*

4. Examination of handwriting on the basis of comparing the outer shapes of letters is known as the _____ method.
   A. holographic
   B. penographic
   C. calligraphic
   D. pedographic

5. An investigator who receives a lead from an anonymous phone caller would generally be BEST advised to
   A. ignore the information as unfounded
   B. tell the informant to call back when he is ready to divulge his identity
   C. determine from the informant the motivation behind his making the call
   D. get all relevant information possible on the assumption he will not hear from the caller again

6. In order to demonstrate his findings to the court, a document examiner must use enlarged, mounted photographs. Which of the following should ALSO be submitted to the court?
   A. Color enlargements, as well as black and white
   B. Normal-size photographs of the enlarged documents
   C. Negatives of the enlarged photographs
   D. Duplicates of the enlarged photographs

7. X, an investigator, has come upon a few documents belonging to Y, a person whom X is investigating. The documents cannot be taken or moved.
   Of the following, the MOST appropriate action for X to take is to
   A. make a record of the documents, making certain to include any names, addresses, and numbers mentioned even though they may appear meaningless at the time of discovery
   B. make a record only of those documents deemed relevant by him at the time of discovery, including names, addresses, and numbers mentioned
   C. leave the documents without making any notes because documents that cannot be moved may not be copied
   D. make a record only of those names, addresses, or numbers mentioned which are clearly relevant to the case

8. Assume that you are interviewing W, a neighbor of N, whom you are investigating. It is important to establish whether or not N uses alcoholic beverages excessively. Which of the following questions is MOST appropriate for obtaining the information you seek?
   A. Have you ever seen N intoxicated?
   B. Can you tell me something about N's habits?
   C. Do you know whether or not N is a patron of nearby bars?
   D. What is N's reputation in the neighborhood?

9. A check may be altered to change the amount, the name, or some other element.
   The one of the following which can BEST be used to discover any changes is
   A. a magnetometer
   B. an ultra-violet lamp
   C. a tensimeter
   D. polarography

10. Z, an investigator, is attempting to interview W concerning an accident witnessed by W. However, W is disinterested and indifferent.
    In order to encourage W's cooperation, Z should
    A. stimulate W's interest by stressing the importance of the information that he possesses
    B. impress upon W that Z is an investigator performing an official function
    C. warn W that the withholding of information may be considered as an obstruction of justice
    D. gain W's sympathy for Z, who is merely trying to do his job

11. Of the following, the three types of ink MOST commonly used in the United States today are:
    A. gallotannic, logwood, and nigrosine
    B. gallotannic, vanadium, and wolfram
    C. wolfram, logwood, and nigrosine
    D. vanadium, logwood, and nigrosine

12. Which of the following BEST describes the science of poroscopy?
    Identification
    A. by the casting of footprints
    B. by the tracing of tools used in a crime
    C. by means of sweat pores indicated on a fingerprint
    D. through the examination of human hairs

13. Which of the following statements concerning the folding of paper is generally ACCURATE?
    A. When uncut paper has been folded, the fibers remain unbroken.
    B. If an ink line is first drawn and the paper is subsequently folded, the line over the fold will not be even and uniform.
    C. If an ink line is written over an already existing fold, the ink will spread over the fold but protruding fibers will not become stained.
    D. It is almost impossible to determine whether a lead pencil line was drawn on a paper before or after it was folded.

14. All of the following are generally good methods of making erased lead-pencil writing visible EXCEPT
    A. examination in non-polarized light
    B. use of iodine fumes
    C. contrast photography
    D. photography in oblique light

15. Following are four statements concerning crime-scene photography that may or may not be valid:
    I. The general procedure of crime-scene photography aims at obtaining views of broad areas of the crime locale, supplemented by closer views of sections containing important detail.
    II. The crime scene should be first photographed in its original, undisturbed state.
    III. Crime-scene photographs are of great value to the investigator because they accurately show the distances between objects.
    IV. If a room is to be photographed, a set of at least four views will be required to show the room adequately.

    Which of the following choices MOST accurately classifies the above into those which are VALID procedures and those which are NOT VALID?
    A. I and II are valid, but III and IV are not valid.
    B. I, II, and IV are valid, but III is not valid.
    C. III and IV are valid, but I and II are not valid.
    D. I, II, and III are valid, but IV is not valid.

16. Following are four statements concerning the erasing of ink which may or may not be valid:
    I. It may be difficult to detect an erasure made with an eradicator, especially after a considerable length of time has elapsed.
    II. When an erasure has been made with a knife or rubber, it is generally easy to detect the area involved, as it is translucent.
    III. The sulfocyanic acid method is inappropriate for the detection of residue of iron-containing inks.
    IV. Examination with ultra-violet rays should not be strongly relied upon because clever forgers have been known to wash away all residue of eradication with distilled water.

    Which of the following choices MOST accurately classifies the above statements into those which are generally VALID and those which are NOT VALID?
    A. I and II are generally valid, but III and IV are not generally valid.
    B. IV is generally valid, but I, II, and III are not generally valid.
    C. I, II, and IV are generally valid, but III is not generally valid.
    D. III and IV are generally valid, but I and II are not generally valid.

17. Following are four statements concerning fingerprints which may or may not be true:
    I. Plastic fingerprints are found on such objects as a bar of soap or ball of melted wax.
    II. Visible fingerprints are left by fingers covered with a colored material such as blood or grease.

    III. The majority of latent fingerprints are relatively invisible and must be developed.
    IV. Dirty surfaces and absorbent materials readily bear prints.

Which of the following choices MOST accurately classifies the above statements into those which are TRUE and those which are NOT TRUE?
   A. I and II are true; III and IV are not true.
   B. I and III are true; II and IV are not true.
   C. I, II, and III are true, and IV is not true.
   D. I, II, and IV are true, and III is not true.

18. Of the following, the method of fingerprint classification MOST commonly used in the United States is the _____ system.
   A. Henry   B. Vucetich   C. Bertillon   D. Pottecher

19. Of the following, the term *curtilage* is MOST appropriately used to refer to
   A. the enclosed space of ground and buildings immediately surrounding a dwelling
   B. a surgical procedure used to induce an abortion
   C. the illegal detention of suspects by law enforcement personnel
   D. a legal action taken by a judge to curtail the irrelevant testimony of witnesses in court

20. Which of the following statements is MOST valid as a guide to investigators in their dealings with informants?
   A. Whether they are agreeable or not, informants should be made available for questioning by other agencies since they may have good information in areas other than those which directly concern you.
   B. Many informants work out of revenge, while some others do it only for money. Therefore, you should evaluate the information they give you with regard to their motivation.
   C. Informants tend to use their connections with law enforcement agencies. From time to time, they must be put in their place by letting them know they are *stool pigeons*.
   D. To cultivate informants, it is a good practice to give them some money in advance so they will be assured of a reward when they have good information.

21. The more meager the evidence against a suspect, the later the suspect should be allowed to know of it.
As a practical rule to guide the investigator during an interrogation, the advice contained in this statement is GENERALLY
   A. *bad*, chiefly because suspects have a right to know the details of the offense being investigated
   B. *good*, chiefly because the interrogator will not look foolish due to his lack of information

C. *bad*, chiefly because the investigator will be unable to develop the proper rapport with the suspect during the interrogation
D. *good*, chiefly because the suspect, not sensing the direction of the interrogation, is more likely to reveal information

22. Following are three statements concerning fingerprinting which may or may not be valid:
    I. The best paper for fingerprinting purposes has a rough surface which will absorb ink.
    II. The subject should roll his fingers on the paper from right to left exercising as much pressure as possible on the paper to make a print.
    III. Fingerprints taken with stamp-pad ink are not usually legible or permanent.
    Which of the following classifies the above statements into thos which are VALID and those which are NOT VALID?
    A. I is valid, but II and III are not valid.
    B. I and II are valid, but III is not valid.
    C. II is valid, but I and III are not valid.
    D. III is valid, but I and II are not valid.

23. All of the following statements concerning fingerprints are true EXCEPT:
    A. There are no two identical fingerprints
    B. Fingerprint patterns are not generally changed by illness
    C. A modern procedure called dactylmogrification has been developed to change the fingerprints of individuals relatively easily
    D. if the skin on the fingertips is wounded, the whole fingerprint pattern will reappear when the wound heals

24. Mechanical erasures on a document produce an abrasion of the paper. Assume that a forger makes an ink writing which crosses an area which has been previously erased. Following are three conditions which might result in the erased area from such an action:
    I. The ink line is brighter.
    II. The ink line is wider.
    III. The ink line tends to run or feather out sideways.
    Which one of the following choices MOST accurately classifies the above statements into those which would result from writing over the erased area and those which would not?
    A. I and II would result, but III would not result.
    B. I and III would result, but II would not result.
    C. II would result, but I and III would not result.
    D. II and III would result, but I would not result.

25. In the investigation of the periodic theft of equipment from stockrooms, the detection of the thieves is USUALLY accomplished by
    A. the use of strict inventory controls
    B. careful background investigation of applicants for the stockroom jobs
    C. issuing photo identification cards to all employees of the agency
    D. the use of intelligent surveillance

KEY (CORRECT ANSWERS)

1. C
2. D
3. C
4. C
5. D

6. B
7. A
8. A
9. B
10. A

11. A
12. C
13. D
14. A
15. B

16. C
17. C
18. A
19. A
20. B

21. D
22. D
23. C
24. D
25. D

EXAMINATION SECTION
TEST 1

DIRECTIONS: Each question or incomplete statement is followed by several suggested answers or completions. Select the one that BEST answers the question or completes the statement. PRINT THE LETTER OF THE CORRECT ANSWER IN THE SPACE AT THE RIGHT.

1. As a superior officer you have the responsibility of deciding whether some of your duties should be delegated to subordinate officers.

    The delegation of certain duties to subordinates is *generally* considered
    A. *inadvisable;* subordinates should not share your responsibilities
    B. *advisable;* this will help to prevent you from getting bogged down with minor details and problems
    C. *inadvisable;* you can probably do all parts of your job better than anyone else can
    D. *advisable;* more time can therefore be devoted to day-to-day operations, and less to long-range planning

1.____

2. Assume that you are a superior officer and that one of your subordinates is careless in the performance of his job.

    Of the following, it would be MOST important for you, when helping this employee, to realize that
    A. punitive methods produce better long-term results than non-punitive methods
    B. most problem officers require strict supervision rather than counseling and training
    C. the superior can often play a large part in changing employee patterns of work
    D. if orders are given in detail, carelessness will be eliminated

2.____

3. One of the key qualities of a good superior officer is his ability to balance his work load against the time available to him to complete the job.

    Of the following, the BEST procedure for a superior to follow in establishing his work priorities is to
    A. organize tasks according to urgency without regard to importance
    B. undertake all important, difficult tasks in any order and delegate the routine work to subordinates
    C. assign all work to various subordinates and guide their handling of the problems
    D. delegate those problems that can be solved by others and personally handle the difficult, most pressing issues first

3.____

4. It is generally *correct* to state that the planning process within an organization
    A. is a management responsibility and should not involve the participation of operating personnel
    B. should include long-range programs and goals, and should not include activities which can be carried out within a few weeks or months
    C. is to be used in order to develop and improve practices and procedures but is not to be used in applying these procedures in actual operations
    D. should be used at all supervisory levels since each superior officer must determine how to accomplish tasks and what resources are needed

5. Assume you are a superior officer and one of your subordinates, who has a low performance rating, has made a good suggestion that will make his job easier.

    The *BEST* course of action for you to take in this situation is to
    A. disregard his suggestion, since he is only trying to do as little work as possible
    B. use his suggestion, since it is a positive suggestion and could motivate him to do better work
    C. use his suggestion, but transfer him to a position where he will not benefit from it
    D. disregard his suggestion, and have a talk with him about his poor performance

6. The use of different criteria to rate employees in different jobs is *generally* considered
    A. *desirable*, chiefly because people should be treated as individuals with varying strengths and weaknesses
    B. *undesirable*, chiefly because the use of different criteria results in unfair evaluations
    C. *desirable*, chiefly because people in different jobs cannot always be rated on the basis of the same criteria
    D. *undesirable*, chiefly because ratings that are standarized cannot be compared

7. In preparing an annual division budget for equipment and supplies, the one of the following methods that is *MOST* appropriate to use is to
    A. combine the previous year's division budget with the estimate of any additional or reduced needs for the coming year
    B. determine what amount the department will approve and use that figure
    C. overestimate division needs by 10% because the department will automatically reduce the figure that is first submitted
    D. underestimate division needs because a reduction in the budget indicates increased efficiency

8. All of the following are objectives of in-service training EXCEPT
    A. discovering and developing skills
    B. providing better service to the public
    C. raising the status of the service
    D. eliminating the need for performance evaluations

9. From a management point of view, the *one* of the following that is the *MOST* important advantage of regular personnel performance appraisals is that they
    A. help an officer to prepare for promotion examinations
    B. pinpoint an officer's personality weaknesses
    C. provide an opportunity for regular discussions, including counseling, between an officer and his superior
    D. provide the setting to explain the reasons for disciplinary actions which an officer might not understand

10. Assume that an officer arrests a man for assaulting a woman in the building he is guarding. Later, while the suspect is being searched, the officer finds a switchblade knife, four bags of heroin and three hypodermic syringes in his clothing.

    In these circumstances, the possession of which of the following items might indicate a violation of some law?
    A. *Only* the heroin
    B. The heroin, the hypodermic syringes, but not the switchblade knife
    C. The switchblade knife, the heroin, but not the hypodermic syringes
    D. The switchblade knife, the heroin, and the hypodermic syringes

11. Upon arriving at the scene of a serious crime, a superior officer *SHOULD* instruct his subordinates to
    A. protect the crime scene
    B. collect, mark, and evaluate evidence
    C. brief the news media on the status of the crime
    D. prevent medical personnel from entering the crime scene

12. In standard police terminology, the term *fugitive warrant* refers to
    A. any type of warrant that is not a local warrant
    B. a written request for the detention of a suspect
    C. a warrant for a person who leaves his local jurisdiction and commits an offense in another jurisdiction
    D. a type of booking made when a person wanted by an out-of-state jurisdiction is arrested by local officers

13. The one of the following actions with respect to an offender that an officer should *NOT* take when an infraction has been committed is to
    A. inform the offender of his rights
    B. punish the offender
    C. warn the offender of possible consequences
    D. apprehend the offender using appropriate force

14. Perimeter barriers, intrusion devices, protective lighting, and a personnel identification system are used for good physical security of a building.

    An objective of personnel identification and control is to
    A. exempt authorized personnel from compliance with annoying entry and departure procedures
    B. detect unauthorized persons who attempt to gain entry
    C. eliminate the need for expensive perimeter barriers and intrusion alarms
    D. allow an increased number of gates and perimeter entrances to be operated at the same time during peak activity hours

15. A *true* copy of the testimony taken in a criminal action is known as a(n)
    A. verdict   B. transcript   C. judgment   D. indictment

16. The process of gathering information during an investigation usually involves interviewing or interrogating witnesses.

    Interviews or interrogations are *primarily* used for all of the following purposes EXCEPT to
    A. establish the facts of a possible crime to provide the investigator with leads
    B. verify information already known to the police
    C. secure evidence that may establish the guilt or complicity of a suspect
    D. prevent the person questioned from giving an account of the incident under investigation to newspaper

17. Of the following, the BEST reason to apprehend a narcotics violator out of view of the public is to
    A. prevent the drug user from becoming violent
    B. allow the suspect to "save face" with his friends
    C. prevent the knowledge of his apprehension from reaching any collaborators
    D. keep the suspect from disposing of evidence

18. Assume that you, a superior officer, are planning the physical security operation at a facility. One of the problems you are faced with is that of casual thievery by staff.

    Of the following, the BEST means of discouraging such thievery is by establishing
    A. an aggressive security education program
    B. adequate inventory control measures
    C. spot search procedures
    D. an effective key control system

19. Under an officer's scope of authority, all of the following actions would be proper EXCEPT
    A. apprehending persons attempting to gain unauthorized access to any work location
    B. enforcing the traffic control rules applicable to the work location
    C. removing persons suspected of theft with a warning to them not to return
    D. responding to protective alarm signals and other warning devices

20. One of the ways of deploying an officer force at the scene of a demonstration is called "strength in reserve." This procedure involves having only a few officers police the demonstration while most are being held in reserve.

    Which one of the following is a DISADVANTAGE of this type of deployment? It
    A. permits the demonstrators to estimate the number of officers available
    B. might result in a delay between a violent outbreak and the arrival of enough officers to handle the situation
    C. prevents the superior officer from deploying his forces
    D. does not permit rotation of the officers confronting the demonstrators

21. Of the following, the MOST important principle to keep in mind when making arrests is that
    A. the absence of force will discourage resistance on the part of the offender
    B. the arresting officer should assume, for his own safety, that the person to be arrested is dangerous
    C. once the offender is arrested he should be kept at the scene of the arrest and questioned
    D. in order to prevent violence, it is better to have too few officers making arrests than too many

22. Of the following steps, the *one* that an officer should take *FIRST* upon discovering a broken electrical power line while on duty is to
    A. notify his supervisor
    B. notify the electrical company
    C. determine whether it is a live wire
    D. take measures to protect and barricade the area

23. Assume you are a superior officer interrogating a suspect.

    The *FIRST* question you ask him should *usually* pertain to
    A. his name and address
    B. a package which he may be carrying
    C. where he has been
    D. where he is going

24. Which one of the following statements concerning the interrogation of a juvenile is *INCORRECT*?
    A. The juvenile should be advised of his rights.
    B. The juvenile should be told as little as possible about the case.
    C. A bond of mutual interest should be established with the juvenile.
    D. The juvenile should be encouraged to ask the interrogator questions.

25. Assume that an intoxicated man has wandered into a center and is begging for money and harassing clients.

    Of the following, the *MOST* effective action to take in this situation would be to
    A. call immediately for police assistance
    B. take the man aside quietly and try to persuade him to move along
    C. ask two or three male clients to help you take the man outside
    D. arrest the man at once so that drunks will know they should stay away

KEY (CORRECT ANSWERS)

1. B	6. C	11. A	16. D	21. B
2. C	7. A	12. D	17. C	22. D
3. D	8. D	13. B	18. C	23. A
4. D	9. C	14. B	19. C	24. D
5. B	10. D	15. B	20. B	25. B

TEST 2

DIRECTIONS: Each question or incomplete statement is followed by several suggested answers or completions. Select the one that *BEST* answers the question or completes the statement. *PRINT THE LETTER OF THE CORRECT ANSWER IN THE SPACE AT THE RIGHT.*

1. Assume that you, a superior officer, have received a communication from one of your subordinates that his center has just received a "ticking" package.

    Of the following steps, the *one* that he should take FIRST is to
    A. notify the Police Department
    B. remove the package and soak it in water
    C. check the contents of the package
    D. evacuate the area

    1.___

2. Assume that an individual suspected of drug abuse is apprehended. The suspect produces a prescription which he claims is for the drug found on his person.

    Which of the following actions should be taken *NEXT*?
    A. The prescription should be disregarded and the suspect should be arrested
    B. Release the individual, but confiscate the drug in order to have a laboratory check its composition
    C. The opinion of a medical doctor should be obtained
    D. The suspect should be released since he has a prescription

    2.___

3. A mob has been defined as a group of individuals who commit lawless acts under the stimulus of intense excitement or agitation.

    All of the following are generally considered characteristics of a mob *EXCEPT*
    A. some degree of organization
    B. one or more leaders
    C. a common motive for action
    D. unemotional behavior

    3.___

4. Which of the following would be *IMPROPER* for an officer to do while apprehending a suspect?
    A. Maintain a quiet voice and manner
    B. Remove the person from the scene as soon as possible in order to avoid conflict with the suspect and bystanders
    C. Allow the suspect to realize that the officer does not like persons who commit crimes
    D. Direct and accompany the person to an appropriate location

    4.___

5. Which of the following is MOST appropriate for an officer to do while testifying as a witness in court?
   A. State the facts only of your own knowledge
   B. Argue with the defense attorney in order to show that your actions were proper
   C. Deny that you have discussed the case outside of court even if you have done so only with close friends
   D. Use as much technical language as possible in order to impress the jury with your knowledge

6. It is sometimes inadvisable to arrest the leaders of an unlawful demonstration immediately.

   Of the following, the BEST reason to delay arresting the leaders of a demonstration is to
   A. permit them to restrain their followers who might threaten violence
   B. avoid unfavorable coverage by the press
   C. determine whether there is more than one charge involved
   D. let them get deeper into trouble so they will receive longer sentences when convicted

7. The one of the following approaches which would BEST foster good human relations when dealing with the public is for an officer to
   A. act very self-assured, thus gaining respect
   B. learn how to appeal to the biases and prejudices of others
   C. treat everyone in exactly the same way since everyone has the same needs
   D. appeal to the positive interests of others

8. The causes of many job complaints come not just from wages and working conditions but also from contacts with people on and off the job and from the officer's background and outlook on life.

   Because of this the BEST of the following ways for a superior officer to handle a complaint from a subordinate is, *generally*, to
   A. talk to the officer for the purpose of getting him to withdraw his complaint
   B. get as much information as possible to try to determine the real causes of the complaint
   C. postpone action on the complaint since conditions change so rapidly that it is useless to try to act quickly on a complaint
   D. handle each complaint as quickly as possible without looking into the motives for the complaint

9. In every unit certain officers are more cooperative than others.   9.___

   The *one* of the following that is *most likely* to occur with regard to supervising such cooperative officers is that they
   A. are more easily intimidated
   B. are often assigned to difficult jobs
   C. are unfriendly to the general public
   D. assume a supervisor's position in dealing with others

10. Assume that you are a superior officer and that one of your subordinate officers comes to you with a complaint about an officer under his command. After listening to a few of the details, you suspect that his complaint is not justified.   10.___

    Considering this, you should do all of the following during this initial conversation EXCEPT
    A. listen with interest until the subordinate officer finishes making his complaint
    B. tell the subordinate officer that you will investigate the matter further
    C. inform the subordinate that his complaint is invalid
    D. ask the subordinate officer further questions about his complaint

11. As a superior officer, you may receive complaints about the department or individual officers from the public.   11.___

    Of the following, the *proper attitude* to take with regard to such complaints is that they
    A. are often helpful in determining how to give the public better service
    B. cause poor morale in the service and should not be revealed to subordinates
    C. are useful as a basis for disciplining officers who have been troublesome in the past
    D. take up too much of an officer's time and should not be accepted

12. One of the people present at a local parent-teacher organization meeting complained about the time it took for him to be taken care of at an agency office. A superior officer, present at the meeting, who was familiar with that office and its operations, stood up and explained to the person and the group that there was no personal discrimination involved because the normal procedures took a while and that everyone spent about the same amount of time in the office.   12.___

In this situation the action of the superior officer was
- A. *proper,* mainly because it will show the group how much he knows about agency operations
- B. *improper,* mainly because he should tell the man who complained to check first with the agency before complaining
- C. *proper,* mainly because he helped to clear up a misunderstanding
- D. *improper,* mainly because the officer should not discuss his agency in public

13. Assume that you are a superior officer and that you have begun a campaign to encourage your subordinates to be prompt in reporting for work. One of your subordinates requests that he be allowed to arrive a half hour late in the morning while his wife is in the hospital as a maternity patient.

    Of the following actions, it would be BEST in this situation for you to
    - A. *refuse* the request, claiming it would be unfair to others to make an exception
    - B. *grant* the request, telling your other subordinates the reason for this exception
    - C. *refuse* the request, blaming the central office for having inflexible rules
    - D. *grant* the request, making it clear to all that this will be the last exception

14. Authorities agree that keeping rumors to a minimum is one of the goals of communication.

    Which of the following is NOT consistent with this goal?
    - A. Distribute information that will tend to make rumors unnecessary
    - B. Reduce the social distance between top management and the lower supervisors
    - C. Stress the development of downward rather than upward channels of communication
    - D. Understand the emotional elements that cause stress

15. Of the following, the MOST important factor in determining the success or failure of communication between officers and the public is the
    - A. attitude of the public toward the officers prior to and during the communication
    - B. use of proper channels of communication within the organization
    - C. use of the mass media to change the public's attitude from negative to positive
    - D. increase in opportunities for personal contact between the officers and the public

16. Assume that you are a superior officer concerned with the effective use of praise and criticism to motivate your subordinates.

    Of the following statements, the one that is EQUALLY TRUE of praise and criticism is that both should, generally, be
    A. directed mainly toward the act instead of the person
    B. given often and with no restrictions
    C. given in public for the greatest effect
    D. directed toward group efforts rather than individual efforts

16.___

17. Which of the following actions on the part of a superior officer is MOST likely to improve *upward* communication between his subordinates and himself?
    A. Delay acting on undesirable working conditions until complaints from subordinates have reached top management
    B. Make the time to listen to subordinates' ideas
    C. Resist becoming involved with the personal problems of subordinates
    D. Discourage communications that indicate which policies may have resulted in poor performance

17.___

18. Assume that you are a recently appointed superior officer and are told that one of your subordinates is a chronic complainer. In this situation, which of the following steps should you take FIRST?
    A. Report your subordinate to higher authority
    B. Discipline your subordinate for his poor performance
    C. Change your subordinate's tour of duty
    D. Ask your subordinate for a list of his complaints

18.___

19. In addition to formal supervision, every group of officers soon develops informal leaders who influence the other members of the group.

    Of the following statements about informal leaders, the *one* that is GENERALLY correct is that they
    A. provide supervision when the regular supervisor is absent
    B. are entitled to special benefits for their services
    C. can be used to help settle disputes between employees
    D. prevent the rapid transmission of orders

19.___

20. The grapevine is a frequently used means of informal communication in any work location.

    The *one* of the following statements that BEST describes the attitude a superior officer should take in relation to the grapevine is that it is
    A. unreliable and should not be trusted
    B. useful and should be recognized
    C. valuable and should be the chief method of transmitting orders
    D. insignificant and should be ignored

20.___

21. As a supervising officer, it may be useful for you to conduct periodic interviews with each of your subordinates to discuss his job performance in broad perspective.

    All of the following are ground rules to follow during such an interview EXCEPT
    A. showing him how he compares in work performance with other supervisors in your district
    B. giving him a chance to talk
    C. focusing on what can be learned from any mistakes discussed rather than on the mistakes themselves
    D. avoiding a discussion of personalities

22. When you, as a superior officer, are correcting the errors of a supervisor in your district, which of the following is NOT a good point to keep in mind?
    A. Find something on which to compliment the supervisor before you correct him
    B. Watch yourself carefully to avoid the mistake of overcorrecting
    C. Correct the supervisor at the same time as you correct other supervisors who make similar mistakes
    D. Induce the supervisor to correct himself if possible

23. Following are four steps to be used when instructing a subordinate in the performance of his job:
    I. Observe the subordinate doing the job.
    II. Compare his performance to established standards.
    III. Explain the purpose of the job to the subordinate.
    IV. Demonstrate each step of the job.

    Which of the following choices lists the CORRECT order in which the above steps should be taken?
    A. III, IV, I, II
    B. IV, III, I, II
    C. III, IV, II, I
    D. IV, III, II, I

24. Of the following leadership characteristics, the one that is *generally* considered PRIMARY for a supervisor is the ability to
    A. achieve good working relations with fellow supervisors
    B. get subordinates to air their personal problems
    C. take action to get the job done
    D. plan his work efficiently

25. A recently appointed supervising officer is placed in charge of a district which includes several senior employees. He finds that while these subordinates are able to learn new tasks and methods, some of them tend to take longer to learn procedural changes than newer, younger workers.

    Of the following, the MAIN reason for this is that senior workers
    A. are embarrassed by younger workers' intelligence
    B. have to "unlearn" what was taught them in the past
    C. form learning blocks when they are supervised by a younger person
    D. are more interested in doing the work than in academic discussions

KEY (CORRECT ANSWERS)

1.	D	11.	A
2.	C	12.	C
3.	D	13.	B
4.	C	14.	C
5.	A	15.	A
6.	A	16.	A
7.	D	17.	B
8.	B	18.	D
9.	B	19.	C
10.	C	20.	B

21. A
22. C
23. A
24. C
25. B

READING COMPREHENSION
UNDERSTANDING AND INTERPRETING WRITTEN MATERIAL
EXAMINATION SECTION
TEST 1

DIRECTIONS: Each question or incomplete statement is followed by several suggested answers or completions. Select the one that BEST answers the question or completes the statement. *PRINT THE LETTER OF THE CORRECT ANSWER IN THE SPACE AT THE RIGHT.*

Questions 1-2.

DIRECTIONS: Questions 1 and 2 are to be answered SOLELY on the basis of the information given in the following paragraph.

It is argued by some that the locale of the trial should be given little or no consideration. Facts are facts, they say, and if presented properly to a jury panel they will be productive of the same results regardless of where the trial is held. However, experience shows great differences in the methods of handling claims by juries. In some counties, large demands in personal injury suits are viewed with suspicion by the jury. In others, the jurors are liberal in dealing with someone else's funds.

1. According to the above paragraph, it would be ADVISABLE for an examiner on a personal injury case to
   A. get information as to the kind of verdicts that are usually awarded by juries in the county of trial
   B. give little or no consideration to the locale of the trial
   C. look for incomplete and improper presentation of facts to the jury if the verdict was not justified by the facts
   D. offer a high but realistic initial settlement figure so that no temptation is left to the claimant to gamble on the jury's verdict

1.___

2. According to the above statement, the argument that the location of a trial in a personal injury suit CANNOT counteract the weight of the evidence is
   A. basically sound
   B. disproven by the differences in awards for similar claims
   C. substantiated in those cases where the facts are properly and carefully presented to the injury
   D. supported by experience which shows great differences in the methods of handling claims by juries

2.___

Questions 3-6.

DIRECTIONS: Questions 3 through 6 are to be answered SOLELY on the basis of the following excerpt from a recorded annual report of the police department. This material should be read first and then referred to in answering these questions.

LEGAL BUREAU

One of the more important functions of this bureau is to analyze and furnish the department with pertinent information concerning Federal and State statutes and local laws which affect the department, law enforcement or crime prevention. In addition, all measure introduced in the State Legislature and the City Council which may affect this department are carefully reviewed by members of the Legal Bureau and, where necessary, opinions and recommendations thereon are prepared.

Another important function of this office is the prosecution of cases in the Criminal Courts. This is accomplished by assignment of attorneys who are members of the Legal Bureau to appear in those cases which are deemed to raise issues of importance to the department or questions of law which require technical presentation to facilitate proper determination; and also in those cases where request is made for such appearances by a judge or magistrate, some other official of the city, or a member of the force.

Proposed legislation was prepared and sponsored for introduction in the State Legislature and, at this writing, one of these proposals has already been enacted into law and five others are presently on the Governor's desk awaiting executive action. The new law prohibits the sale or possession of a hypodermic syringe or needle by an unauthorized person. The bureau's proposals awaiting executive action pertain to an amendment to the Criminal Procedure Law prohibiting desk officers from taking bail in gambling cases or in cases mentioned in the Criminal Procedure Law, including confidence men and swindlers as jostlers in the Penal Law; prohibiting the sale of switchblade knives of any size to children under 16 and bills extending the licensing period of gunsmiths.

The Legal Bureau has regularly cooperated with the Corporation Counsel and the District Attorneys in respect to matters affecting this department, and has continued to advise and represent the Police Athletic League, the Police Sports Association, the Police Relief Fund, and the Police Pension Fund.

3. Members of the Legal Bureau frequently appear in Criminal Court for the purpose of
    A. defending members of the Police Force
    B. raising issues of important to the Police Department
    C. prosecuting all offenders arrested by members of the Force
    D. facilitating proper determination of questions of law requiring technical presentation

4. The Legal Bureau sponsored a bill that would 4.___
   A. extend the licenses of gunsmiths
   B. prohibit the sale of switchblade knives to children of any size
   C. place confidence men and swindlers in the same category as jostlers in the Penal Law
   D. prohibit desk officers from admitting gamblers, confidence men, and swindlers to bail

5. One of the functions of the Legal Bureau is to 5.___
   A. review and make recommendations on proposed Federal laws affecting law enforcement
   B. prepare opinions on all measures introduced in the State Legislature and the City Council
   C. furnish the Police Department with pertinent information concerning all new Federal and State laws
   D. analyze all laws affecting the work of the Police Department

6. The one of the following that is NOT a function of the Legal Bureau is 6.___
   A. law enforcement and crime prevention
   B. prosecution of all cases in Women's Court
   C. advise and represent the Police Sports Association
   D. lecturing at the Police Academy

7. It is usual in public service for recruits to serve a probationary period before they receive tenured positions. The objective of this is to observe them in actual service, to teach them the duties of their position, and to provide a means for eliminating those who prove they are not suited for this kind of work. During this period, firings may be made at the discretion of the chief. 7.___
   Which one of the following is BEST supported by the above selection?
   A. Demonstrated fitness for the job is the basis for retention of probationary employees.
   B. Trial appointments protect the appointee from unfair dismissal practices.
   C. Public service employees need experience and instruction before permanent appointment.
   D. Exams must be given to determine the ability of probationary employees.

8. As the fundamental changes sought to be brought about in the inmates of a correctional institution can be accomplished only under good leadership, it follows that the quality of the staff whose duty it is to influence and guide the inmates in the right direction is more important than the physical facilities of the institution. 8.___
   Of the following, the MOST accurate conclusion based on the preceding statement is that
   A. the development of leadership is the fundamental change brought about in inmates by good quality staff

B. the physical facilities of an institution are not very important in bringing about fundamental changes in the inmates
C. with proper training the entire staff of a correctional institution can be developed into good leaders
D. without good leadership the basic changes desired in the inmates of a correctional institution cannot be brought about

Questions 9-11.

DIRECTIONS: Questions 9 through 11 are to be answered SOLELY on the basis of the following paragraph.

The law enforcement agency is one of the most important agencies in the field of juvenile delinquency prevention. This is so not because of the social work connected with this problem, however, for this is not a police matter, but because the officers are usually the first to come in contact with the delinquent. The manner of arrest and detention makes a deep impression upon him and affects his life-long attitude toward society and the law. The juvenile court is perhaps the most important agency in this work. Contrary to the general opinion, however, it is not primarily concerned with putting children into correctional schools. The main purpose of the juvenile court is to save the child and to develop his emotional make-up in order that he can grow up to be a decent and well-balanced citizen. The system of probation is the means whereby the court seeks to accomplish these goals.

9. According to this paragraph, police work is an important part of a program to prevent juvenile delinquency because
    A. social work is no longer considered important in juvenile delinquency prevention
    B. police officers are the first to have contact with the delinquent
    C. police officers jail the offender in order to be able to change his attitude toward society and the law
    D. it is the first step in placing the delinquent in jail

10. According to this paragraph, the CHIEF purpose of the juvenile court is to
    A. punish the child for his offense
    B. select a suitable correctional school for the delinquent
    C. use available means to help the delinquent become a better person
    D. provide psychiatric care for the delinquent

11. According to this paragraph, the juvenile court directs the development of delinquents under its care CHIEFLY by
    A. placing the child under probation
    B. sending the child to a correctional school
    C. keeping the delinquent in prison
    D. returning the child to his home

Questions 12-14.

DIRECTIONS: Questions 12 through 14 are to be answered on the basis of the following paragraph.

An assassination is an act that consists of a plotted, attempted or actual murder of a prominent political figure by an individual who performs this act in other than a governmental role. This definition draws a distinction between political execution and assassination. An execution may be regarded as a political killing, but it is initiated by the organs of the state, while an assassination can always be characterized as an illegal act. A prominent figure must be the target of the killing, since the killing of lesser members of the political community is included within a wider category of internal political turmoil, namely, terrorism. Assassination is also to be distinguished from homicide. The target of the aggressive act must be a political figure rather than a private person. The killing of a prime minister by a member of an insurrectionist or underground group clearly qualifies as an assassination. So does an act by a deranged individual who tries to kill not just any individual, but the individual in his political role - as President, for example.

12. Assume that a nationally prominent political figure is charged with treason by the state, tried in a court of law, found guilty, and hanged by the state.
    According to the above passage, it would be MOST appropriate to regard his death as a(n)
    A. assassination   B. execution
    C. aggressive act   D. homicide   12.___

13. According to the above passage, which of the following statements is CORRECT?   13.___
    A. The assassination of a political figure is an illegal act.
    B. A private person may be the target of an assassination attempt.
    C. The killing of an obscure member of a political community is considered an assassination event.
    D. An execution may not be regarded as a political killing.

14. Of the following, the MOST appropriate title for this passage would be   14.___
    A. ASSASSINATION - LEGAL ASPECTS
    B. POLITICAL CAUSES OF ASSASSINATION
    C. ASSASSINATION - A DEFINITION
    D. CATEGORIES OF ASSASSINATION

Questions 15-17.

DIRECTIONS: Questions 15 through 17 are to be answered SOLELY on the basis of the following paragraph.

    All applicants for an original license to operate a catering establishment shall be fingerprinted. This shall include the officers, employees, and stockholders of the company and the members of a partnership. In case of a change, by addition or substitution, occurring during the existence of a license, the person added or substituted shall be fingerprinted. However, in the case of a hotel containing more than 200 rooms, only the officer or manager filing the application is required to be fingerprinted. The police commissioner may also, at his discretion, exempt the employees and stockholders of any company. The fingerprints shall be taken on one copy of Form C.E. 20 and on two copies of C.E. 21. One copy of Form C.E. 21 shall accompany the application. Fingerprints are not required with a renewal application.

15. According to the above paragraph, an employee added to the payroll of a licensed catering establishment which is not in a hotel must be fingerprinted
    A. always
    B. unless he has been previously fingerprinted for another license
    C. unless exempted by the police commissioner
    D. only if he is the manager or an officer of the company

16. According to the above paragraph, it would be MOST accurate to state that
    A. Form C.E. 20 must accompany a renewal application
    B. Form C.E. 21 must accompany all applications
    C. Form C.E. 21 must accompany an original application
    D. both Forms C.E. 20 and C.E. 21 must accompany all applications

17. A hotel of 270 rooms has applied for a license to operate a catering establishment on the premises. According to the instructions for fingerprinting given in the above paragraph, the _____ shall be fingerprinted.
    A. officers, employees, and stockholders
    B. officers and the manager
    C. employees
    D. officer filing the application

Questions 18-24.

DIRECTIONS: Read the following two paragraphs. Then answer the
questions by selecting the answer
A - if the paragraphs indicate it is TRUE
B - if the paragraphs indicate it is PROBABLY true
C - if the paragraphs indicate it is PROBABLY false
D - if the paragraphs indicate it is FALSE

The fallacy underlying what some might call the eighteenth and nineteenth century misconceptions of the nature of scientific investigations seems to lie in a mistaken analogy. Those who said they were investigating the structure of the universe imagined themselves as the equivalent of the early explorers and map makers. The explorers of the fifteenth and sixteenth centuries had opened up new worlds with the aid of imperfect maps; in their accounts of distant lands, there had been some false and many ambiguous statements. But by the time everyone came to believe the world was round, the maps of distant continents were beginning to assume a fairly consistent pattern. By the seventeenth century, methods of measuring space and time had laid the foundations for an accurate geography.

On this basic issue there is far from complete agreement among philosophers of science today. You can, each of you, choose your side and find highly distinguished advocates for the point of view you have selected. However, in view of the revolution in physics, anyone who now asserts that science is an exploration of the universe must be prepared to shoulder a heavy burden of proof. To my mind, the analogy between the map maker and the scientist is false. A scientific theory is not even the first approximation to a map; it is not a need; it is a policy -- an economical and fruitful guide to action, by scientific investigators.

18. The author thinks that 18th and 19th century science followed the same technique as the 15th century geographers.   18.___

19. The author disagrees with the philosophers who are labelled realists.   19.___

20. The author believes there is a permanent structure to the universe.   20.___

21. A scientific theory is an economical guide to exploring what cannot be known absolutely.   21.___

22. Philosophers of science accept the relativity implications of recent research in physics.   22.___

23. It is a matter of time and effort before modern scientists will be as successful as the geographers.   23.___

24. The author believes in an indeterminate universe. 24.____

25. Borough X reports that its police force makes fewer 25.____
    arrests per thousand persons than any of the other
    boroughs.
    From this statement, it is MOST probable that
    A. sufficient information has not been given to warrant
       any conclusion
    B. the police force of Borough X is less efficient
    C. fewer crimes are being committed in Borough X
    D. fewer crimes are being reported in Borough X

KEY (CORRECT ANSWERS)

1. A
2. B
3. D
4. C
5. D

6. A
7. A
8. D
9. B
10. C

11. A
12. B
13. A
14. C
15. C

16. C
17. D
18. D
19. B
20. D

21. A
22. D
23. D
24. B
25. A

TEST 2

DIRECTIONS: Each question or incomplete statement is followed by several suggested answers or completions. Select the one that BEST answers the question or completes the statement. *PRINT THE LETTER OF THE CORRECT ANSWER IN THE SPACE AT THE RIGHT.*

Questions 1-2.

DIRECTIONS: Questions 1 and 2 are to be answered on the basis of the information given in the following passage.

Assume that a certain agency is having a problem at one of its work locations because a sizable portion of the staff at that location is regularly tardy in reporting to work. The management of the agency is primarily concerned about eliminating the problem and is not yet too concerned about taking any disciplinary action. An investigator is assigned to investigate to determine, if possible, what might be causing this problem.

After several interviews, the investigator sees that low morale created by poor supervision at this location is at least part of the problem. In addition, there is a problem of tardiness and lack of interest.

1. Given the goals of the investigation and assuming that the investigator was using a non-directive approach in this interview, of the following, the investigator's MOST effective response should be:
    A. You know, you are building a bad record of tardiness
    B. Can you tell me more about this situation?
    C. What kind of person is your superior?
    D. Do you think you are acting fairly towards the agency by being late so often?

1.___

2. Given the goals of the investigation and assuming the investigator was using a directed approach in this interview, of the following, the investigator's response should be:
    A. That doesn't seem like much of an excuse to me
    B. What do you mean by saying that you've lost interest?
    C. What problems are there with the supervision you are getting?
    D. How do you think your tardiness looks in your personnel record?

2.___

Questions 3-5.

DIRECTIONS: Questions 3 through 5 are to be answered SOLELY on the basis of the following passage.

As investigators, we are more concerned with the utilitarian than the philosophical aspects of ethics and ethical standards, procedures, and conduct. As a working consideration, we might view ethics as the science of doing the right thing at the right time in the right manner in conformity with the normal, everyday standards imposed by society; and in conformity with the judgment society would be expected to make concerning the rightness or wrongness of what we have done.

An ethical code might be considered a basic set of rules and regulations to which we must conform in the performance of investigative duties. Ethical standards, procedures, and conduct might be considered the logical workings of our ethical code in its everyday application to our work. Ethics also necessarily involves morals and morality. We must eventually answer the self-imposed question of whether or not we have acted in the right way in conducting our investigative activities in their individual and total aspects.

3. Of the following, the MOST suitable title for the above passage is
   A. THE IMPORTANCE OF RULES FOR INVESTIGATORS
   B. THE BASIC PHILOSOPHY OF A LAWFUL SOCIETY
   C. SCIENTIFIC ASPECTS OF INVESTIGATIONS
   D. ETHICAL GUIDELINES FOR THE CONDUCT OF INVESTIGATIONS

4. According to the above passage, ethical considerations for investigators involve
   A. special standards that are different from those which apply to the rest of society
   B. practices and procedures which cannot be evaluated by others
   C. individual judgments by investigators of the appropriateness of their own actions
   D. regulations which are based primarily upon a philosophical approach

5. Of the following, the author's PRINCIPAL purpose in writing the above passage seems to have been to
   A. emphasize the importance of self-criticism in investigative activities
   B. explain the relationship that exists between ethics and investigative conduct
   C. reduce the amount of unethical conduct in the area of investigations
   D. seek recognition by his fellow investigators for his academic treatment of the subject matter

Questions 6-8.

DIRECTIONS: Questions 6 through 8 are to be answered SOLELY on the basis of the following passage.

The investigator must remember that acts of omission can be as effective as acts of commission in affecting the determination of disputed issues. Acts of omission, such as failure to obtain available information or failure to verify dubious information, manifest themselves in miscarriages of justice and erroneous adjudications. An incomplete investigation is an erroneous investigation because a conclusion predicated upon inadequate facts is based on quicksand.

When an investigator throws up his hands and admits defeat, the reason for this action does not necessarily lie in his possible laziness and ineptitude. It is more likely that the investigator has made his conclusions after exhausting only those avenues of investigation of which he is aware. He has exercised good faith in his belief that nothing else can be done.

This tendency must be overcome by all investigators if they are to operate at top efficiency. If no suggestion for new or additional action can be found in any authority, an investigator should use his own initiative to cope with a given situation. No investigator should ever hesitate to set precedents. It is far better in the final analysis to attempt difficult solutions, even if the chances of error are obviously present, than it is to take refuge in the spineless adage: If you don't do anything, you don't do it wrong.

6. Of the following, the MOST suitable title for the above passage is
   A. THE NEED FOR RESOURCEFULNESS IN INVESTIGATIONS
   B. PROCEDURES FOR COMPLETING AN INVESTIGATION
   C. THE DEVELOPMENT OF STANDARDS FOR INVESTIGATORS
   D. THE CAUSES OF INCOMPLETE INVESTIGATIONS

7. Of the following, the author of this passage considers that the LEAST important consideration in developing new investigative methods is
   A. efficiency   B. caution
   C. imagination   D. thoroughness

8. According to this passage, which of the following statements is INCORRECT?
   A. Lack of creativity may lead to erroneous investigations.
   B. Acts of omission are sometimes as harmful as acts of commission.
   C. Some investigators who give up on a case are lazy or inept.
   D. An investigator who gives up on a case is usually not acting in good faith.

Questions 9-12.

DIRECTIONS: Questions 9 through 12 are to be answered on the basis of the following paragraph.

A report of investigation should not be weighed down by a mass of information which is hardly material or only remotely relevant, or which fails to prove a point, clarify an issue, or aid the inquiry even by indirection. Some investigative agencies, however, value the report for its own sake, considering it primarily as a justification of the investigative activity contained therein. Every step is listed to show that no logical measure has been overlooked and to demonstrate that the reporting agent is beyond criticism. This system serves to provide reviewing authorities with a ready means of checking subordinates and provides order, method, and routine to investigative activity. In addition, it may offer supervisors and investigators a sense of security; the investigator would know within fairly exact limits what is expected of him and the supervisor may be comforted by the knowledge that his organization may not be reasonably criticized in a particular case on the grounds of obvious omissions or inertia. To the state's attorney and others, however, who must take administrative action on the basis of the report, the irrelevant and immaterial information thwarts the purpose of the investigation by dimming the issues and obscuring the facts that are truly contributory to the proof.

9. From the point of view of the supervising investigator, a drawback of having the investigator prepare the type of report which the state's attorney would like is that it
    A. gives a biased and one-sided view of what should have been an impartial investigation
    B. has only limited usefulness as an indication that all proper investigative methods were used by the investigator
    C. overlooks logical measures, removing the responsibility for taking those measures which the investigator should otherwise have been expected to take
    D. sets fairly exact limits to what the supervisor can expect of the investigator

10. District attorneys do not like reports of investigations in which every step is listed because
    A. their administrative action is then based on irrelevant and immaterial information
    B. it places the investigator beyond criticism, making the responsibility of the district attorney that much greater
    C. of the difficulty of finding among the mass of information the portion which is meaningful and useful
    D. the inclusion of indirect or hardly material information is not in accord with the order in which the steps were taken

11. As expressed in the above paragraph, the type of report which MOST investigators prefer to prepare is
    A. a step-by-step account of their activities, including both fruitful and unfruitful steps, since to do so provides order and method and gives them a sense of security
    B. not made clear, even though current practice in some agencies is to include every step taken in the investigation
    C. one from which useless and confusing information has been excluded because it is not helpful and is poor practice
    D. one not weighed down by a mass of irrelevant information but one which shows within fairly exact limits what was expected of them

12. With regard to the type of information which an investigator should include in his report, the above paragraph expresses the opinion that
    A. it is best to include in the report only that information which supports the conclusions of the investigator
    B. reports should include all relevant and clarifying information and exclude information on inquiries which had no productive result
    C. reports should include sufficient information to demonstrate that the investigator has been properly attending to his duties and all the information which contributes toward proof of what occurred in the case
    D. the most logical thing to do is to list every step in the investigation and its result

Questions 13-17.

DIRECTIONS: Questions 13 through 17 are to be answered SOLELY on the basis of the following paragraph.

Those statutes of limitations which are of interest to a claim examiner are the ones affecting third party actions brought against an insured covered by a liability policy of insurance. Such statutes of limitations are legislative enactments limiting the time within which such actions at law may be brought. Research shows that such periods differ from state to state and vary within the states with the type of action brought. The laws of the jurisdiction in which the action is brought govern and determine the period within which the action may be instituted, regardless of the place of the cause of action or the residence of the parties at the time of cause of action. The period of time set by a statute of limitations for a tort action starts from the moment the alleged tort is committed. The period usually extends continuously until its expiration, upon which legal action may no longer be brought. However, there is a suspension of the running of the period when a defendant has concealed himself in order to avoid service of legal process. The suspension continues until the defendant discontinues his concealment and then the period starts running again. A defendant may, by his agreement or conduct, be legally barred from asserting the statute of limitations as a defense to an action. The insurance carrier for the defendant may, by the misrepresentation of the claims man, cause such a bar against use of the statute of limitations by the defendant. If the claim examiner of the insurance carrier has by his conduct or assertion lulled the plaintiff into a false sense of security by false representations, the defendant may be barred from setting up the statute of limitations as a defense.

13. Of the following, the MOST suitable title for the above paragraph is
    A. FRAUDULENT USE OF THE STATUTE OF LIMITATIONS
    B. PARTIES AT INTEREST IN A LAWSUIT
    C. THE CLAIM EXAMINER AND THE LAW
    D. THE STATUTE OF LIMITATIONS IN CLAIMS WORK

14. The period of time during which a third party action may be brought against an insured covered by a liability policy depends on
    A. the laws of the jurisdiction in which the action is brought
    B. where the cause of action which is the subject of the suit took place
    C. where the claimant lived at the time of the cause of action
    D. where the insured lived at the time of the cause of action

15. Time limits in third party actions which are set by the statutes of limitations described above are
    A. determined by claimant's place of residence at start of action
    B. different in a state for different actions
    C. the same from state to state for the same type of action
    D. the same within a state regardless of type of action

16. According to the above paragraph, grounds which may be legally used to prevent a defendant from using the statute of limitations as a defense in the action described are
    A. defendant's agreement or concealment; a charge of liability for death and injury
    B. defendant's agreement or conduct; misrepresentation by the claims man
    C. fraudulent concealment by claim examiner; a charge of liability for death or injury; defendant's agreement
    D. misrepresentation by claim examiner of carrier; defendant's agreement; plaintiff's concealment

17. Suppose an alleged tort was commited on January 1, 1978
and that the period in which action may be taken is set
at three years by the statute of limitations. Suppose
further that the defendant, in order to avoid service of
legal process, had concealed himself from July 1, 1980
through December 31, 1980.
In this case, the defendant may not use the statute of
limitations as a defense unless action is brought by the
plaintiff after _____, 1981.
   A. January 1
   B. February 28
   C. June 30
   D. August 1

Questions 18-20.

DIRECTIONS: Questions 18 through 20 are to be answered SOLELY on the basis of information contained in the following passage.

No matter how well the interrogator adjusts himself to the witness and how precisely he induces the witness to describe his observations, mistakes still can be made. The mistakes made by an experienced interrogator may be comparatively few, but as far as the witness is concerned, his path is full of pitfalls. Modern *witness psychology* has shown that even the most honest and trustworthy witnesses are apt to make grave mistakes in good faith. It is, therefore, necessary that the interrogator get an idea of the weak links in the testimony in order to check up on them in the event that something appears to be strange or not quite satisfactory.

Unfortunately, modern witness psychology does not yet offer any means of directly testing the credibility of testimony. It lacks precision and method, in spite of worthwhile attempts on the part of learned men. At the same time, witness psychology, through the gathering of many experiences concerning the weaknesses of human testimony, has been of invaluable service. It shows clearly that only evidence of a technical nature has absolute value as proof.

Testimony may be separated into the following stages: (1) perception, (2) observation, (3) mind fixation of the observed occurrences, in which fantasy, association of ideas, and personal judgment participate, and (4) expression in oral or written form, where the testimony is transferred from one witness to another or to the interrogator.

Each of these stages offers innumerable possibilities for the distortion of testimony.

18. The above passage indicates that having witnesses talk to each other before testifying is a practice which is GENERALLY
   A. *desirable*, since the witnesses will be able to correct each other's errors in observation before testimony

B. *undesirable*, since the witnesses will collaborate on one story to tell the investigator
C. *undesirable*, since one witness may distort his testimony because of what another witness may erroneously say
D. *desirable*, since witnesses will become aware of discrepancies in their own testimony and can point out the discrepancies to the investigator

19. According to the above passage, the one of the following which would be the MOST reliable for use as evidence would be the testimony of a
    A. handwriting expert about a signature on a forged check
    B. trained police officer about the identity of a criminal
    C. laboratory technician about an accident he has observed
    D. psychologist who has interviewed any witnesses who relate conflicting stories

20. Concerning the validity of evidence, it is CLEAR from the above passage that
    A. only evidence of a technical nature is at all valuable
    B. the testimony of witnesses is so flawed that it is usually valueless
    C. an investigator, by knowing modern witness psychology, will usually be able to perceive mistaken testimony
    D. an investigator ought to expect mistakes in even the most reliable witness testimony

Questions 21-22.

DIRECTIONS: Questions 21 and 22 are to be answered SOLELY on the basis of the information contained in the passage below. This passage represents a report prepared by a subordinate superior concerning a school demonstration.

On April 1, a group of students, each holding an anti-apartheid sign, was involved in a demonstration on the grounds of Columbia University. The students began by locking the main entrance doors to the Administration Building and preventing faculty and students from entering or leaving the building.

The C.O. of the police detail at the scene requested additional assistance of four female detectives, an Emergency Service van, and a police photographer equipped with a Polaroid instamatic camera.

When the additional assistance arrived, the Commanding Officer directed the students to disperse. His justification for the order was that the demonstrators were violating the rights of other students and certain faculty members by denying them access to the Administration Building. The students ignored the order to disperse and the Commanding Officer of the police detail ordered them to be removed.

Another group of students who had been standing in front of the library were sympathetic toward the demonstrators and charged the police. Several police officers were injured during the ensuing hostilities.

Eventually, order was restored. That evening, the television coverage presented a neutral and fairly accurate account of the incident.

21. Which of the following statements MOST clearly and accurately reflects the contents of the report? 21.___
    A. A large group of students, all of whom were holding anti-apartheid signs, was involved in a demonstration on the grounds of Columbia University.
    B. A large group of students, some of whom were holding anti-apartheid signs, was involved in a demonstration on the grounds of Columbia University.
    C. Each of a group of Columbia students carrying anti-apartheid signs was involved in a demonstration on the grounds of Columbia University.
    D. Each of the students involved in the demonstration on the grounds of Columbia University was holding an anti-apartheid sign.

22. Which of the following statements MOST clearly and accurately reflects the contents of the report? 22.___
    A. The Commanding Officer of the police detail justified his order that the demonstrators disperse when the additional assistance arrived.
    B. When the additional assistance arrived, the Commanding Officer of the police detail justified his order that the demonstrators disperse.
    C. The Commanding Officer of the police detail directed the students to disperse when the additional assistance arrived.
    D. The Commanding Officer of the police detail requested additional assistance because the student demonstrators were violating the rights of other students and certain faculty members.

23. Which of the following statements MOST clearly and accurately reflects the contents of the report? 23.___
    A. Another group of students charged the police because they were sympathetic toward the police.
    B. The evening television coverage of the demonstration was fair and accurate.
    C. The group of students who had been standing in front of the library was sympathetic toward the demonstrators.
    D. Several police officers were injured during the hostilities which took place in front of the library.

Questions 24-25.

DIRECTIONS: Questions 24 and 25 are to be answered SOLELY on the basis of the information given in the following paragraph.

Credibility of a witness is usually governed by his character and is evidenced by his reputation for truthfulness. Personal or financial reasons or a criminal record may cause a witness to give false information to avoid being implicated. Age, sex, physical and mental abnormalities, loyalty, revenge, social and economic status, indulgence in alcohol, and the influence of other persons are some of the many factors which may affect the accuracy, willingness, or ability with which witnesses observe, interpret, and describe occurrences.

24. According to the above paragraph, a witness may, for personal reasons, give wrong information about an occurrence because he
    A. wants to protect his reputation for truthfulness
    B. wants to embarrass the investigator
    C. doesn't want to become involved
    D. doesn't really remember what happened

25. According to the above paragraph, factors which influence the witness of an occurrence may affect
    A. not only what he tells about it but what he was able and wanted to see of it
    B. only what he describes and interprets later but not what he actually sees at the time of the event
    C. what he sees but not what he describes
    D. what he is willing to see but not what he is able to see

KEY (CORRECT ANSWERS)

1. B	6. A	11. B	16. B	21. D
2. C	7. B	12. B	17. C	22. C
3. D	8. D	13. D	18. C	23. C
4. C	9. B	14. A	19. A	24. C
5. B	10. C	15. B	20. D	25. A

RECORD KEEPING
EXAMINATION SECTION
TEST 1

DIRECTIONS: Each question or incomplete statement is followed by several suggested answers or completions. Select the one that BEST answers the question or completes the statement. *PRINT THE LETTER OF THE CORRECT ANSWER IN THE SPACE AT THE RIGHT.*

Questions 1-15.

DIRECTIONS: Questions 1 through 15 are to be answered on the basis of the following list of company names below. Arrange a file alphabetically, word-by-word, disregarding punctuation, conjunctions, and apostrophes. Then answer the questions.

    A Bee C Reading Materials
    ABCO Parts
    A Better Course for Test Preparation
    AAA Auto Parts Co.
    A-Z Auto Parts, Inc.
    Aabar Books
    Abbey, Joanne
    Boman-Sylvan Law Firm
    BMW Autowerks
    C Q Service Company
    Chappell-Murray, Inc.
    E&E Life Insurance
    Emcrisco
    Gigi Arts
    Gordon, Jon & Associates
    SOS Plumbing
    Schmidt, J.B. Co.

1. Which of these files should appear FIRST?   1.___
   A. ABCO Parts
   B. A Bee C Reading Materials
   C. A Better Course for Test Preparation
   D. AAA Auto Parts Co.

2. Which of these files should appear SECOND?   2.___
   A. A-Z Auto Parts, Inc.
   B. A Bee C Reading Materials
   C. A Better Course for Test Preparation
   D. AAA Auto Parts Co.

3. Which of these files should appear THIRD?   3.___
   A. ABCO Parts
   B. A Bee C Reading Materials
   C. Aabar Books
   D. AAA Auto Parts Co.

4. Which of these files should appear FOURTH?   4.___
    A. ABCO Parts
    B. A Bee C Reading Materials
    C. Abbey, Joanne
    D. AAA Auto Parts Co.

5. Which of these files should appear LAST?   5.___
    A. Gordon, Jon & Associates
    B. Gigi Arts
    C. Schmidt, J.B. Co.
    D. SOS Plumbing

6. Which of these files should appear between A-Z Auto Parts,   6.___
   Inc. and Abbey, Joanne?
    A. A Bee C Reading Materials
    B. AAA Auto Parts Co.
    C. Aabar Books
    D. A Better Course for Test Preparation

7. Which of these files should appear between ABCO Parts and   7.___
   Aabar Books?
    A. A Bee C Reading Materials
    B. Abbey, Joanne
    C. Aabar Books
    D. A-Z Auto Parts

8. Which of these files should appear between Abbey, Joanne   8.___
   and Boman-Sylvan Law Firm?
    A. A Better Course for Test Preparation
    B. BMW Autowerks
    C. A-Z Auto Parts, Inc.
    D. Aabar Books

9. Which of these files should appear between Abbey, Joanne   9.___
   and C Q Service?
    A. A-Z Auto Parts, Inc.   B. BMW Autowerks
    C. Choices A and B   D. Chappell-Murray, Inc.

10. Which of these files should appear between C Q Service   10.___
    Company and Emcrisco?
    A. Chappell-Murray, Inc.   B. E&E Life Insurance
    C. Gigi Arts   D. Choices A and B

11. Which of these files should NOT appear between C Q Service 11.___
    Company and E&E Life Insurance?
    A. Gordon, Jon & Associates
    B. Emcrisco
    C. Gigi Arts
    D. Choices A and C

12. Which of these files should appear between Chappell-Murray 12.___
    Inc., and Gigi Arts?
    A. CQ Service Inc.   E&E Life Insurance, and Emcrisco
    B. Emcrisco, E&E Life Insurance, and Gordon, Jon &
       Associates

C. E&E Life Insurance and Emcrisco
D. Emcrisco and Gordon, Jon & Associates

13. Which of these files should appear between Gordon, Jon & Associates and SOS Plumbing? 13.___
    A. Gigi Arts   B. Schmidt, J.B. Co.
    C. Choices A and B   D. None of the above

14. Which of the choices lists the four files in their proper alphabetical order? 14.___
    A. E&E Life Insurance; Gigi Arts; Gordon, Jon & Associates; SOS Plumbing
    B. E&E Life Insurance; Emcrisco; Gigi Arts; SOS Plumbing
    C. Emcrisco; Gordon, Jon & Associates; Schmidt, J.B. Co.; SOS Plumbing
    D. Emcrisco; Gigi Arts; Gordon, Jon & Associates; SOS Plumbing

15. Which of the choices lists the four files in their proper alphabetical order? 15.___
    A. Gigi Arts; Gordon, Jon & Associates; SOS Plumbing; Schmidt, J.B. Co.
    B. Gordon, Jon & Associates; Gigi Arts; Schmidt, J.B. Co.; SOS Plumbing
    C. Gordon, Jon & Associates; Gigi Arts; SOS Plumbing; Schmidt, J.B. Co.
    D. Gigi Arts; Gordon, Jon & Associates; Schmidt, J.B. Co.; SOS Plumbing

16. The alphabetical filing order of two businesses with identical names is determined by the 16.___
    A. length of time each business has been operating
    B. addresses of the businesses
    C. last name of the company president
    D. none of the above

17. In an alphabetical filing system, if a business name includes a number, it should be 17.___
    A. disregarded
    B. considered a number and placed at the end of an alphabetical section
    C. treated as though it were written in words and alphabetized accordingly
    D. considered a number and placed at the beginning of an alphabetical section

18. If a business name includes a contraction (such as *don't* or *it's*), how should that word be treated in an alphabetical filing system? 18.___
    A. Divide the word into its separate parts and treat it as two words.
    B. Ignore the letters that come after the apostrophe.
    C. Ignore the word that contains the contraction.
    D. Ignore the apostrophe and consider all letters in the contraction.

19. In what order should the parts of an address be considered when using an alphabetical filing system? 19.___
   A. City or town; state; street name; house or building number
   B. State; city or town; street name; house or building number
   C. House or building number; street name; city or town; state
   D. Street name; city or town; state

20. A business record should be cross-referenced when a(n) 20.___
   A. organization is known by an abbreviated name
   B. business has a name change because of a sale, incorporation, or other reason
   C. business is known by a *coined* or common name which differs from a dictionary spelling
   D. all of the above

21. A geographical filing system is MOST effective when 21.___
   A. location is more important than name
   B. many names or titles sound alike
   C. dealing with companies who have offices all over the world
   D. filing personal and business files

Questions 22-25.

DIRECTIONS: Questions 22 through 25 are to be answered on the basis of the list of items below, which are to be filed geographically. Organize the items geographically and then answer the questions.

   1. University Press at Berkeley, U.S.
   2. Maria Sanchez, Mexico City, Mexico
   3. Great Expectations Ltd. in London, England
   4. Justice League, Cape Town, South Africa, Africa
   5. Crown Pearls Ltd. in London, England
   6. Joseph Prasad in London, England

22. Which of the following arrangements of the items is composed according to the policy of: *Continent, Country, City, Firm or Individual Name*? 22.___
   A. 5, 3, 4, 6, 2, 1   B. 4, 5, 3, 6, 2, 1
   C. 1, 4, 5, 3, 6, 2   D. 4, 5, 3, 6, 1, 2

23. Which of the following files is arranged according to the policy of: *Continent, Country, City, Firm or Individual Name*? 23.___
   A. South Africa. Africa. Cape Town. Justice League
   B. Mexico. Mexico City. Maria Sanchez
   C. North America. United States. Berkeley. University Press
   D. England. Europe. London. Prasad, Joseph

24. Which of the following arrangements of the items is composed according to the policy of: *Country, City, Firm or Individual Name*?
    A. 5, 6, 3, 2, 4, 1
    B. 1, 5, 6, 3, 2, 4
    C. 6, 5, 3, 2, 4, 1
    D. 5, 3, 6, 2, 4, 1

25. Which of the following files is arranged according to a policy of: *Country, City, Firm or Individual Name*?
    A. England. London. Crown Pearls Ltd.
    B. North America. United States. Berkeley. University Press
    C. Africa. Cape Town. Justice League
    D. Mexico City. Mexico. Maria Sanchez

26. Under which of the following circumstances would a phonetic filing system be MOST effective?
    A. When the person in charge of filing can't spell very well
    B. With large files with names that sound alike
    C. With large files with names that are spelled alike
    D. All of the above

Questions 27-29.

DIRECTIONS: Questions 27 through 29 are to be answered on the basis of the following list of numerical files.

    1. 391-023-100
    2. 361-132-170
    3. 385-732-200
    4. 381-432-150
    5. 391-632-387
    6. 361-423-303
    7. 391-123-271

27. Which of the following arrangements of the files follows a consecutive-digit system?
    A. 2, 3, 4, 1
    B. 1, 5, 7, 3
    C. 2, 4, 3, 1
    D. 3, 1, 5, 7

28. Which of the following arrangements follows a terminal-digit system?
    A. 1, 7, 2, 4, 3
    B. 2, 1, 4, 5, 7
    C. 7, 6, 5, 4, 3
    D. 1, 4, 2, 3, 7

29. Which of the following lists follows a middle-digit system?
    A. 1, 7, 2, 6, 4, 5, 3
    B. 1, 2, 7, 4, 6, 5, 3
    C. 7, 2, 1, 3, 5, 6, 4
    D. 7, 1, 2, 4, 6, 5, 3

Questions 30-31.

DIRECTIONS: Questions 30 and 31 are to be answered on the basis of the following information.

1. Reconfirm Laura Bates appointment with James Caldecort on December 12 at 9:30 A.M.
2. Laurence Kinder contact Julia Lucas on August 3 and set up a meeting for week of September 23 at 4 P.M.
3. John Lutz contact Larry Waverly on August 3 and set up appointment for September 23 at 9:30 A.M.
4. Call for tickets for Gerry Stanton August 21 for New Jersey on September 23, flight 143 at 4:43 P.M.

30. A chronological file for the above information would be
    A. 4, 3, 2, 1   B. 3, 2, 4, 1
    C. 4, 2, 3, 1   D. 3, 1, 2, 4

31. Using the above information, a chronological file for the date of September 23 would be
    A. 2, 3, 4   B. 3, 1, 4   C. 3, 2, 4   D. 4, 3, 2

Questions 32-34.

DIRECTIONS: Questions 32 through 34 are to be answered on the basis of the following information.

1. Call Roger Epstein, Ashoke Naipaul, Jon Anderson, and Sarah Washington on April 19 at 1:00 P.M. to set up meeting with Alika D'Ornay for June 6 in New York
2. Call Martin Ames before noon on April 19 to confirm afternoon meeting with Bob Greenwood on April 20th
3. Set up meeting room at noon for 2:30 P.M. meeting on April 19th
4. Ashley Stanton contact Bob Greenwood at 9:00 A.M. on April 20 and set up meeting for June 6 at 8:30 A.M.
5. Carol Guiland contact Shelby Van Ness during afternoon of April 20 and set up meeting for June 6 at 10:00 A.M.
6. Call airline and reserve tickets on June 6 for Roger Epstein trip to Denver on July 8
7. Meeting at 2:30 P.M. on April 19th

32. A chronological file for all of the above information would be
    A. 2, 1, 3, 7, 5, 4, 6   B. 3, 7, 2, 1, 4, 5, 6
    C. 3, 7, 1, 2, 5, 4, 6   D. 2, 3, 1, 7, 4, 5, 6

33. A chronological file for the date of April 19th would be
    A. 2, 3, 7, 1   B. 2, 3, 1, 7
    C. 7, 1, 3, 2   D. 3, 7, 1, 2

34. Add the following information to the file, and then   34.___
    create a chronological file for April 20th:
    8. April 20: 3:00 P.M. meeting between Bob Greenwood
    and Martin Ames.
       A. 4, 5, 8   B. 4, 8, 5   C. 8, 5, 4   D. 5, 4, 8

35. The PRIMARY advantage of computer records filing over   35.___
    a manual system is
       A. speed of retrieval   B. accuracy
       C. cost   D. potential file loss

KEY (CORRECT ANSWERS)

1. B	11. B	21. A	31. C
2. C	12. C	22. B	32. D
3. D	13. D	23. C	33. B
4. A	14. D	24. D	34. A
5. C	15. A	25. A	35. A
6. C	16. B	26. B	
7. D	17. C	27. C	
8. B	18. D	28. D	
9. B	19. A	29. A	
10. D	20. D	30. B	

PREPARING WRITTEN MATERIAL
EXAMINATION SECTION
TEST 1

Questions 1-15.

DIRECTIONS: For each of Questions 1 through 15, select from the options given below the MOST applicable choice, and mark your answer accordingly.

    A. The sentence is correct.
    B. The sentence contains a spelling error *only*.
    C. The sentence contains an English grammar error *only*.
    D. The sentence contains both a spelling error and an English grammar error.

1. He is a very dependable person whom we expect will be an asset to this division.

2. An investigator often finds it necessary to be very diplomatic when conducting an interview.

3. Accurate detail is especially important if court action results from an investigation.

4. The report was signed by him and I since we conducted the investigation jointly.

5. Upon receipt of the complaint, an inquiry was begun.

6. An employee has to organize his time so that he can handle his workload efficiantly.

7. It was not apparant that anyone was living at the address given by the client.

8. According to regulations, there is to be at least three attempts made to locate the client.

9. Neither the inmate nor the correction officer was willing to sign a formal statement.

10. It is our opinion that one of the persons interviewed were lying.

11. We interviewed both clients and departmental personel in the course of this investigation.

12. It is concievable that further research might produce additional evidence.

13. There are too many occurences of this nature to ignore.

14. We cannot accede to the candidate's request. 14.___

15. The submission of overdue reports is the reason that 15.___
there was a delay in completion of this investigation.

Questions 16-25.

DIRECTIONS: Each of Questions 16 through 25 may be classified under one of the following four categories:

A. Faulty because of incorrect grammar or sentence structure
B. Faulty because of incorrect punctuation
C. Faulty because of incorrect spelling
D. Correct

Examine each sentence carefully to determine under which of the above four options it is best classified. Then, in the space at the right, write the letter preceding the option which is the BEST of the four suggested above. Each incorrect sentence contains but one type of error. Consider a sentence to be correct if it contains none of the types of errors mentioned, even though there may be other correct ways of expressing the same thought.

16. Although the department's supply of scratch pads and 16.___
stationary have diminished considerably, the allotment
for our division has not been reduced.

17. You have not told us whom you wish to designate as your 17.___
secretary.

18. Upon reading the minutes of the last meeting, the new 18.___
proposal was taken up for consideration.

19. Before beginning the discussion, we locked the door as a 19.___
precautionery measure.

20. The supervisor remarked, "Only those clerks, who perform 20.___
routine work, are permitted to take a rest period."

21. Not only will this duplicating machine make accurate 21.___
copies, but it will also produce a quantity of work equal
to fifteen transcribing typists.

22. "Mr. Jones," said the supervisor, "we regret our inability 22.___
to grant you an extention of your leave of absence."

23. Although the employees find the work monotonous and 23.___
fatigueing, they rarely complain.

24. We completed the tabulation of the receipts on time despite the fact that Miss Smith our fastest operator was absent for over a week. 24.___

25. The reaction of the employees who attended the meeting, as well as the reaction of those who did not attend, indicates clearly that the schedule is satisfactory to everyone concerned. 25.___

KEY (CORRECT ANSWERS)

1. D
2. A
3. A
4. C
5. A

6. B
7. B
8. C
9. A
10. C

11. B
12. B
13. B
14. A
15. C

16. A
17. D
18. A
19. C
20. B

21. A
22. C
23. C
24. B
25. D

TEST 2

Questions 1-15.

DIRECTIONS: Questions 1 through 15 consist of two sentences. Some are correct according to ordinary formal English usage. Others are incorrect because they contain errors in English usage, spelling, or punctuation. Consider a sentence correct if it contains no errors in English usage, spelling, or punctuation, even if there may be other ways of writing the sentence correctly.
Mark your answer:

A. If only sentence I is correct
B. If only sentence II is correct
C. If sentences I and II are correct
D. If neither sentence I nor II is correct

1. I. The influence of recruitment efficiency upon administrative standards is readily apparant.
    II. Rapid and accurate thinking are an essential quality of the police officer.　　　1.___

2. I. The administrator of a police department is constantly confronted by the demands of subordinates for increased personnel in their respective units.
    II. Since a chief executive must work within well-defined fiscal limits, he must weigh the relative importance of various requests.　　　2.___

3. I. The two men whom the police arrested for a parking violation were wanted for robbery in three states.
    II. Strong executive control from the top to the bottom of the enterprise is one of the basic principals of police administration.　　　3.___

4. I. When he gave testimony unfavorable to the defendant loyalty seemed to mean very little.
    II. Having run off the road while passing a car, the patrolman gave the driver a traffic ticket.　　　4.___

5. I. The judge ruled that the defendant's conversation with his doctor was a priviliged communication.
    II. The importance of our training program is widely recognized; however, fiscal difficulties limit the program's effectiveness.　　　5.___

6. I. Despite an increase in patrol coverage, there were less arrests for crimes against property this year.
    II. The investigators could hardly have expected greater cooperation from the public.　　　6.___

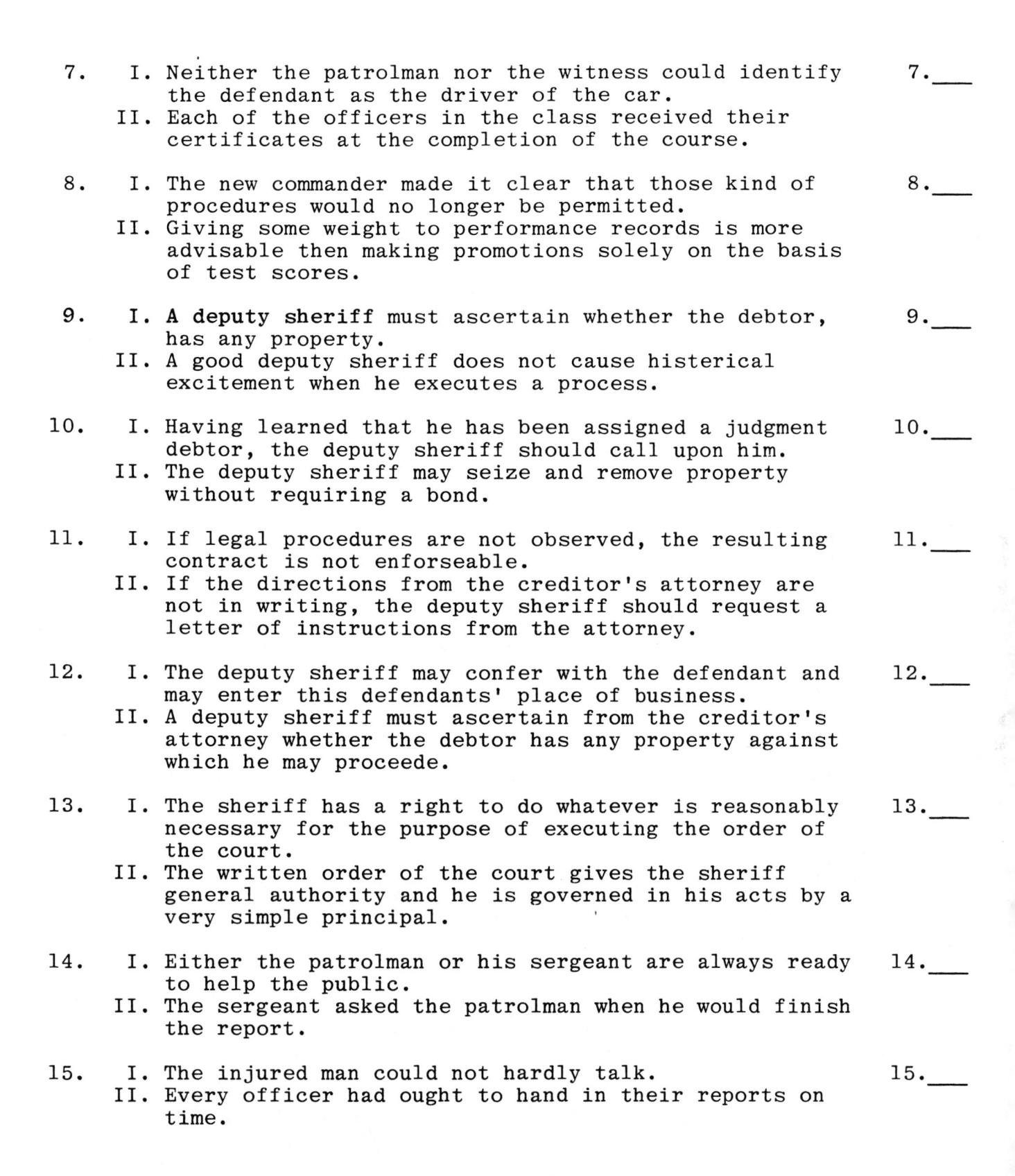

7. I. Neither the patrolman nor the witness could identify the defendant as the driver of the car.
    II. Each of the officers in the class received their certificates at the completion of the course.

8. I. The new commander made it clear that those kind of procedures would no longer be permitted.
    II. Giving some weight to performance records is more advisable then making promotions solely on the basis of test scores.

9. I. A deputy sheriff must ascertain whether the debtor, has any property.
    II. A good deputy sheriff does not cause histerical excitement when he executes a process.

10. I. Having learned that he has been assigned a judgment debtor, the deputy sheriff should call upon him.
    II. The deputy sheriff may seize and remove property without requiring a bond.

11. I. If legal procedures are not observed, the resulting contract is not enforseable.
    II. If the directions from the creditor's attorney are not in writing, the deputy sheriff should request a letter of instructions from the attorney.

12. I. The deputy sheriff may confer with the defendant and may enter this defendants' place of business.
    II. A deputy sheriff must ascertain from the creditor's attorney whether the debtor has any property against which he may proceede.

13. I. The sheriff has a right to do whatever is reasonably necessary for the purpose of executing the order of the court.
    II. The written order of the court gives the sheriff general authority and he is governed in his acts by a very simple principal.

14. I. Either the patrolman or his sergeant are always ready to help the public.
    II. The sergeant asked the patrolman when he would finish the report.

15. I. The injured man could not hardly talk.
    II. Every officer had ought to hand in their reports on time.

Questions 16-25.

DIRECTIONS: For each of the sentences given below, numbered 16 through 25, select from the following choices the MOST correct choice and print your choice in the space at the right. Select as your answer:

A. If the statement contains an unnecessary word or expression
B. If the statement contains a slang term or expression ordinarily not acceptable in government report writing
C. If the statement contains an old-fashioned word or expression, where a concrete, plain term would be more useful
D. If the statement contains no major faults

16. Every one of us should try harder   16.___

17. Yours of the first instant has been received.   17.___

18. We will have to do a real snow job on him.   18.___

19. I shall contact him next Thursday.   19.___

20. None of us were invited to the meeting with the community.   20.___

21. We got this here job to do.   21.___

22. She could not help but see the mistake in the checkbook.   22.___

23. Don't bug the Director about the report.   23.___

24. I beg to inform you that your letter has been received.   24.___

25. This project is all screwed up.   25.___

KEY (CORRECT ANSWERS)

1. D	6. B	11. B	16. D	21. B
2. C	7. A	12. D	17. C	22. D
3. A	8. D	13. A	18. B	23. B
4. D	9. D	14. D	19. D	24. C
5. B	10. C	15. D	20. D	25. B

TEST 3

DIRECTIONS: Questions 1 through 25 are sentences taken from reports. Some are correct according to ordinary formal English usage. Others are incorrect because they contain errors in English usage, spelling, or punctuation. Consider a sentence correct if it contains no errors in English usage, spelling, or punctuation, even if there may be other ways of writing the sentence correctly.
Mark your answer:

A. If only sentence I is correct
B. If only sentence II is correct
C. If sentences I and II are correct
D. If neither sentence I nor II is correct.

1.
   I. The Neighborhood Police Team Commander and Team Patrolmen are encouraged to give to the public the widest possible verbal and written disemination of information regarding the existence and purposes of the program.
   II. The police must be vitally interelated with every segment of the public they serve.

2.
   I. If social gambling, prostitution, and other vices are to be prohibited, the law makers should provide the manpower and method for enforcement.
   II. In addition to checking on possible crime locations such as hallways, roofs yards and other similar locations, Team Patrolmen are encouraged to make known their presence to members of the community.

3.
   I. The Neighborhood Police Team Commander is authorized to secure, the cooperation of local publications, as well as public and private agencies, to further the goals of the program.
   II. Recruitment from social minorities is essential to effective police work among minorities and meaningful relations with them.

4.
   I. The Neighborhood Police Team Commander and his men have the responsibility for providing patrol service within the sector territory on a twenty-four hour basis.
   II. While the patrolman was walking his beat at midnight he noticed that the clothing stores' door was partly open.

5.
   I. Authority is granted to the Neighborhood Police Team to device tactics for coping with the crime in the sector.
   II. Before leaving the scene of the accident, the patrolman drew a map showing the positions of the automobiles and indicated the time of the accident as 10 A.M. in the morning.

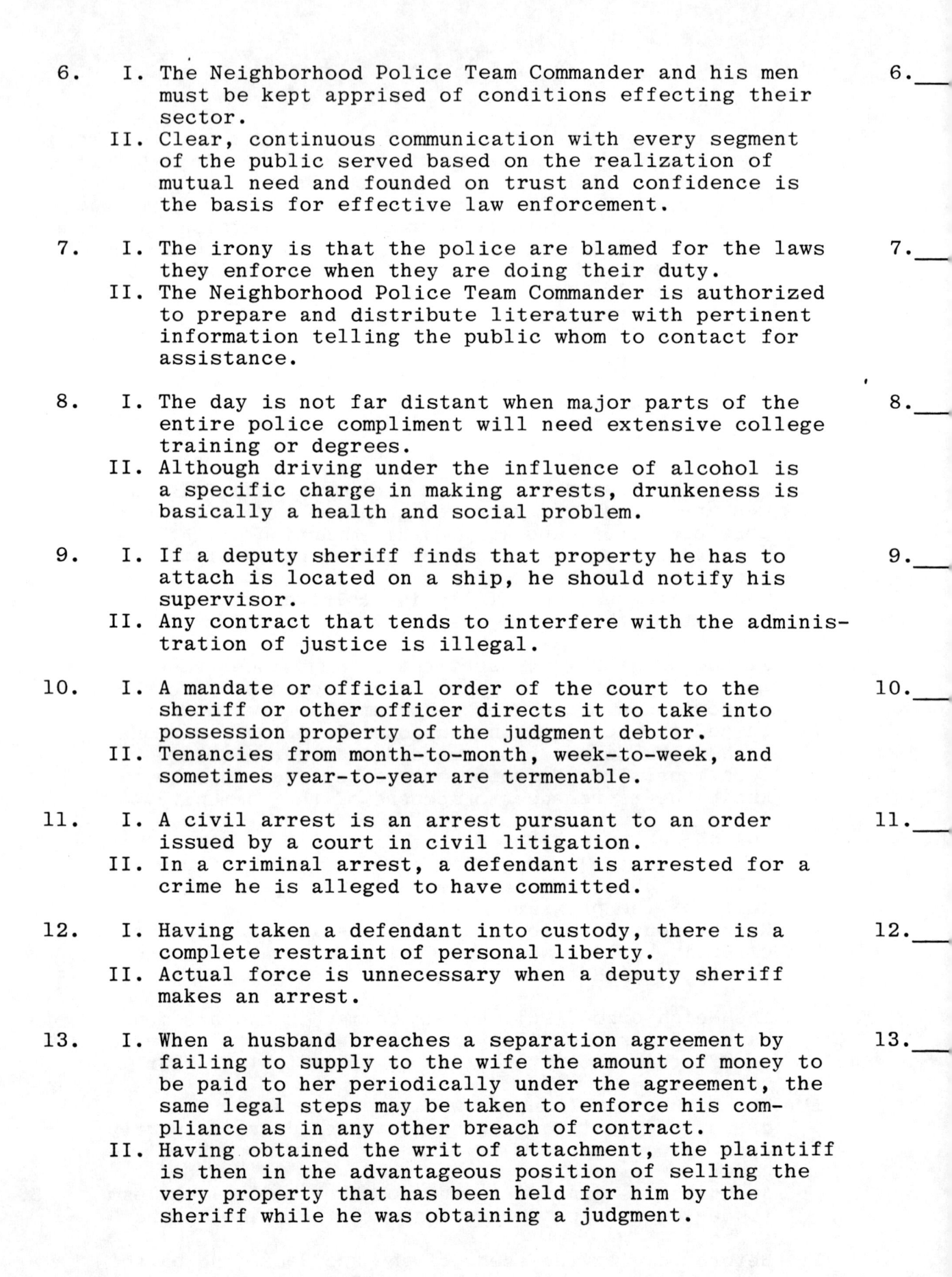

6. I. The Neighborhood Police Team Commander and his men must be kept apprised of conditions effecting their sector.
   II. Clear, continuous communication with every segment of the public served based on the realization of mutual need and founded on trust and confidence is the basis for effective law enforcement.

6.___

7. I. The irony is that the police are blamed for the laws they enforce when they are doing their duty.
   II. The Neighborhood Police Team Commander is authorized to prepare and distribute literature with pertinent information telling the public whom to contact for assistance.

7.___

8. I. The day is not far distant when major parts of the entire police compliment will need extensive college training or degrees.
   II. Although driving under the influence of alcohol is a specific charge in making arrests, drunkenness is basically a health and social problem.

8.___

9. I. If a deputy sheriff finds that property he has to attach is located on a ship, he should notify his supervisor.
   II. Any contract that tends to interfere with the administration of justice is illegal.

9.___

10. I. A mandate or official order of the court to the sheriff or other officer directs it to take into possession property of the judgment debtor.
    II. Tenancies from month-to-month, week-to-week, and sometimes year-to-year are termenable.

10.___

11. I. A civil arrest is an arrest pursuant to an order issued by a court in civil litigation.
    II. In a criminal arrest, a defendant is arrested for a crime he is alleged to have committed.

11.___

12. I. Having taken a defendant into custody, there is a complete restraint of personal liberty.
    II. Actual force is unnecessary when a deputy sheriff makes an arrest.

12.___

13. I. When a husband breaches a separation agreement by failing to supply to the wife the amount of money to be paid to her periodically under the agreement, the same legal steps may be taken to enforce his compliance as in any other breach of contract.
    II. Having obtained the writ of attachment, the plaintiff is then in the advantageous position of selling the very property that has been held for him by the sheriff while he was obtaining a judgment.

13.___

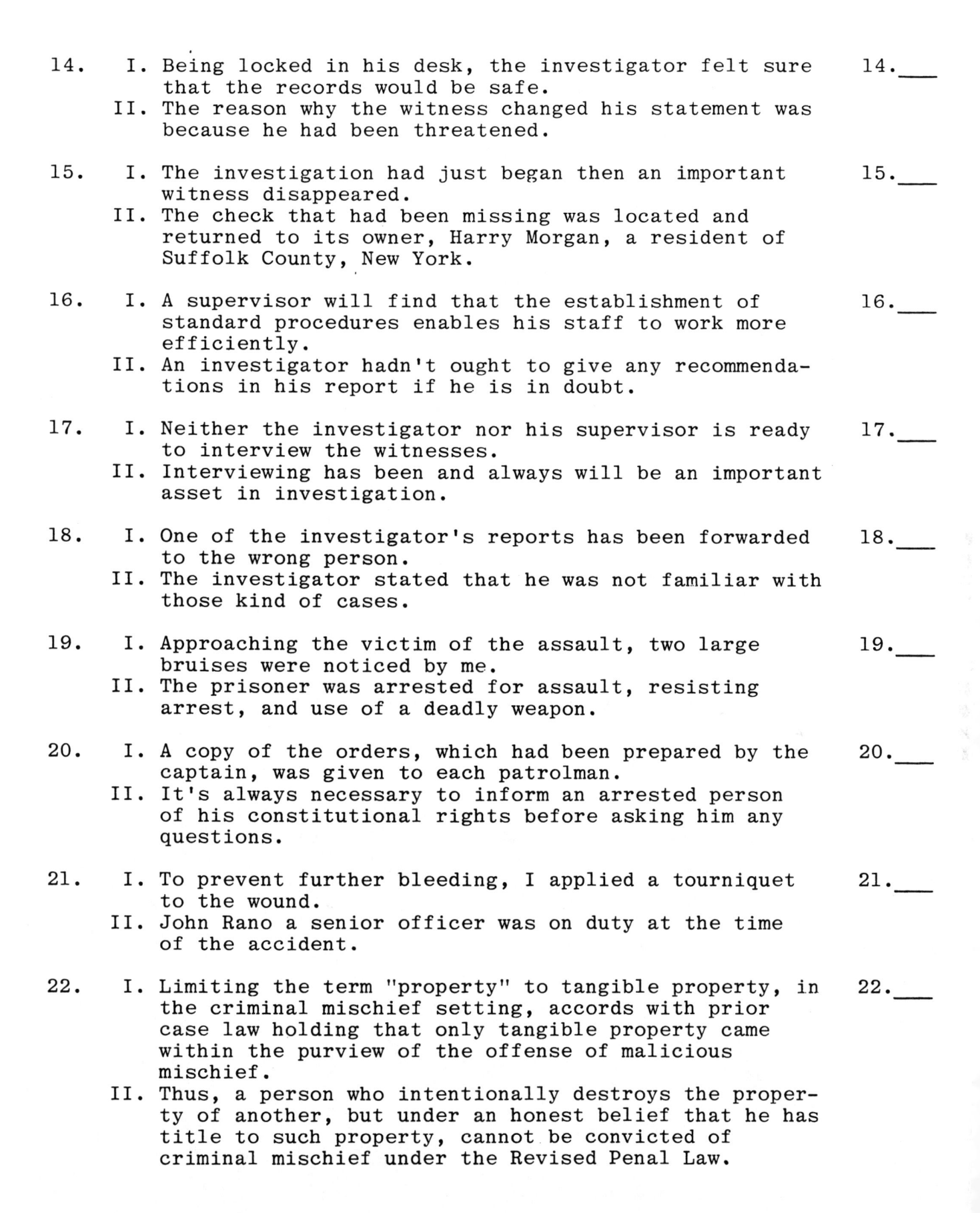

14. I. Being locked in his desk, the investigator felt sure that the records would be safe.
    II. The reason why the witness changed his statement was because he had been threatened.

14.___

15. I. The investigation had just began then an important witness disappeared.
    II. The check that had been missing was located and returned to its owner, Harry Morgan, a resident of Suffolk County, New York.

15.___

16. I. A supervisor will find that the establishment of standard procedures enables his staff to work more efficiently.
    II. An investigator hadn't ought to give any recommendations in his report if he is in doubt.

16.___

17. I. Neither the investigator nor his supervisor is ready to interview the witnesses.
    II. Interviewing has been and always will be an important asset in investigation.

17.___

18. I. One of the investigator's reports has been forwarded to the wrong person.
    II. The investigator stated that he was not familiar with those kind of cases.

18.___

19. I. Approaching the victim of the assault, two large bruises were noticed by me.
    II. The prisoner was arrested for assault, resisting arrest, and use of a deadly weapon.

19.___

20. I. A copy of the orders, which had been prepared by the captain, was given to each patrolman.
    II. It's always necessary to inform an arrested person of his constitutional rights before asking him any questions.

20.___

21. I. To prevent further bleeding, I applied a tourniquet to the wound.
    II. John Rano a senior officer was on duty at the time of the accident.

21.___

22. I. Limiting the term "property" to tangible property, in the criminal mischief setting, accords with prior case law holding that only tangible property came within the purview of the offense of malicious mischief.
    II. Thus, a person who intentionally destroys the property of another, but under an honest belief that he has title to such property, cannot be convicted of criminal mischief under the Revised Penal Law.

22.___

23.   I. Very early in it's history, New York enacted statutes from time to time punishing, either as a felony or as a misdemeanor, malicious injuries to various kinds of property: piers, booms, dams, bridges, etc.
     II. The application of the statute is necessarily restricted to trespassory takings with larcenous intent: namely with intent permanently or virtually permanently to "appropriate" property or "deprive" the owner of its use.

24.   I. Since the former Penal Law did not define the instruments of forgery in a general fashion, its crime of forgery was held to be narrower than the common law offense in this respect and to embrace only those instruments explicitly specified in the substantive provisions.
     II. After entering the barn through an open door for the purpose of stealing, it was closed by the defendants.

25.   I. The use of fire or explosives to destroy tangible property is proscribed by the criminal mischief provisions of the Revised Penal Law.
     II. The defendant's taking of a taxicab for the immediate purpose of affecting his escape did not constitute grand larceny.

KEY (CORRECT ANSWERS)

1. D
2. D
3. B
4. A
5. D

6. D
7. C
8. D
9. C
10. D

11. C
12. B
13. C
14. D
15. B

16. A
17. C
18. A
19. B
20. C

21. A
22. C
23. B
24. A
25. A

TEST 4

Questions 1-4.

DIRECTIONS: Each of the two sentences in Questions 1 through 4 may be correct or may contain errors in punctuation, capitalization, or grammar.
Mark your answer:

    A. If there is an error only in sentence I
    B. If there is an error only in sentence II
    C. If there is an error in both sentences I and II
    D. If both sentences are correct.

1. I. It is very annoying to have a pencil sharpener, which is not in working order.
   II. Patrolman Blake checked the door of Joe's Restaurant and found that the lock has been jammed.

2. I. When you are studying a good textbook is important.
   II. He said he would divide the money equally between you and me.

3. I. Since he went on the city council a year ago, one of his primary concerns has been safety in the streets.
   II. After waiting in the doorway for about 15 minutes, a black sedan appeared.

Questions 5-9.

DIRECTIONS: Each of the sentences in Questions 5 through 9 may be classified under one of the following four categories:
    A. Faulty because of incorrect grammar
    B. Faulty because of incorrect punctuation
    C. Faulty because of incorrect capitalization or incorrect spelling
    D. Correct

Examine each sentence carefully to determine under which of the above four options it is BEST classified. Then, in the space at the right, print the capitalized letter preceding the option which is the BEST of the four suggested above. Each faulty sentence contains but one type of error. Consider a sentence to be correct if it contains none of the types of errors mentioned, even though there may be other correct ways of expressing the same thought.

5. They told both he and I that the prisoner had escaped.

6. Any superior officer, who, disregards the just complaints of his subordinates, is remiss in the performance of his duty.

7. Only those members of the national organization who 7.___
   resided in the Middle west attended the conference in
   Chicago.

8. We told him to give the investigation assignment to who- 8.___
   ever was available.

9. Please do not disappoint and embarass us by not appearing 9.___
   in court.

Questions 10-14.

DIRECTIONS: Each of Questions 10 through 14 consists of three
sentences lettered A, B, and C. In each of these
questions, one of the sentences may contain an error
in grammar, sentence structure, or punctuation, or all
three sentences may be correct. If one of the sentences
in a question contains an error in grammar, sentence
structure, or punctuation, print in the space at the
right the capital letter preceding the sentence which
contains the error. If all three sentences are
correct, print the letter D.

10. A. Mr. Smith appears to be less competent than I in 10.___
       performing these duties.
    B. The supervisor spoke to the employee, who had made
       the error, but did not reprimand him.
    C. When he found the book lying on the table, he immedi-
       ately notified the owner.

11. A. Being locked in the desk, we were certain that the 11.___
       papers would not be taken.
    B. It wasn't I who dictated the telegram; I believe it
       was Eleanor.
    C. You should interview whoever comes to the office today.

12. A. The clerk was instructed to set the machine on the 12.___
       table before summoning the manager.
    B. He said that he was not familiar with those kind of
       activities.
    C. A box of pencils, in addition to erasers and blotters,
       was included in the shipment of supplies.

13. A. The supervisor remarked, "Assigning an employee to the 13.___
       proper type of work is not always easy."
    B. The employer found that each of the applicants were
       qualified to perform the duties of the position.
    C. Any competent student is permitted to take this course
       if he obtains the consent of the instructor.

14. A. The prize was awarded to the employee whom the judges believed to be most deserving.
    B. Since the instructor believes this book is the better of the two, he is recommending it for use in the school.
    C. It was obvious to the employees that the completion of the task by the scheduled date would require their working overtime.

Questions 15-21.

DIRECTIONS: In answering Questions 15 through 21, choose the sentence which is BEST from the point of view of English usage suitable for a business report.

15. A. The client's receiving of public assistance checks at two different addresses were disclosed by the investigation.
    B. The investigation disclosed that the client was receiving public assistance checks at two different addresses.
    C. The client was found out by the investigation to be receiving public assistance checks at two different addresses.
    D. The client has been receiving public assistance checks at two different addresses, disclosed the investigation.

16. A. The investigation of complaints are usually handled by this unit, which deals with internal security problems in the department.
    B. This unit deals with internal security problems in the department usually investigating complaints.
    C. Investigating complaints is this unit's job, being that it handles internal security problems in the department.
    D. This unit deals with internal security problems in the department and usually investigates complaints.

17. A. The delay in completing this investigation was caused by difficulty in obtaining the required documents from the candidate.
    B. Because of difficulty in obtaining the required documents from the candidate is the reason that there was a delay in completing this investigation.
    C. Having had difficulty in obtaining the required documents from the candidate, there was a delay in completing this investigation.
    D. Difficulty in obtaining the required documents from the candidate had the affect of delaying the completion of this investigation.

18. A. This report, together with documents supporting our
        recommendation, are being submitted for your approval.
     B. Documents supporting our recommendation is being
        submitted with the report for your approval.
     C. This report, together with documents supporting our
        recommendation, is being submitted for your approval.
     D. The report and documents supporting our recommendation
        is being submitted for your approval.

19. A. The chairman himself, rather than his aides, has
        reviewed the report.
     B. The chairman himself, rather than his aides, have
        reviewed the report.
     C. The chairmen, not the aide, has reviewed the report.
     D. The aide, not the chairmen, have reviewed the report.

20. A. Various proposals were submitted but the decision is
        not been made.
     B. Various proposals has been submitted but the decision
        has not been made.
     C. Various proposals were submitted but the decision is
        not been made.
     D. Various proposals have been submitted but the decision
        has not been made.

21. A. Everyone were rewarded for his successful attempt.
     B. They were successful in their attempts and each of
        them was rewarded.
     C. Each of them are rewarded for their successful attempts.
     D. The reward for their successful attempts were made to
        each of them.

22. The following is a paragraph from a request for departmental recognition consisting of five numbered sentences submitted to a Captain for review. These sentences may or may not have errors in spelling, grammar, and punctuation:

   1. The officers observed the subject Mills surreptitiously remove a wallet from the woman's handbag and entered his automobile. 2. As they approached Mills, he looked in their direction and drove away. 3. The officers pursued in their car. 4. Mills executed a series of complicated manuvers to evade the pursuing officers. 5. At the corner of Broome and Elizabeth Streets, Mills stopped the car, got out, raised his hands and surrendered to the officers.

   Which one of the following BEST classifies the above with regard to spelling, grammar and punctuation?
     A. 1, 2, and 3 are correct, but 4 and 5 have errors.
     B. 2, 3, and 5 are correct, but 1 and 4 have errors.
     C. 3, 4, and 5 are correct, but 1 and 2 have errors.
     D. 1, 2, 3, and 5 are correct, but 4 has errors.

23. The one of the following sentences which is grammatically PREFERABLE to the others is:
    A. Our engineers will go over your blueprints so that you may have no problems in construction.
    B. For a long time he had been arguing that we, not he, are to blame for the confusion.
    C. I worked on this automobile for two hours and still cannot find out what is wrong with it.
    D. Accustomed to all kinds of hardships, fatigue seldom bothers veteran policemen.

24. The MOST accurate of the following sentences is:
    A. The commissioner, as well as his deputy and various bureau heads, were present.
    B. A new organization of employers and employees have been formed.
    C. One or the other of these men have been selected.
    D. The number of pages in the book is enough to discourage a reader.

25. The MOST accurate of the following sentences is:
    A. Between you and me, I think he is the better man.
    B. He was believed to be me.
    C. Is it us that you wish to see?
    D. The winners are him and her.

KEY (CORRECT ANSWERS)

1. C	11. A
2. A	12. B
3. C	13. B
4. B	14. D
5. A	15. B
6. B	16. D
7. C	17. A
8. D	18. C
9. C	19. A
10. B	20. D

21. B
22. B
23. A
24. D
25. A

POLICE SCIENCE NOTES

DETENTION PROCEDURES

Introduction

Generally detention is thought of as confinement of a prisoner in a jail facility from his formal booking to his formal release. This includes a period of time when he is merely held for bail or court appearance, when he is held after trial for formal sentencing, and when he is actually serving time in a jail or prison. Actually his arrest restricts or removes his freedom and places him under official restraint; thus, it is at this point that his actual detention begins.

Responsibility for the prisoner before booking may be solely that of the arresting officer or it may be given over to jail personnel assigned to transport him to the detention facility. We are concerned, therefore, as a practical matter with the entire time the prisoner is in official custody beginning with his arrest and ending with his release from custody.

Security is the essence of detention and implies assurance against escape or rescue of the prisoner. It also implies a full measure of personal safety for the officers, the prisoner himself, other inmates and visitors and other citizens.

Although it has been implied, and is true in fact, that our concern is with persons arrested for the commission of crimes, our responsibility is a broader one. The more broad responsibility will be increasingly important in time of natural disaster or civil defense emergency. The latter includes the "holding" for safekeeping of the mentally and physically incompetent, children without parents or who are lost or abandoned, persons who are threatened by mobs or individuals, and those who must be held as material witnesses. While legal and procedural provisions must be made to handle each of the above, this is a local matter not detailed here.

Transportation

Usually an arresting officer makes a search of his prisoner at the time of arrest for dangerous weapons, means of self-destruction, and less frequently, for evidence of a crime. Officers should be trained and required to make this search. Nonetheless, since it is often made under unusual conditions of stress, transporting and booking officers should also conduct searches with final responsibility lying with the booking officer. Adequate search is a protection to police and jailers, to the prisoner and other inmates, and to visitors and other citizens.

The search, however, only removes one kind of danger; the security measure of adequate restraint must be provided to avoid loss of the prisoner by his own actions or those of others. The restraint is also provided, of course, as another means of preventing injury to the prisoner and to others.

Transportation should be considered as any means used to get the prisoner from one point to another which is usually considered to be from the location of arrest to the place of detention. Transportation, however, is also involved in taking the prisoner to court, in moving him from one place of detention to another, and in taking him to the site of work details or assignments. For our purposes we must assume that transportation may mean moving the prisoner on foot, in a special or regular police automobile, in a special prisoner vehicle (paddywagon or prisoner van) or by other means including aircraft or boats.

The same general precautions apply to all means of transport because the need for security and restraint exists in all. Transport by walking should only be considered in the absence of a proper vehicle, for very short distances, or when physical circumstances may require it, as in moving the prisoner from a detention facility to a court. The number of officers required varies according to apparent need but also according to prescribed regulations. Only one officer is required in the transport of noncriminal nonviolent persons in protective custody and these include children, the aged, minor offenders, and others. Two officers should be used normally for a person under criminal arrest if there is even a nominal possibility of escape or rescue. Three or more officers should be used in serious criminal cases, cases involving a violent prisoner, or where there is likely to be a serious attempt to escape, rescue, or attack the prisoner.

Two officers should almost always be used in prisoner transport by vehicle except in minor cases when the prisoner is placed in a separate, secure and specially designed section of the vehicle screened off from the driver. When a vehicle is used all doors should be locked and inside handles removed from the prisoner section, as in the rear of an automobile.

Minimal restraint is required when the prisoner is in a secure and separate section of the vehicle unless conflict among prisoners may develop. Reasonable restraint should be used otherwise and will usually involve the use of handcuffs. Whenever handcuffs and other restraining devices are required public display of their use should be avoided.

Special precautions should be used at the place of detention because this is the most likely point of escape or rescue. It is important that detention officers assist transporting officers in placing prisoners in the detention facility. Although the prisoner has been under restraint since his arrest, detention in a formal sense begins when he is placed in the detention facility. Properly booking and admitting the prisoner is of utmost importance and carefully prescribed admittance procedures should be established and followed. The latter, of course, must conform to State and local legal requirements. A prisoner's property, and evidence also, must be properly identified, receipted, and secured. Identification of property should be witnessed under most circumstances and especially when the prisoner is unable to sign for it. Securing property implies controlling it so that it may be returned intact on the prisoner's release.

Fingerprinting and photographing of each prisoner should be required in all criminal cases and in emergency conditions where accurate identification is important as when the prisoner is suffering from amnesia. Exceptions to this practice may be established, i.e., if the prisoner had been previously arrested and his identification established prior to the present arrest.

A final detailed and complete search must be made. The search should be for evidence if this is appropriate under the circumstances; however, the principal purpose at this point is probably to remove offensive weapons and means of self-destruction. Before a prisoner is placed in a cell it should be carefully searched also.

Capabilities for medical examination of incoming prisoners, especially those who are sick or injured, should be provided. This is not only humane but may prevent serious problems later including criticism for failure to provide proper care. Under some circumstances a detailed medical examination for all prisoners may be practicable. In this case, by formal regulation, prisoners falling in certain categories must be examined. Categories should include any person over 60 years of age as this age group will usually contain a much higher percentage of persons requiring care than would those who are younger; any person with a history of illness or disability known to the officers by prior acquaintance with the person or through medical records he carries on his person; any person who is apparently, although not necessarily obviously, ill or injured; any prisoner who complains of illness or injury; and any person who is unconscious or comatose.

It is standard practice in detention facilities to provide for separation of prisoners by age and sex. Quite obviously juveniles and adults should not be quartered together, nor should men be placed with women. Those who have communicable diseases or who may have been exposed to them should be placed in quarantine sections. Those who are perverts or who exhibit tendencies to perversion should be separated from others, particularly children. Those who are mentally deranged, or who apparently become so, must also be isolated. This may be an especially important consideration under emergency conditions. Less serious offenders should be separated from the more serious offenders to avoid recruiting prisoners to the ranks of major criminals. The use of psychiatrists and medical personnel is recommended to assist in determining necessary separation in the case of perversion and mental derangement.

Providing adequate security is essential. All offensive weapons and means of self-destruction must be physically protected and adequately guarded. None should be within reach of any prisoner. Guards should not carry firearms while in any prisoner section. Full control of all means of entrance and exit must be provided. No guard should have on his person a set of keys which would allow escape from or admittance to the full facility or a series of its sections. All tools require close control because they may be used as weapons, escape devices, or provide the means to make such items. Prisoners being returned to cells from corridors, shops, and dining rooms should be searched.

Medical supplies must be carefully controlled. Their possession by prisoners provide means of self-destruction and barter. Under some circumstances prisoners would maliciously destroy essential medical provisions.

On a frequent, intermittent basis, quarters and inmates must be inspected and prisoners counted.

To avoid emotional problems, provide exercise, and for other reasons prisoners who warrant the trust can be given some freedom in the facility and be put to minor but productive tasks. Classification of prisoners as "trusties" or available for light work must be carefully done to avoid escapes and other problems.

All security measures must be established on a basis that allows prompt implementation of plans for evacuation of prisoners in the event of fire or facility destruction by other means. Planning must also provide full means of protection against the consequences of riot and mob attempts at rescue or attack. This may require provisions to quickly and inconspicuously move key prisoners to other detention.

Detention When Jails Unavailable

Most shelters and relocation facilities are not designed for detention purposes. This will require imaginative improvisation of both quarters and procedures. Two things must be provided in spite of adverse circumstances: (1) Basic security for prisoners, officers, and other occupants; and (2) separation of various categories of prisoners.

Large rooms, of course, can be used for group detention if adequate security is provided and if the need for separation is minimal or absent. Such use of space, however, may require the use of additional guards constantly on the alert to avoid altercations or plotting for escape.

In shelters the problems of security and separation may require unusual use of restraining devices and materials. Individual prisoners can be handcuffed to pipes, doorknobs, stanchions, or window bars. If this is done, adequate free space around the prisoner should be provided to avoid improper and dangerous contact with other prisoners or occupants of the shelter. Two prisoners can be secured with a single set of handcuffs merely by passing the cuffs behind a pipe set close to a wall or the floor, or behind a bar in a barred window or door.

Ropes, belts, and similar material may be used in lieu of handcuffs, but require unusual care to avoid injury or escapes. Although it may be necessary to occasionally check handcuffs to see that they are not too tight for the comfort or safety of the prisoner, frequent inspection of rope and other nonmetallic material is essential. These may quickly become either too tight and thus cause injury, or too loose and thus permit escape. Restraints of material must also be checked if they become wet, or dry out after being wet.

Sedatives may be used under unusual circumstances by a doctor or by a nurse under his direction. Sedatives have a particular value when handling a violent person and may be used both as a restraint and treatment in many cases.

Expensive, but necessary on occasion, will be the use of guards or officers on the basis of one guard to a prisoner. This should be avoided if possible because of the excessive drain it puts on available personnel.

Conclusion

It should be said once again that security is the essence of detention. The safety of officers, prisoners, and others is dependent on strict adherence to carefully prepared procedures.

CRIMINAL INVESTIGATION

TECHNIQUE OF INTERVIEWS AND INTERROGATION

CONTENTS

	Page
1. General	1
2. Purpose of Interview	2
3. Preparation for Interview	2
4. Time of Interview	3
5. Place of Interview	3
6. Introduction of the Investigator	3
7. Control over Interviews	4
8. Rights of Person Interviewed	4
9. Attitude and Demeanor of Investigator	4
10. Types of Approaches	5
11. Interview of Complainants	6
12. Interview of Victims	6
13. Interview of Witnesses	7
14. Types of Witnesses	7
15. Assistance to Witnesses in Descriptions	8
16. Credibility of Witnesses	9
17. Evaluation During Interview	9
18. Interview Notes	10
19. Purpose of Interrogation	10
20. Preparation for Interrogation	11
21. Classification of Suspects	12
22. Length of Interrogation	13
23. Persons at Interrogation	13
24. Interrogation Checklist	14
25. Introduction of Investigator	14
26. Rights of Person being Interrogated	15
27. Attitude of Investigator	15
28. Types of Approach	16
29. Interrogation Notes	19
30. Scientific Aids to Interrogation	19
31. Lie Detecting Set	19
32. Narco-Analysis	20

CRIMINAL INVESTIGATION
TECHNIQUE OF INTERVIEWS AND INTERROGATION

1. GENERAL

The successful investigation of criminal offenses depends in a great measure upon the effective questioning of complainants, witnesses, informants, suspects, and other persons encountered during the course of an investigation. Questioning is divided into two broad classifications: *interviews*, which are conducted to learn facts from persons who may have knowledge of a wrongful act but who are not themselves implicated; and *interrogations*, which are conducted to learn facts and to obtain admissions or confessions of wrongful acts from persons who are implicated in a wrongful act. Persons who have been interviewed may later be interrogated. An interrogation is not necessarily confined to individuals suspected of criminal acts, but may include persons who may have been accessories, or who may have knowledge of the crime which, for various motives, they are reluctant to admit. It is usually advisable to take statements from persons being interviewed or interrogated. When an interview or interrogation develops information which will have definite value as evidence, that information or evidence must be recorded in a written, signed, and witnessed statement, or preserved through mechanical recording.

2. PURPOSE OF INTERVIEW

An interview is an informal questioning to learn facts. The successful investigation of crime requires that the investigator be able to learn, through personal questioning, what the person interviewed has observed through his five senses: sight, hearing, taste, smell, and touch. Each individual interviewed is presumed to possess certain information that may lead to the solution of a crime. Effective interviewing requires that the interviewer make full use of all the knowledge of human nature he possesses, so that the individual interviewed will disclose all that he knows about the matter in question. If a person does not possess knowledge of the crime, the interview should establish that fact. Pertinent negative evidence is as much a part of a complete investigation as positive information.

3. PREPARATION FOR INTERVIEW

Interviews other than those conducted at the scene of the crime should be planned carefully and thoroughly to prevent repetition of the interview. The investigator must review thoroughly all developments in the investigation prior to the interview. He must also consider the relationship of the person to be interviewed to the investigation; i. e., complainant, victim, witness, or informant. An effective interviewer combines his knowledge of human nature with all available information about the person to be interviewed, such as education, character, reputation, associates, habits, and past criminal record. This background information is used advantageously in the interview. The investigator should estimate the extent and kind of information which he may expect to elicit. He should prepare, by noting pertinent facts to be developed, to detect inconsistencies and discrepancies in the statements of the person being interviewed, to evaluate them, and to require their clarification. The investigator should prepare a plan for the interview which takes into consideration the information available to him about the person to be interviewed; the time, place, and environment for the interview; as well as the legal proof to be developed in the crime.

4. TIME OF INTERVIEW

An interview should be conducted as soon as possible after the discovery of a crime. The investigator should take as much time as is required for a complete and thorough interview.

5. PLACE OF INTERVIEW

When possible, the place of the interview should be so selected as to assure a favorable environment. When possible, the interview should be conducted in a comfortable room and in an environment familiar to the person interviewed. The person to be interviewed should never be brought to the investigator.

6. INTRODUCTION OF THE INVESTIGATOR

Usually the investigator and the person to be interviewed are strangers. The investigator should introduce himself, present his credentials (when appropriate), and begin by making a general statement regarding the purpose of the interview. The introduction should be made in such a manner as to establish a cordial relationship between the investigator and the person being interviewed.

7. CONTROL OVER INTERVIEWS

An investigator must maintain absolute control of the interview at all times. He must be careful not to elicit false information through improper questioning. He may permit digression or discussion of matters seemingly unrelated to the crime in order to place the person interviewed at ease but he must not permit the person being interviewed to become evasive. If the person interviewed should become so evasive as to obscure the purpose of the interview, effective results may be obtained by a more formal type of questioning, taking notes, or by the aggressiveness of the investigator.

8. RIGHTS OF PERSON INTERVIEWED

Although an investigator has no legal power to compel a person being interviewed to divulge information, he may, if he is clever and alert, induce him to disclose what he knows. When an interview develops into an interrogation, the investigator must warn the person being interviewed of his rights (par. 26).

9. ATTITUDE AND DEMEANOR OF INVESTIGATOR

The attitude and demeanor of an investigator contributes immeasurably to the success or failure of an interview. The investigator should be friendly, yet businesslike. He should endeavor to lead the person being interviewed into talkativeness. He should then direct the conversation toward the investigation. The individual being interviewed should be permitted to give an uninterrupted account while the investigator makes mental notes of omissions, inconsistencies, or discrepancies that require clarification by later questioning. The investigator should strive to turn to advantage the subject's prejudices. He rarely reveals the precise objective of an interview, and usually obtains a more accurate account from the person interviewed if he claims only to be attempting to establish facts. He should avoid a clash of personalities; acts of undue familiarity: the use of profanity or violent expressions such as "kill," "steal," "confess," "murder"; improbable stories; or distracting mannerisms such as pacing the floor or fumbling with objects.

10. TYPES OF APPROACHES

The *indirect* approach employed in interviewing consists of discussion carried on in a conversational tone that permits the person being interviewed to talk without having to answer direct questions. The *direct* approach consists of direct questioning as in interrogations (par. 28a). The use of interrogation technique often succeeds when the person interviewed fears or dislikes police officers, fears retribution from a criminal, desires to protect a friend or relative, is impudent, or, for diverse reasons, is unwilling to cooperate with the investigator. Unreliable persons or liars should always be permitted to give their version of an incident. They may, through contradiction or denial, trip themselves into admissions through which the true facts may be obtained. When interviewing shy or nervous persons, the investigator may be obliged to obtain information piecemeal. He should interview in the normal environment of such persons and should be as casual and calm as possible. The talkative person should be allowed to speak freely and to use his own expressions, but should be confined to the subject by appropriate questions. When persons pretend to know nothing about an incident, the investigator should ask many questions, any one which, if answered, will refute their claim that they know nothing at all. Disinterested persons may divulge more information if their personal interest can be aroused by an indirect approach. Investigators should always attempt to put uneducated witnesses at ease and to help them express themselves as best they can, but should not put words into their mouths. Flattery is most often successful when alcoholics or braggarts are interviewed. Information gained from such individuals must be corroborated.

11. INTERVIEW OF COMPLAINANTS

In interviewing complainants, the investigator should be considerate, understanding, tactful, and impartial, regardless of the motive for the complaint, and should inform the complainant that appropriate action will be initiated promptly.

12. INTERVIEW OF VICTIMS

When interviewing victims, the investigator must consider their emotional state, particularly in crimes of violence. Frequently, victims have unsupported beliefs regarding the circumstances connected with the crime. Their observations may be partial and imperfect because of excitement and tension. It is imperative that the investigator obtain from the victim an accurate account of the circumstances that existed immediately before, during, and after the incident. The investigator should consider the reputation of the victim in determining the credibility of his complaint.

13. INTERVIEW OF WITNESSES

The investigator must frequently assist witnesses to recall and relate facts exactly as they observed them. He must know what may affect a person's ability to observe and describe acts, articles, or circumstances related to a crime (ch. 3). He should lead witnesses toward accurate statements of fact by assisting them to recall in detail their experiences.

14. TYPES OF WITNESSES

In general, children from 7 to 12 years of age are good observers, although their testimony may be inadmissible in court. Teen-age children are also good observers but may exaggerate. Young adults are often poor witnesses; middle-aged and older persons are the best witnesses. Persons differ in their physical and mental characteristics as well as in their experience and training. These differences may cause them to notice only those aspects of a situation in which they may have had a particular experience. As a consequence, they differ in their observations, interpretations, and descriptions. If a witness cannot recall what he has observed, poor memory may be the cause. Preoccupation of a witness may often prevent him from recalling exactly what occurred. Lack of education may make it difficult for a witness to describe what he observed; such a person is sometimes reluctant to divulge information because of embarrassment over his diction. That which has been observed, because of exaggeration, misrepresentation, or inaccurate interpretation, may result in faulty information; i. e., a squeal of joy may be misinterpreted as a scream of terror. The emotions of witnesses before, during, and after an incident, and when interviewed, greatly affect their recall of events as they actually occurred. A frightened witness may recall events differently than a calm, unruffled person. Witnesses may exaggerate more each time their observations are repeated.

15. ASSISTANCE TO WITNESSES IN DESCRIPTIONS

The investigator should provide certain indexes to assist witnesses in describing size, height, weight, distance, and colors. The eye-level method of determining height may be used as standard. By asking a witness to tell how far another person's eyes were above or below his own, the investigator may obtain an estimate of height. Speed is difficult to estimate accurately; even opinions based on long experience may be subject to influence by noise, light, weather, and other conditions. Age is difficult for witnesses to judge because of differences among races, nationalities, and individuals; if selected individuals are used for comparison, they must be chosen carefully. In situations which are strange or which involve unusual circumstances, the witness may have no standards or associations on which to base his judgment and may be unable to utilize the standards presented for comparison. A detailed review or reconstruction of events will sometimes help the witness to recall events, but the investigator must be careful to avoid confusing the actual event with the reconstruction.

16. CREDIBILITY OF WITNESSES

Credibility of a witness is usually governed by his character and is evidenced by his reputation for veracity. Personal or financial reason or previous criminal activity may cause a witness to give false information to avoid being implicated. Hope of gain by informants or prisoners; political, racial, or religious factors; and hatred for the police or the suspect are some of the reasons why a witness may make a false statement. Age, sex, physical and mental abnormalities, loyalty, revenge, social and economic status, indulgence in alcohol, and the influence of other persons are some of the many factors which may affect the accuracy, willingness, or ability with which witnesses observe, interpret, and describe occurrences.

17. EVALUATION DURING INTERVIEW

During an interview, the investigator must evaluate continuously the mannerisms and the emotional state of the person in terms of the information developed. The manner in which a person relates his story or answers questions may indicate that he is not telling the truth or is concealing information. Evasiveness, hesitation, or unwillingness to discuss situations may signify a lack of cooperation. The relation of body movements to the emotional state of persons must be carefully considered by the investigator. A dry mouth indicated by the wetting of the lips, fidgeting, or vague movements of the hands may indicate nervousness or deception. A "cold sweat" or pale face may indicate fear. A slight gasp, holding the breath, or an unsteady voice may indicate that the knowledge of the investigator has shocked the person being interviewed. The pumping of the heart may be observed by the pulse in the neck. A ruddy or flushed face may be an indication of anger or embarrassment, not necessarily guilt, and may also indicate that the matter under discussion is of vital importance, or that some information is being withheld. Although such symptoms are not necessarily valid indications of guilt or innocence and may be a manifestation of the physical condition or health of the individual, they are often related to the emotional state of the person.

18. INTERVIEW NOTES

Complete notes are essential to effective investigation and reporting. Normally, most people have no objection to note-taking; however, the investigator should not take notes until he has had an opportunity to gage the person's reactions, since note-taking may create a reluctance to divulge information. If he does not take notes, the investigator should record, at the first opportunity after the interview, all pertinent information while it is fresh in his mind. Notes on interviews should contain the case number; hour, date, and place of interview; complete identification of the person interviewed; names of other persons present; and a resumé of the interview.

19. PURPOSE OF INTERROGATION

The interrogation should take place immediately if the suspect is surprised or apprehended in the act of committing a crime. In all other instances, interrogation should be conducted only after sufficient information has been secured and the background of the suspect has been thoroughly explored. The purpose of interrogation of a suspect is to obtain an admission or confession of his wrongful acts and a written, signed, and witnessed statement, and to establish the facts of a crime or to develop information which will enable the investigator to obtain direct, physical, or other evidence to prove or disprove the truth of an admission or confession. A confession is an acknowledgment of guilt, whereas an admission is a self-incriminatory statement falling short of an acknowledgment of guilt. The securing of confessions or acknowledgments of guilt does not complete the investigation of a crime. A statement made by one conspirator during the conspiracy and in pursuance of it is admissible in evidence against his co-conspirators as tending to prove the fact of the matter stated. In interrogation, the investigator seeks to learn the identity of accomplices and details of any other crime in which the suspect may have been involved.

20. PREPARATION FOR INTERROGATION

a. Preparation for interrogation should be thorough. The investigator should base his plan for interrogation on background data, information, or direct evidence received from victims and witnesses, physical evidence, and reconstruction of the crime scene. The plan, which should be written, should take into consideration the various means for testing the truthfulness of the suspect and for gaining a psychological advantage over him through the use of known facts and proper use of time, place, and environment. Unless the investigator interrogates a suspect immediately following the commission of a crime, or desires to question him without previous notification, he should be interrogated at criminal investigation headquarters, where recordings may be made or stenographic notes may be taken.

b. During interrogation, the subject should be seated in a plain chair placed where his movements and physical reactions may be observed easily. The interrogation room should be plainly but comfortably furnished, without items which may cause distraction. Recording devices, one-way mirrors, and similar equipment should appear as normal furnishings. Tables, desks, and other furnishings should be located where they will not impair the interrogator's observation of the suspect.

21. CLASSIFICATION OF SUSPECTS

Background information and the facts established in an investigation enable the investigator to classify persons to be interrogated as follows:

a. Known offenders, whose guilt is reasonably certain on the basis of the evidence available.

b. Persons whose guilt is doubtful or uncertain because of the evidence or lack of evidence.

c. Material witnesses, accessories, and persons who have knowledge of the crime but may not themselves be guilty of a crime. Persons to be interrogated may be further classified as those readily influenced by sympathy or understanding; and those readily influenced by the use of an attitude of suspicion and obvious disbelief.

22. LENGTH OF INTERROGATION

No time limit is placed on the duration of interrogation except that it shall not be so long and under such conditions as to amount to duress. Questioning for many hours without food, sleep, or under glaring lights has been held to constitute such duress as to invalidate a confession. The suspect may be questioned at length in an attempt to break down his resistance, or he may be questioned for short periods daily as a test of his consistency. The interrogator should always consider the physical condition of the person being interrogated as well as his emotional stability. Once the suspect has begun to reveal pertinent information, the interrogation should not be interrupted.

23. PERSONS AT INTERROGATION

An interrogation usually should be conducted in complete privacy. A person under interrogation is not inclined to reveal confidences to a public gathering. Witnesses to a confession may be called in to hear the reading of the statement and the declaration that it is the subject's statement, to witness the signing by the subject, and to affix their own signatures. Some investigative agencies advocate the presence of a witness at all times during an interrogation, particularly during the period of warning of rights and at such other periods when corroborative testimony might be needed or desirable. When a woman is questioned, the interrogator should provide witnesses, preferably women, in order to avoid charges of compromise which an unscrupulous woman may later interject as mitigating circumstance.

24. INTERROGATION CHECKLIST

Before beginning an interrogation, the investigator should check his preparation against the following questions:

a. Has the crime scene been carefully and adequately searched for real evidence?

b. Have all persons known to have knowledge of the crime been questioned?

c. Has all possible evidence been obtained?

d. Has the person to be interrogated been searched?

e. Have all files been checked for pertinent information?

f. Is background investigation complete?

g. Is the interrogation room properly prepared for the interrogation?

h. Is the interrogation plan complete?

i. Have the elements of legal proof been checked?

j. Are all details of the investigation firmly fixed in the investigator's mind?

k. What information should be elicited from the individual to be interrogated?

25. INTRODUCTION OF INVESTIGATOR

Prior to any interrogation, the investigator may introduce and identify himself by presenting his credentials if the person to be interrogated questions the authority of the investigator. After the introduction, the person to be interrogated should be informed in general terms of the nature of the investigation being conducted. The investigator, however, should not disclose his knowledge of the case, nor should he prematurely disclose any fact of the case.

26. RIGHTS OF PERSON BEING INTERROGATED

The investigator should begin interrogation by explaining to the person to be questioned his rights under the Fifth Amendment to the Constitution of the United States, if he is a civilian, and under Article 31 of the Uniform Code of Military Justice, if he is a military person. The person to be questioned is informed that he need not answer any question which may tend to incriminate him but that, if he chooses to answer any question, such answer may be used in testimony against him. Throughout the questioning the investigator must refrain from threats, violence, or promise of reward. In response to a request by the person being questioned for legal counsel, the investigator should courteously but firmly refuse and state that the Uniform Code of Military Justice does not provide for counsel prior to charges being preferred against a soldier.

27. ATTITUDE OF INVESTIGATOR

Because of the importance of admissions or confessions, the investigator must become skilled in the art of interrogation. He must master a variety of questioning techniques, learn to judge the psychological strength or weakness of others, and learn to take advantage of his own particular abilities in questioning any suspect or reluctant witness. He must not presume guilt of the persons being interrogated without sufficient proof. He must act as naturally as possible under the circumstances. If a suspect begins admitting criminal acts, the investigator must not become overeager or condescending. The interrogator should, when it is necessary to stir the emotions of another to confess a wrongful act, permit his own emotions to be stirred.

28. TYPES OF APPROACH

He adapts his approach to the character and background of the person to be interrogated, the known facts of the crime, and the real evidence available. The investigator may use any of the following type approaches or any combination of them:

a. The *direct approach* is normally employed where guilt is reasonably certain. The investigator assumes an air of confidence concerning the guilt of the offender and points out the evidence indicative of guilt. He outwardly sympathizes with the offender and indicates that anyone else might have done the same thing under similar circumstances. He urges the offender to tell the whole truth, avoids threatening words or insinuation, and develops a detailed account of the crime from premeditation to commission. He may ask questions such as the following: "Tell me all you know about this. When did you get the idea of doing it? Why did you do it? How did you do that? Where did you get the money?" In dealing with habitual criminals whose guilt is reasonably certain and who apparently have no feeling of wrongdoing, the investigator must convince them that their guilt can be or is established by the testimony of witnesses or available evidence. Investigators must never make promises of leniency or clemency as these promises might vitiate confessions obtained as a result of the interrogation.

b. The *indirect approach* is normally employed in interrogating a person who has knowledge of the crime. The investigator must proceed cautiously.

He requests the individual being interrogated to tell all he knows about the incident. He then requires an explanation of discrepancies or distortions and endeavors to lead the individual being interrogated into admissions of truth. When facts indicative of guilt are developed, the investigator casually asks questions to determine through the offender's reactions whether he will acknowledge or deny guilt. When guilt appears probable, the investigator reverts to direct questioning to obtain an admission or confession.

c. The *emotional approach* is designed to arouse any play upon the emotions of a person. Body actions may indicate the presence of nervous tension. The investigator points out these signs of nervous tension to the person under interrogation. The investigator may discuss the moral seriousness of the offense, emphasize the penalty, and appeal to the suspect's pride or ego, fear, like or dislike, or his hate and desire for revenge. This approach may lead to emotional breakdown and a confession.

d. Subterfuge is employed to induce guilty persons to confess when all other approaches have failed. Considerable care should be exercised in the employment of subterfuge. If the person to be interrogated recognizes the approach as subterfuge, further efforts to obtain an admission or confession may be futile. Examples of subterfuge are:

    (1) *Hypothetical story.* A fictitious crime, varying only in minute details from the offense of which the subject is suspected, is related to him. The investigator later visits the subject and asks him to write out details of the hypothetical story as related. If the

subject is guilty, he often includes details of the crime under investigation, but not mentioned by the investigator in his fictitious story. When confronted with these inconsistencies, the suspect may make a confession.

(2) *Signed false statement.* When evidence indicates, but is not conclusive, that a certain person may be guilty of a crime, he may be requested to make a sworn written statement. After he has made a false written statement, the discrepancies contained therein are pointed out to him in an attempt to gain a true confession.

(3) '*Cold shoulder.*" This term designates a technique of subterfuge keynoted by indifference. The person suspected is invited to come to the investigator's office. If he accepts the invitation, he is taken either to the office or the crime scene. The investigator, or those accompanying the person subjected to this type of interrogation, say nothing to him or to each other, and await his reactions. This technique may cause the suspect to surmise that the investigator has evidence adequate to prove his guilt.

(4) *Playing one suspect against another.* When two or more persons are suspected of having been involved in a crime, the person believed to have the weakest character is interrogated first. The others are interrogated separately and informed that their partner has accused them of the crime. A confession, shown to the others involved, may influence

them to attempt to protect themselves by confessing.

(5) *Contrasting personalities.* This technique employs two investigators, one determined and the other sympathetic and understanding. The interrogation is so arranged that the person under interrogation will play into the hands of one or the other.

29. INTERROGATION NOTES

The taking of notes during an interrogation may be essential in order to record all pertinent information; however, the effect of note-taking on the success of the interrogation must be considered. If notes are not taken during the interrogation, the investigator should record all pertinent data immediately after the interrogation.

30. SCIENTIFIC AIDS TO INTERROGATION

Scientific aids are available to the investigator to assist in the investigation of criminal offenses. These aids are normally employed to develop information from persons who are suspected of committing a crime. They may also be used to check the validity and completeness of information given by complainants, witnesses, and victims.

31. LIE DETECTING SET

Lie detecting set examinations can be conducted only by operators trained in the use of the instrument. The lie detecting set is an instrument which records the body changes that accompany emotions and is used to develop information, to determine if a person has knowledge of an offense, and to obtain an admission or confession of guilt. The provisions of Article 31, Uniform Code of Military Justice, and the Fifth Amendment to the Constitution of the United States apply to persons who are requested to submit to an examination by a lie detecting set. Investigators should obtain written consent from all persons subjected to lie detecting set examinations, acknowledging that they have been informed of their rights and that they agree to submit voluntarily to such an examination. A copy of this statement should be included in the case file folder. In general, graphs obtained during a lie detecting set examination are not admissible as evidence in court. However, the operator is usually permitted to testify relative to the questions asked, and the answers given. Oral or written admissions or confessions obtained as a consequence of the examination may be admitted into evidence, if they meet legal requirements.

32. NARCO-ANALYSIS

Narco-analysis is the term employed to define the questioning of a person under the influence of drugs (truth serums). Scopolamine, sodium amytal, and sodium pentathol are the drugs most commonly used. When properly administered, these drugs tend to overcome inhibitions. The use of narco-analysis as an investigative technique has not found general acceptance. Admissions or confessions obtained through the use of truth serums are not admissible as evidence in court. The information obtained may be used only to develop the investigation. The subject must be warned of his rights, and a written statement obtained wherein the subject acknowledges the warning and voluntarily agrees to the narco-analysis. *No person may be compelled to submit to such an examination. It must be conducted only when a qualified medical officer is available to administer the drugs and to witness the examination.*

ANSWER SHEET

TEST NO. _____ PART _____ TITLE OF POSITION _____
(AS GIVEN IN EXAMINATION ANNOUNCEMENT - INCLUDE OPTION, IF ANY)

PLACE OF EXAMINATION _____ DATE _____
(CITY OR TOWN)   (STATE)

RATING

USE THE SPECIAL PENCIL.   MAKE GLOSSY BLACK MARKS.

	A B C D E		A B C D E		A B C D E		A B C D E		A B C D E
1	⁞ ⁞ ⁞ ⁞ ⁞	26	⁞ ⁞ ⁞ ⁞ ⁞	51	⁞ ⁞ ⁞ ⁞ ⁞	76	⁞ ⁞ ⁞ ⁞ ⁞	101	⁞ ⁞ ⁞ ⁞ ⁞
2	⁞ ⁞ ⁞ ⁞ ⁞	27	⁞ ⁞ ⁞ ⁞ ⁞	52	⁞ ⁞ ⁞ ⁞ ⁞	77	⁞ ⁞ ⁞ ⁞ ⁞	102	⁞ ⁞ ⁞ ⁞ ⁞
3	⁞ ⁞ ⁞ ⁞ ⁞	28	⁞ ⁞ ⁞ ⁞ ⁞	53	⁞ ⁞ ⁞ ⁞ ⁞	78	⁞ ⁞ ⁞ ⁞ ⁞	103	⁞ ⁞ ⁞ ⁞ ⁞
4	⁞ ⁞ ⁞ ⁞ ⁞	29	⁞ ⁞ ⁞ ⁞ ⁞	54	⁞ ⁞ ⁞ ⁞ ⁞	79	⁞ ⁞ ⁞ ⁞ ⁞	104	⁞ ⁞ ⁞ ⁞ ⁞
5	⁞ ⁞ ⁞ ⁞ ⁞	30	⁞ ⁞ ⁞ ⁞ ⁞	55	⁞ ⁞ ⁞ ⁞ ⁞	80	⁞ ⁞ ⁞ ⁞ ⁞	105	⁞ ⁞ ⁞ ⁞ ⁞
6	⁞ ⁞ ⁞ ⁞ ⁞	31	⁞ ⁞ ⁞ ⁞ ⁞	56	⁞ ⁞ ⁞ ⁞ ⁞	81	⁞ ⁞ ⁞ ⁞ ⁞	106	⁞ ⁞ ⁞ ⁞ ⁞
7	⁞ ⁞ ⁞ ⁞ ⁞	32	⁞ ⁞ ⁞ ⁞ ⁞	57	⁞ ⁞ ⁞ ⁞ ⁞	82	⁞ ⁞ ⁞ ⁞ ⁞	107	⁞ ⁞ ⁞ ⁞ ⁞
8	⁞ ⁞ ⁞ ⁞ ⁞	33	⁞ ⁞ ⁞ ⁞ ⁞	58	⁞ ⁞ ⁞ ⁞ ⁞	83	⁞ ⁞ ⁞ ⁞ ⁞	108	⁞ ⁞ ⁞ ⁞ ⁞
9	⁞ ⁞ ⁞ ⁞ ⁞	34	⁞ ⁞ ⁞ ⁞ ⁞	59	⁞ ⁞ ⁞ ⁞ ⁞	84	⁞ ⁞ ⁞ ⁞ ⁞	109	⁞ ⁞ ⁞ ⁞ ⁞
10	⁞ ⁞ ⁞ ⁞ ⁞	35	⁞ ⁞ ⁞ ⁞ ⁞	60	⁞ ⁞ ⁞ ⁞ ⁞	85	⁞ ⁞ ⁞ ⁞ ⁞	110	⁞ ⁞ ⁞ ⁞ ⁞

Make only ONE mark for each answer.   Additional and stray marks may be counted as mistakes.   In making corrections, erase errors COMPLETELY.

	A B C D E		A B C D E		A B C D E		A B C D E		A B C D E
11	⁞ ⁞ ⁞ ⁞ ⁞	36	⁞ ⁞ ⁞ ⁞ ⁞	61	⁞ ⁞ ⁞ ⁞ ⁞	86	⁞ ⁞ ⁞ ⁞ ⁞	111	⁞ ⁞ ⁞ ⁞ ⁞
12	⁞ ⁞ ⁞ ⁞ ⁞	37	⁞ ⁞ ⁞ ⁞ ⁞	62	⁞ ⁞ ⁞ ⁞ ⁞	87	⁞ ⁞ ⁞ ⁞ ⁞	112	⁞ ⁞ ⁞ ⁞ ⁞
13	⁞ ⁞ ⁞ ⁞ ⁞	38	⁞ ⁞ ⁞ ⁞ ⁞	63	⁞ ⁞ ⁞ ⁞ ⁞	88	⁞ ⁞ ⁞ ⁞ ⁞	113	⁞ ⁞ ⁞ ⁞ ⁞
14	⁞ ⁞ ⁞ ⁞ ⁞	39	⁞ ⁞ ⁞ ⁞ ⁞	64	⁞ ⁞ ⁞ ⁞ ⁞	89	⁞ ⁞ ⁞ ⁞ ⁞	114	⁞ ⁞ ⁞ ⁞ ⁞
15	⁞ ⁞ ⁞ ⁞ ⁞	40	⁞ ⁞ ⁞ ⁞ ⁞	65	⁞ ⁞ ⁞ ⁞ ⁞	90	⁞ ⁞ ⁞ ⁞ ⁞	115	⁞ ⁞ ⁞ ⁞ ⁞
16	⁞ ⁞ ⁞ ⁞ ⁞	41	⁞ ⁞ ⁞ ⁞ ⁞	66	⁞ ⁞ ⁞ ⁞ ⁞	91	⁞ ⁞ ⁞ ⁞ ⁞	116	⁞ ⁞ ⁞ ⁞ ⁞
17	⁞ ⁞ ⁞ ⁞ ⁞	42	⁞ ⁞ ⁞ ⁞ ⁞	67	⁞ ⁞ ⁞ ⁞ ⁞	92	⁞ ⁞ ⁞ ⁞ ⁞	117	⁞ ⁞ ⁞ ⁞ ⁞
18	⁞ ⁞ ⁞ ⁞ ⁞	43	⁞ ⁞ ⁞ ⁞ ⁞	68	⁞ ⁞ ⁞ ⁞ ⁞	93	⁞ ⁞ ⁞ ⁞ ⁞	118	⁞ ⁞ ⁞ ⁞ ⁞
19	⁞ ⁞ ⁞ ⁞ ⁞	44	⁞ ⁞ ⁞ ⁞ ⁞	69	⁞ ⁞ ⁞ ⁞ ⁞	94	⁞ ⁞ ⁞ ⁞ ⁞	119	⁞ ⁞ ⁞ ⁞ ⁞
20	⁞ ⁞ ⁞ ⁞ ⁞	45	⁞ ⁞ ⁞ ⁞ ⁞	70	⁞ ⁞ ⁞ ⁞ ⁞	95	⁞ ⁞ ⁞ ⁞ ⁞	120	⁞ ⁞ ⁞ ⁞ ⁞
21	⁞ ⁞ ⁞ ⁞ ⁞	46	⁞ ⁞ ⁞ ⁞ ⁞	71	⁞ ⁞ ⁞ ⁞ ⁞	96	⁞ ⁞ ⁞ ⁞ ⁞	121	⁞ ⁞ ⁞ ⁞ ⁞
22	⁞ ⁞ ⁞ ⁞ ⁞	47	⁞ ⁞ ⁞ ⁞ ⁞	72	⁞ ⁞ ⁞ ⁞ ⁞	97	⁞ ⁞ ⁞ ⁞ ⁞	122	⁞ ⁞ ⁞ ⁞ ⁞
23	⁞ ⁞ ⁞ ⁞ ⁞	48	⁞ ⁞ ⁞ ⁞ ⁞	73	⁞ ⁞ ⁞ ⁞ ⁞	98	⁞ ⁞ ⁞ ⁞ ⁞	123	⁞ ⁞ ⁞ ⁞ ⁞
24	⁞ ⁞ ⁞ ⁞ ⁞	49	⁞ ⁞ ⁞ ⁞ ⁞	74	⁞ ⁞ ⁞ ⁞ ⁞	99	⁞ ⁞ ⁞ ⁞ ⁞	124	⁞ ⁞ ⁞ ⁞ ⁞
25	⁞ ⁞ ⁞ ⁞ ⁞	50	⁞ ⁞ ⁞ ⁞ ⁞	75	⁞ ⁞ ⁞ ⁞ ⁞	100	⁞ ⁞ ⁞ ⁞ ⁞	125	⁞ ⁞ ⁞ ⁞ ⁞

ANSWER SHEET

TEST NO. _____ PART _____ TITLE OF POSITION _____
(AS GIVEN IN EXAMINATION ANNOUNCEMENT - INCLUDE OPTION, IF ANY)

PLACE OF EXAMINATION _____ DATE _____
(CITY OR TOWN)   (STATE)

RATING

USE THE SPECIAL PENCIL.   MAKE GLOSSY BLACK MARKS.

	A	B	C	D	E		A	B	C	D	E		A	B	C	D	E		A	B	C	D	E		A	B	C	D	E
1	∷	∷	∷	∷	∷	26	∷	∷	∷	∷	∷	51	∷	∷	∷	∷	∷	76	∷	∷	∷	∷	∷	101	∷	∷	∷	∷	∷
2	∷	∷	∷	∷	∷	27	∷	∷	∷	∷	∷	52	∷	∷	∷	∷	∷	77	∷	∷	∷	∷	∷	102	∷	∷	∷	∷	∷
3	∷	∷	∷	∷	∷	28	∷	∷	∷	∷	∷	53	∷	∷	∷	∷	∷	78	∷	∷	∷	∷	∷	103	∷	∷	∷	∷	∷
4	∷	∷	∷	∷	∷	29	∷	∷	∷	∷	∷	54	∷	∷	∷	∷	∷	79	∷	∷	∷	∷	∷	104	∷	∷	∷	∷	∷
5	∷	∷	∷	∷	∷	30	∷	∷	∷	∷	∷	55	∷	∷	∷	∷	∷	80	∷	∷	∷	∷	∷	105	∷	∷	∷	∷	∷
6	∷	∷	∷	∷	∷	31	∷	∷	∷	∷	∷	56	∷	∷	∷	∷	∷	81	∷	∷	∷	∷	∷	106	∷	∷	∷	∷	∷
7	∷	∷	∷	∷	∷	32	∷	∷	∷	∷	∷	57	∷	∷	∷	∷	∷	82	∷	∷	∷	∷	∷	107	∷	∷	∷	∷	∷
8	∷	∷	∷	∷	∷	33	∷	∷	∷	∷	∷	58	∷	∷	∷	∷	∷	83	∷	∷	∷	∷	∷	108	∷	∷	∷	∷	∷
9	∷	∷	∷	∷	∷	34	∷	∷	∷	∷	∷	59	∷	∷	∷	∷	∷	84	∷	∷	∷	∷	∷	109	∷	∷	∷	∷	∷
10	∷	∷	∷	∷	∷	35	∷	∷	∷	∷	∷	60	∷	∷	∷	∷	∷	85	∷	∷	∷	∷	∷	110	∷	∷	∷	∷	∷

Make only ONE mark for each answer.   Additional and stray marks may be counted as mistakes.   In making corrections, erase errors COMPLETELY.

	A	B	C	D	E		A	B	C	D	E		A	B	C	D	E		A	B	C	D	E		A	B	C	D	E
11	∷	∷	∷	∷	∷	36	∷	∷	∷	∷	∷	61	∷	∷	∷	∷	∷	86	∷	∷	∷	∷	∷	111	∷	∷	∷	∷	∷
12	∷	∷	∷	∷	∷	37	∷	∷	∷	∷	∷	62	∷	∷	∷	∷	∷	87	∷	∷	∷	∷	∷	112	∷	∷	∷	∷	∷
13	∷	∷	∷	∷	∷	38	∷	∷	∷	∷	∷	63	∷	∷	∷	∷	∷	88	∷	∷	∷	∷	∷	113	∷	∷	∷	∷	∷
14	∷	∷	∷	∷	∷	39	∷	∷	∷	∷	∷	64	∷	∷	∷	∷	∷	89	∷	∷	∷	∷	∷	114	∷	∷	∷	∷	∷
15	∷	∷	∷	∷	∷	40	∷	∷	∷	∷	∷	65	∷	∷	∷	∷	∷	90	∷	∷	∷	∷	∷	115	∷	∷	∷	∷	∷
16	∷	∷	∷	∷	∷	41	∷	∷	∷	∷	∷	66	∷	∷	∷	∷	∷	91	∷	∷	∷	∷	∷	116	∷	∷	∷	∷	∷
17	∷	∷	∷	∷	∷	42	∷	∷	∷	∷	∷	67	∷	∷	∷	∷	∷	92	∷	∷	∷	∷	∷	117	∷	∷	∷	∷	∷
18	∷	∷	∷	∷	∷	43	∷	∷	∷	∷	∷	68	∷	∷	∷	∷	∷	93	∷	∷	∷	∷	∷	118	∷	∷	∷	∷	∷
19	∷	∷	∷	∷	∷	44	∷	∷	∷	∷	∷	69	∷	∷	∷	∷	∷	94	∷	∷	∷	∷	∷	119	∷	∷	∷	∷	∷
20	∷	∷	∷	∷	∷	45	∷	∷	∷	∷	∷	70	∷	∷	∷	∷	∷	95	∷	∷	∷	∷	∷	120	∷	∷	∷	∷	∷
21	∷	∷	∷	∷	∷	46	∷	∷	∷	∷	∷	71	∷	∷	∷	∷	∷	96	∷	∷	∷	∷	∷	121	∷	∷	∷	∷	∷
22	∷	∷	∷	∷	∷	47	∷	∷	∷	∷	∷	72	∷	∷	∷	∷	∷	97	∷	∷	∷	∷	∷	122	∷	∷	∷	∷	∷
23	∷	∷	∷	∷	∷	48	∷	∷	∷	∷	∷	73	∷	∷	∷	∷	∷	98	∷	∷	∷	∷	∷	123	∷	∷	∷	∷	∷
24	∷	∷	∷	∷	∷	49	∷	∷	∷	∷	∷	74	∷	∷	∷	∷	∷	99	∷	∷	∷	∷	∷	124	∷	∷	∷	∷	∷
25	∷	∷	∷	∷	∷	50	∷	∷	∷	∷	∷	75	∷	∷	∷	∷	∷	100	∷	∷	∷	∷	∷	125	∷	∷	∷	∷	∷